Manager's Toolkit

The Harvard Business Essentials Series

The Harvard Business Essentials series is designed to provide comprehensive advice, personal coaching, background information, and guidance on the most relevant topics in business. Drawing on rich content from Harvard Business School Publishing and other sources, these concise guides are carefully crafted to provide a highly practical resource for readers with all levels of experience. To assure quality and accuracy, each volume is closely reviewed by a specialized content adviser from a world-class business school. Whether you are a new manager interested in expanding your skills or an experienced executive looking for a personal resource, these solution-oriented books offer reliable answers at your fingertips.

Other books in the series:

Finance for Managers
Hiring and Keeping the Best People
Managing Change and Transition
Negotiation
Business Communication
Managing Creativity and Innovation
Managing Projects Large and Small
Creating Teams with an Edge

HARVARD
BUSINESS
ESSENTIALS

Manager's Toolkit

The 13 Skills Managers Need to Succeed

Harvard Business School Press | *Boston, Massachusetts*

Copyright 2007 Harvard Business School Publishing Corporation

All rights reserved

Printed in the United States of America

11 10 09 08 07   5 4 3 2 1

978-1-4221-1868-9 (Hardcover edition ISBN 13)

Library of Congress Cataloging-in-Publication Data
Harvard business essentials : manager's toolkit :
the 13 skills managers need to succeed.
p. cm. — (Harvard business essentials series)
Includes bibliographical references.
ISBN 1-59139-289-6
1. Management. 2. Supervision of employees.
I. Title. II. Series
HD31.H3496 2004
658—dc22
2003016384

Contents

Manager's Toolkit

Introduction

If you are a manager, it's likely that you got that position because you were an excellent individual contributor. As an individual contributor you developed useful skills. You did good work and got it done on time. Now, as a manager, you've been asked to play a larger role. Some of the qualities and know-how that accounted for your earlier success will help you very little in that new role. The technical expertise and workplace skills you gained earlier remain important but no longer define your role. Your job as a manager is to get results through the creativity, expertise, and energy of others. For example, your sales skills may have gotten you promoted to the rank of district sales manager. Those skills can help you coach your subordinates. But your success as a manager will be determined by other capabilities: your ability to hire and retain good people; to motivate and develop the potential of each member of your team; to create winning plans; to control your budget; to make good decisions; to fire people who cannot or will not do their work; to help promotable people move up; and on and on. It's a new game with different measures of success, and it requires new skills.

Whether you are new to management or a seasoned pro, this book will help you learn and improve the thirteen essential skills that all effective managers must master. Each chapter draws on reliable sources of expertise and offers plenty of practical advice, personal coaching, and background information that you can apply every day.

What's Ahead

This book is divided into three parts. Part I addresses five basic but essential skills needed to build the foundation of a powerful and high-performing manager. Chapter 1 is about setting goals that others will pursue. It explains why unit goals must be aligned with the strategic objectives of the enterprise, describes the characteristics of effective goals, and provides tips on how you can develop powerful goals for your unit and yourself.

Chapters 2 and 3 address two related skills: hiring and retaining good employees. Good employees well-managed are the key to your success. In chapter 2 you'll learn the latest about defining job requirements, recruiting, and a five-step approach for hiring people who can and will do the job. Chapter 3 explains why retention matters to companies and their managers, why people stay, and why they leave. Unlike many sources, this chapter does not look upon employee turnover as bad in itself. Instead, it takes the position that turnover is only a problem when it involves people who are expensive to recruit and train, and who add real value to customers and to your company. It urges managers to differentiate between employee segments and individual employees; some are worth more to the business than others. Managers should focus their retention efforts on those employees with the highest value. Knowing who the valued employees are is a skill all managers need to keep developing.

Delegating is the subject of chapter 4. This is a bedrock skill. A person who cannot delegate effectively cannot be an effective manager. This chapter points to warning signs that you should do more delegating and provides guidelines for doing it right. Chapter 5 deals with a related issue: time management. Managers who fail to delegate find their calendars overloaded. But there are plenty of other reasons for time binds; this chapter identifies them and explains what you can do to get rid of time-wasters and regain control of your time.

Part II moves on to more challenging managerial skills. Chapter 6 is on team-based work, which many experienced managers, accustomed to being bosses, find difficult to handle. Here you'll get the basics of when and why to use teams, how to create them, how to lead them and handle problems, and how to evaluate their performance.

Chapter 7 is on improving performance through appraisal and coaching. Both activities provide opportunities for the essential feedback that managers must maintain with their subordinates. And though appraisal is an infrequent activity, coaching is a skill you can use every day. On a somewhat related note, chapter 8 addresses the subject that every manager dreads: the problem employee. The bad behavior and poor performance of some employees can be brought into line through motivation and feedback, as explained here. Others, however, either cannot or will not do their jobs, which usually leads to dismissal. Dismissals are difficult for all concerned and, if not handled correctly, can damage the company's reputation and result in lawsuits against it. The chapter spells out what to do and what *not* to do in these situations.

Has your mainframe computer ever gone up in smoke? No? Have you planned what you'd do if it did? Every business is eventually slammed with a crisis of one type or another. The CEO is in a car wreck that leaves him in traction for three months. Customers find rodent droppings in jars of your company's premium grade pickles. Ugh! The possibilities for disaster are practically endless. Chapter 9 explains how you can avoid some crises through planning and prepare for others that cannot be avoided. It provides practical advice for containing crises when and if they happen, resolving them effectively, and learning from them. Crisis management is about the furthest thing from most managers' minds—until the crisis happens. So be smart. Think about it now.

Chapter 10 provides practical ideas for making the most of your career. It will help you identify your core business interests, work values, and skills. Once you have a handle on these, you'll be better prepared to identify the career path that's best for you. But career development isn't just for you. As a manager, one of your responsibilities is to develop the careers of the people who work for you. You can do that using the approaches described in this chapter.

In many respects, the ultimate challenge of every manager is to develop leadership. As chapter 11 makes clear, the boundary between managing and leading is blurry. Managers must be able to lead and leaders must be able to manage. To help you develop leadership skills, this chapter identifies the characteristics of effective leaders, indicates how they balance the tensions typically found in organizations, and how they create a vision that others will follow. Real leaders also act as agents of change, challenging complacency where they find it.

Strategy is the subject of chapter 12. In many respects, strategy formulation is a leadership skill, since it identifies a direction for the rest of the organization. As described in this chapter, strategy is a deliberate search for a plan of action that will give the organization a competitive advantage over its rivals. Drawing on the writings of Michael Porter, Clayton Christensen, and other leading thinkers on the subject, this chapter identifies the different approaches a business can take to differentiate itself and capture an advantage. It presents a five-step process for formulating strategy and aligning the activities of the business with it.

Part III covers the specific financial tools that every mid- to higher-level manager should understand and learn to apply. Financial skill is a necessary complement to the people know-how that dominates so much of the management literature. The topics covered in this part include budgeting (chapter 13), the ability to read and interpret financial statements (chapter 14), net present value analysis and internal rate of return (chapter 15), and breakeven analysis (chapter 16). These tools help managers to take the pulse of the business, provide control, and make better decisions.

The various skills offered in this book have unique vocabularies. This is particularly true of finance. Simply understanding the terminology can help you master the subject matter and be more effective in communicating with other managers and technical professionals. To that end you will find a glossary of all key terms at the back of this book. Each key term is italicized when first introduced in the text, indicating that its definition can be found in the glossary.

A section titled "For Further Reading" can also be found at the end of the book. There you'll find references to recent books and articles—many of them classics—that provide either much more material or unique insights into the topics covered in these chapters. If you'd like to learn more about any of the topics we've included in the book, these references will help you. In addition, the official Harvard Business Essentials Web site, www.elearning.hbsp.org/businesstools, offers free interactive versions of tools, checklists, and worksheets cited in this book and other books in the Essentials series.

Part One

Learning
the Basics

Setting Goals That Others Will Pursue

Committing to an Outcome

Key Topics Covered in This Chapter

- *Why goals must originate in the strategic objective of the enterprise*

- *Top-down and bottom-up goal setting*

- *The characteristics of effective goals*

- *Developing goals for the unit and oneself*

- *Setting priorities*

- *A four-step process for accomplishing goals*

- *After-action review*

GOAL SETTING is a process for defining targets you plan to achieve. It is one of the essential functions of management. When you set goals, you commit to outcomes that you can accomplish personally or through your subordinates. Goal setting makes it possible to focus limited resources and time on the things that matter most. It sets the course of action.

By setting goals and measuring their achievement you can focus on what is most important, waste less energy on noncritical tasks, and achieve greater results. As a manager, you are responsible for setting goals for your unit and for yourself. This chapter explains how to do it right.[1]

Begin with Strategy

Goals should emerge from the strategy of the enterprise. If the strategy is to become the market share leader through rapid product introductions, for example, unit and individual goals should serve that strategy. There should be, in fact, a cascading of linked and aligned goals from top to bottom, as described in figure 1-1. In this figure, the enterprise's strategic goal is at the top. Each operating unit has goals that directly support that strategic objective. Within the operating units, teams and individuals are assigned goals that directly support those of their units. The real power of these cascading goals is their alignment with the highest purposes of the organization. Ideally, every employee would understand his or her goal, how it serves

FIGURE 1 - 1

Goal Alignment

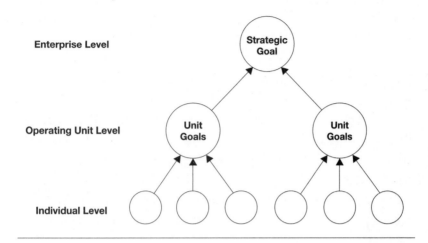

the goal of the unit, and how the unit's activities contribute to the strategic objective of the enterprise.

Top–Down or Bottom–Up?

The two common approaches to goal setting are top-down and bottom-up. In top-down goal setting, management sets broad goals and each employee is assigned objectives that are aligned with and support those broad goals. This approach is most appropriate when rank-and-file employees need close supervision, are new to the organization, or aren't familiar with unit or company goals.

In the bottom–up method, employees develop their own goals, and their manager integrates them into larger organizational goals. This bottom–up approach is most appropriate when employees are fairly self-directed and when they clearly understand the strategy of the business, customer needs, and their own roles in the larger scheme of things.

In both approaches, goal setting is most effective when employees are involved in the process. Involvement increases buy-in, ensures that objectives are understood, and fosters accountability at every level. This involvement may not be possible in the top-down approach. After all, the manager chooses the goals and allocates them. However, buy-in can be secured if the manager communicates the purpose of the individual employee's assigned goals, why they are important, and how they fit in with the organization's larger strategy.

In most cases, a company's goals are determined through a process that subsumes both approaches. Management does not dictate objectives to employees without consultation, nor do employees have a free hand in determining their own goals. Instead, unit and individual goals are determined through a negotiating process in which what is necessary and what is feasible are discussed by management and employees.

Characteristics of Effective Goals

No matter which approach you take to goal setting, those goals must be effective. And to be effective they must be

- recognized by everyone as important;

- clear and easy to understand;

- written down in specific terms;

- measurable and framed in time;

- aligned with organizational strategy;

- achievable but challenging;

- supported by appropriate rewards.

Consider this example of a sales manager assigning goals to a field sales person:

It's very important that our company increase its sales revenues during the coming calendar year. We've made sizeable investments in training and manufacturing lately, and senior management expects us to cover those investments with higher revenues. If we can do that, the company's financial situation will be greatly improved and it will be in a better competitive position for the future. And that means more job security and higher bonuses for everybody.

The company's goal is to increase sales revenues by $15 million over the coming year, and everyone in the sales force is expected to contribute to that goal. Your piece of the goal is to increase sales in your territory from $2 million to $2.2 million for the year—a 10 percent increase. I'll follow up with a written statement to that effect.

A 10 percent increase won't be easy given the outstanding job you've done already, but there's still plenty of opportunity in your territory. I'm confident that you can achieve that goal, and I'll back you up in any way I can.

Notice how this manager touched on every one of the characteristics of effective goals.

Two Mistakes to Avoid

Many organizations make two mistakes in setting goals:

1. They fail to create performance metrics. Performance metrics provide objective evidence of goal achievement—or progress toward it. Output per machine, errors per thousand units produced, and time-to-market for new products are all examples of performance metrics. Whichever metrics you use, be sure that they are linked to the goal outcomes you seek.

2. They fail to align goals and rewards. Many companies change their goals but do not follow up with a realignment of rewards. Even when they try, they often get it wrong, and end up rewarding the wrong things. Misaligned rewards encourage employees to put their energy into the wrong activities.

Developing Unit Goals

In a typical day, you probably think about how your unit can operate more smoothly, which new responsibilities it should assume, how people can work better as a team, or how operating expenses can be reduced. Each one of these areas contains potential goals. Your challenge is to sort through them and identify those that are achievable, linked to organizational goals, and likely to create the most value.

So every six or twelve months you should review your unit's diverse activities, and try to identify opportunities to make a big difference in performance. And since several brains are better than one, call your team together—preferably on a regular basis—to brainstorm possible goals. Ask questions such as these:

- What initiatives need to be accomplished to ensure success?

- What standards are we striving for?

- Where can productivity and efficiency be improved by 10 percent or more?

- What are our customers expecting from us?

- Are customer specifications changing? How can we respond?

Don't worry about constraints or execution as you're brainstorming. Also, don't forget to reexamine existing goals that may need to be revised because of changes in customer requirements and the competitive environment.

Many managers approach goal setting with apprehension. On the one hand, they know that goals should address the most important challenges facing their organizations. But these, almost by definition, are difficult and involve above-average risk. As a result, there's a natural temptation to avoid them or to avoid setting the bar too high. After all, difficult goals may generate grumbling among subordinates. There is also a higher likelihood of failure and the career penalties that go with it. You could avoid these problems by making goals less challenging. But that might not be what's best for the organization or for you and your subordinates. The best course is to communicate frankly with your subordinates. Explain why these challenging goals were selected and why achieving them is so important, both for the organization and for them as individuals. Make sure that they see a personal benefit.

Prioritizing

Some goals are critical to future success. Others are simply nice to have. Because resources are limited, you have to differentiate between critical and "nice to have" goals. Thus, once you have a list of goal ideas, narrow the list and select only the most important ones. Start by identifying criteria that will help you distinguish high-priority goals from low-priority ones. For example:

- Which goals do your organization value most?

- Which will have the greatest impact on performance or profitability?

- Which are most challenging?

- Which goals are your team best situated—by talent or training—to tackle?

Some goals are bound to overlap. When this happens, consolidate them into a single, larger goal. Next, review your list of goals and use your criteria to rank them as A-, B-, or C-level priorities:

Priority A: High value and primary concern.

Priority B: Medium value and secondary importance.

Priority C: Little value and minor importance.

Eliminate all Priority C goals, then look again at the B goals. Are they worth your time or not? If they deserve to be A goals, move them into that batch. Downgrade the rest to C status. The goals now on your Priority A list are your high-level goals. But you're not yet finished. Because resources are always limited, you must prioritize once again. As a last step, review your Priority A goals and rank them according to importance, then commit your final Priority A list to writing.

Your Goals as Manager

You, too, need individual goals. These may include unit goals, or components of unit goals that require your specific skills—things you cannot delegate. They may reflect your contributions to your team members' goals. In some cases, your goals will be handed to you by someone higher in the chain of command: a general manager or the CEO.

Your goals may also include some not specifically related to your unit. For example, you may serve on a task force to revamp company-wide healthcare benefits. In that case, one of your goals would be linked to that activity, even though it is not directly connected to the work done by your unit.

Whatever the focus of your goals, work with your own manager to reach agreement on them, build a shared understanding of the expected outputs, and secure the support and training you need to be successful. In addition, be sure that your team members are aware of your personal goals. If they understand your priorities and how the team's activities fit into them, everyone will work together more smoothly.

Four Steps to Accomplishing Goals

Creating a clear set of goals is important, but that is obviously not the end of the road. Goals in isolation are pointless. They are only meaningful when matched with practical plans to achieve them. Converting goals into realities involves four steps:

1. Break each goal down into specific tasks—with clear outcomes.

2. Plan the execution of those tasks—with timetables.

3. Gather the necessary resources.

4. Execute your plan.

> **Step 1.** In the first step you must determine which tasks are needed to accomplish your goals. Some of these tasks may have to be completed sequentially—such as, task A must be completed before you can begin task B. If this is the case, put

the tasks in the right order. It's likely that other tasks can be completed simultaneously—you can assign some people to task A while another team attacks task B. If a task appears overwhelming, break it into smaller parts.

Step 2. Plan out each task, and give each a start and finish date. You might want to use a *Gantt chart* or some other time-scaled task diagram to make this clear to all. Gantt charts are the basic bar chart familiar to most people. They are easy to read and clearly communicate what needs to be done in a particular time frame (see figure 1-2 for an example). Notice in the figure that key tasks are listed in the left-hand column, with the start and finish times represented in each of the horizontal bars. As you make up a Gantt chart, pay particular attention to the relationships between difficult tasks. For example, "Modify design" is something that cannot be done until the "Customer tests" task has been completed, since modification is no doubt dependent on the outcome of those tests. Some tasks, like "Materials research" may proceed in parallel with others. You should use the most important tasks in your plan as milestones along the long road that leads to

FIGURE 1 - 2

Gantt Chart Example

Product Development Project

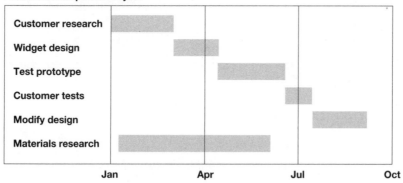

your goals. Milestones break up a long journey into shorter, more manageable chunks, giving people greater assurance that they can get the job done.

Step 3. As you schedule, remember that many efforts fail when planners overlook a significant part of the work or underestimate the time and resources required to complete them. So once you've planned how each task will be executed, check your resources. Do you have the money to get the job done? Do you have the *right* people in terms of training and reliability?

Step 4. An experienced salesperson once described his secret for success this way: "First, plan your day—then work your plan." Working your plan is what's involved in this step. This is where talk and good intentions must be transformed into real work.

Obstacles to Success

If you've done a thorough job of planning your efforts, you will have identified the serious hurdles and planned how to overcome them. Not every obstacle can be anticipated, but you can prevent them from totally disrupting progress toward your goals. So before you begin executing, consider the potential obstacles that might pop up between you and each goal. Then think of possible solutions for each obstacle. The following two strategies may be helpful: If your team members are having trouble completing a task, break it into smaller, more easily handled pieces. If team members appear to be losing their motivation, remind them of the payoff for success.

Finally, don't make yourself an obstacle to success. According to Robert Schaffer, some managers create obstacles to achievement of unit goals when they[2]

- convince themselves that employees are already doing their best;

- focus on procedures instead of results, which enables managers to hope for better results without having to demand them of employees;

- frame ambitious goals in vague terms, which makes it impossible to know when goals are achieved.

Don't make these mistakes.

Keeping On Track

Always know where you stand relative to your goals. Are sales ahead or behind schedule? Is the Web site task force moving forward according to plan, or is it stuck on some technical problem? Progress monitoring allows you to intervene before projects get too far off track. Here are few tips for progress monitoring:

Don't Confuse Activities with Results

Writing in *Harvard Business Review*, Robert Schaffer and Harvey Thomson warned managers not to confuse well-intended activities with results. Most corporate improvement efforts, they say, have negligible impact because they bear little relationship to a company's goals and have long, indeterminate time horizons. Moreover, they equate measures of activities with actual improvements in performance. An activity-centered program confuses ends with means, processes with outcomes. It assumes, for example, that once the company has benchmarked its performance against the competition, assessed customers' expectations, and trained its staff in problem solving, that quality, sales, and profits will automatically improve.

A results-driven approach, in contrast, bypasses lengthy preparations. Its focus is on specific, measurable goals for performance improvement that can be achieved in the short term. By committing to measurable change, managers can not only see results faster, they can also determine more quickly what's working and what isn't.

SOURCE: Robert H. Schaffer and Harvey A. Thomson, "Successful Change Programs Begin with Results," *Harvard Business Review,* January–February 1992.

- Update your people regularly; let them know where they currently stand relative to each goal.

- If progress stalls, get people to face the problem and brainstorm for solutions. Revise completion dates when necessary, but only as a last resort.

- Check off and celebrate milestones as they are reached.

Periodic Review

As you work toward your goals, step back periodically and review them. Are they still realistic? Are they still timely? Are they still important? You should be very cautious about shifting or modifying goals in midstream. Doing so can create confusion in the ranks. And you should not change course simply because you've run into obstacles.

But if the organizational or external environment has changed, and pursuing an assigned goal no longer makes sense, it is both appropriate and necessary to redirect your resources. As John Maynard Keynes told one of his critics, "When the facts change, I change. What do you do, sir?" When you do need to change a goal, it's your job as manager to justify it. Get buy-in from your team, upper management, and other involved groups before proceeding.

After–Action Review

Once you have accomplished a goal, celebrate your team's success and publicly recognize the people who did the work. Celebration and praise will reenergize people and prepare them mentally for future initiatives. But reaching a goal is not the end of the process. You and your team should use the lull that typically follows goal achievement to review how you planned for and executed your tasks. Ask yourself and your team questions like these—and record the answers:

- What worked and what didn't?

- Has reaching the goal produced the payoff we anticipated?

- If we had to do this again, what would we do differently?

- Was the team given sufficient resources and authority to do the job well?

- What lessons from this task can be carried over to future tasks to make them faster, better, or less expensive?

The lessons learned from after-action reviews are extremely valuable. Get people on your team to talk about and internalize them. Then apply those lessons as you develop new goals. Also consider these points as you move forward. If the previous goal was too easily achieved, make future goals more challenging. If the old goal took too much effort, make new goals a little easier. If you noticed a skill deficit while pursuing a goal, make attaining those skills a goal for the future. If a goal was unrealistic, make sure that new goals better reflect organizational realities and time constraints.

Summing Up

- Goals should emerge from and be aligned with the strategy of the enterprise.

- Some organizations take a top-down approach to goal setting; others use a bottom-up approach. Yet most merge the two.

- Effective goals must be recognized as important, clear, specific, measurable, aligned with strategy, achievable but challenging, and supported by appropriate rewards.

- Prioritize. Focus people and other resources on goals that represent the greatest value.

- Convert goals into realities through four steps: (1) break each goal into specific tasks; (2) plan the execution; (3) gather the resources you need; and (4) execute the plan.

- Be results-oriented.

- Once you've accomplished a goal, celebrate; then learn from your experience.

Hiring the Best

The Role of Human Assets

Key Topics Covered in This Chapter

- *Defining job requirements*

- *Recruiting promising candidates*

- *Interviewing*

- *Evaluating candidates*

- *Making the decision and offer*

EW MANAGERIAL DECISIONS are as important as
hiring. In a world where human assets have become the
key differentiator between competing firms, the quality
and capabilities of the people you bring onto your team will determine it success—and yours as a manager.

The character and effectiveness of the unit you manage will be
determined by the people you hire. Hire a bunch of C-level individuals and you will preside over a C-level organization. Even if you
coach them and send them to expensive training programs, you are
not likely to improve the overall tenor of your unit. Hire nothing but
A- and B-level performers, however, and you'll have the makings of
a powerful team.

Like many other activities undertaken by organizations, hiring is
a business process—a set of activities that turn inputs into outputs.
This process compiles information about job requirements, the ap-
plications of various candidates, and the deliberations of decision
makers, and produces an outcome: new people on the payroll. This
chapter describes a five-step hiring process. Execute these steps well,
and not only will the quality of your hires improve, but you will also
be more confident that you are hiring the *right* people.[1]

Defining Job Requirements

Before you can make a good hire, you need to know what you
are hiring for. You also need to determine which skills and personal

attributes will be a good "fit" with the requirements of the job and the organization. To define the job and its requirements, you need to understand the following:

- The primary responsibilities and tasks involved in the job

- The background characteristics needed to perform the job (education and experience)

- The personal characteristics required (for example, does the individual need to have strong interpersonal skills or be highly intelligent?)

- The key features of your organization's culture (for example, team orientation, degree of conformity, reward systems)

- Your managerial style (for example, authoritative, coercive, democratic) and its implications for an effective working relationship

Primary Responsibilities and Tasks

If you're looking to rehire for an existing job, look at what the current incumbent is now doing and evaluate that person's job description, if one exists. But don't simply accept either of these perspectives as definitive. Use the hiring opportunity to reevaluate the primary responsibilities and tasks of the job. Make sure you can answer the question, "What does the employee have to do in this job?"

Education and Experience

Education and experience are the two most critical background characteristics to consider when evaluating candidates. In the case of education, you may wish to specify a certain type of degree, or a certain level. Be sure to ask yourself whether a specific educational background is truly necessary. Can you be flexible in this area, or can relevant experience be substituted for a certain educational background?

Experience requirements should be based on a thorough analysis of the specific tasks and responsibilities of the position. Which would be most desirable:

- Industry experience?

- Functional experience?

- Large- versus small-company experience?

Industry and functional experience are particularly important for externally oriented positions requiring knowledge of products and competitors. However, if a good candidate has not been exposed to everything required, consider whether he or she can learn what is needed and how long that learning will take. Various tests, for example, are available to measure an individual's dexterity with numerical data, spatial acumen, mechanical ability, and so forth. Also, determine whether the organization can afford the time needed for on-the-job learning.

Personal Characteristics

Personal characteristics indicate how the candidate will approach the job and how he or she might relate to coworkers (see "Create Consensus on Personal Characteristics"). Evaluate the following personal characteristics relative to the tasks and responsibilities you've listed for the job opening:

- **Analytical and creative abilities.** A candidate's abilities in these two areas determine how he or she assesses problems and comes up with new approaches to solving them.

- **Decision-making style.** This is very individual. Some people are extremely structured, analytical, and fact-based; others rely more on intuition. Some make decisions quickly, while others ponder them for a long time. Some seek consensus, while others keep their own counsel. It is critical to determine whether a particular style is required for success in the job and, if so, what it is.

- **Interpersonal skills.** Since interpersonal skills and behavior are intimately connected, understanding a candidate's interpersonal skills is an important part of the hiring decision process. To determine which interpersonal skills are most appropriate for a given position, think about the set of tasks that will be performed in the position. Which traits will translate into good performance, especially in view of the superiors, peers, and

Create Consensus on Personal Characteristics

Many hiring decisions start off on the wrong foot because the company hasn't clarified exactly what it wants in the new hire. For example, the different people with whom the new hire will interact (or who have a say in the hiring decision) may have their own ideas about the perfect job candidate.

Consider the hypothetical case of a company that wants to fill a product-designer position, but hasn't reached a consensus about key hiring factors. The design director wants a seasoned individual who has gained extensive design experience at one of the firm's toughest competitors. The head of finance prefers a bright new (and more affordable) college graduate. The marketing director is pressing for someone with marketing experience in the kinds of product lines the company currently offers. Meanwhile, the new hire's immediate supervisor is looking for someone with "people skills."

Pity the poor job applicants who walk into this situation! To avoid this type of confusion, try this procedure:

- Ask everyone who will interact with the new hire to privately write down *exactly* what they would consider the attributes of the ideal candidate.

- Meet and openly discuss differences in the various wish lists.

- Decide *together* which requirements have priority.

- Create a new list of requirements that everyone agrees on.

- Stick to that list when evaluating candidates.

direct reports with whom the person will interact? For example, a controller should ideally be patient and formal, demonstrating careful, cautious, detail-oriented behavior. For a sales manager, high extroversion, competitiveness, and low formality may be desirable.

- **Motivation.** A candidate's personal goals, interests, energy level, and job progression often demonstrate his or her level of motivation. So ask yourself, Does this job match the candidate's personal aspirations? Would he or she do the job with enthusiasm and energy?

- **Attitude and interest.** In many situations, a person with the right attitude and interest is a far better catch than other candidates with more education, skills, and even relevant experience. Southwest Airlines provides a very striking example of a successful enterprise that puts attitude and interest at the top of its hiring agenda. It only hires people who have a sense of humor, a sense of teamwork, and a desire to make customers happy. As founder and former CEO Herb Kelleher once put it, "If you don't have a good attitude, we don't want you, no matter how skilled you are. We can change skill levels through training. We can't change attitude." [2]

Develop a Job Description

Once you understand the position's requirements, you are ready to create a job description. A job description is a profile of the job, its essential functions, reporting relationships, hours, and required credentials. This description will make it possible for you to explain the job both to potential candidates and to any recruiters you may be using to identify candidates. In some cases, your organization may have a required format or a standard job description to use as a model.

A clearly written, results-oriented job description can shape the beginning of the employee relationship, and can help everyone understand the mission, culture, needs, and goals of the company. It can also form the basis of a legal termination of employment should that become necessary. Your job description should include the following:

- Job title, business unit, and the name of the organization

- Job responsibilities and tasks

- Hiring manager and reporting manager

- Summary of the job tasks, responsibilities, and objectives

- Compensation, hours, and location

- Background characteristics required

- Personal characteristics required

Many of these items will have to be cleared with the human resource department.

Developing the job description can be an opportunity to re-design a job, instead of just filling the one you already have. For example, the last person who held the position may have had a strong strategic focus, but if you decide that a more hands-on manager is now needed, then re-create the job description accordingly. As you go through the exercise of describing the job, observe the following:

- Distinguish between knowledge, skills, and abilities. Some jobs require advanced degrees. Some require special skills, such as knowing how to program in Java. Others require physical abilities, such as hand-eye coordination, or mental abilities, such as the ability to work with numbers. Figure out what you need in each area.

- Take the time needed to do it right. Yes, you need that new employee to start next week, but the cost of getting rid of the wrong employee will more than outweigh the cost of time spent finding the right one.

- Comply with all legal restrictions. In the United States at least, stated job requirements must be clearly related to getting the job done and must not unfairly prevent racial minorities, women, people with disabilities, or other "protected classes" from getting hired. (U.S. readers should see "Legal Landmines in Hiring" in Appendix B.)

Recruiting Promising Candidates

Gaining access to qualified candidates is critical to the success of your hiring effort (see "Tips for Finding the Right Person"). You can accomplish this by getting the word out through as many appropriate channels as possible. However, the word "qualified" is important. A large pool of mediocre candidates isn't nearly as valuable as a small pool of *qualified* candidates. Utilizing targeted, relevant channels to get the word out about your position can help ensure that the proportion of qualified candidates in your pool is as high as possible.

Typical channels include recruiting agencies, newspaper ads, referrals from colleagues, trade publications, professional associations, networking, campus recruiting, and the Internet. In addition, you can enhance the pipeline of qualified candidates through programs

---

Tips for Finding the Right Person

- Consider current employees.

- Look outside your organization to bring in new outlooks, skills, and experiences.

- Know what kind of person you're looking for in order to locate a good fit.

- Remember that a person's past job performance is the surest guide to future performance.

- Remember that the right education + the right experience + a compatible personality = a good fit.

- Beware of the "just like me" trap. This trap encourages managers to favor candidates who share similar educational backgrounds, are of the same age, gender, or race, and who enjoy the same pastimes. To avoid the trap, focus on the objective requirements of the job and the candidate's qualifications.

such as internships and partnerships with colleges, universities, and community organizations.

Personal referrals from current employees are another favored method of expanding the candidate pool, and many companies encourage this through the payment of "rewards" to employees whose referrals are actually hired. In general, this practice is much less costly than others, and often produces more satisfactory new hires, since it's unlikely that current employees will suggest a candidate who is unqualified or likely to be a bad employee.

Screening Résumés

A sizeable pool of applicants ensures that you will have choices in the hiring process; it also means that you'll have more sifting to do in finding the best choice. And that sifting begins with résumé screening.

The cover letter and résumé are the candidate's first introduction to you. In order to merit your further attention, they should convey the qualities you seek. When you have a large number of résumés to review, use a two-pass process to make the task more manageable. In the first pass, eliminate candidates who fail to meet the basic requirements of the job. In the second pass, look for résumés that include

- signs of achievement and results; for example, a profit orientation, stability, or progressive career momentum;

- a career goal in line with the job being offered (be on your guard here, as applicants are often coached to tailor their purported career goals to match those of jobs to which they're applying);

- a strong overall construction and clean appearance.

In this pass, also consider the subtler differences among qualified candidates—for example, years and quality of experience; technical versus managerial backgrounds; the quality of the companies they have worked for; and so forth. Then develop a list of the strongest candidates.

When reviewing résumés, be on the alert for red flags that may indicate areas of weakness, such as the following:

- A lengthy description of the applicant's education (possibly not much job experience)

- Employment gaps (what was the applicant doing during these gaps?)

- A pattern of short-term employment, especially after the applicant has been in the work force for more than a few years

- No logical job progression

- Too much personal information (possibly not much job experience)

- Descriptions of jobs and positions only, with no descriptions of results or accomplishments

Interviewing

A hiring interview has one primary purpose: To provide the interviewer and the job candidate with an opportunity to obtain the information that both need to make the best possible decision. Since the time spent with any particular candidate is limited, a well-organized approach will make the most of that time.

When selecting someone for an important position, you will probably go through at least two of the following stages for every job opening. In some cases, you may even go through all three.

1. **Telephone-screening interview.** This may be done by you, a recruiting agency, your human resource department, or someone else in your own department. Its purpose is to confirm that the candidate meets the qualifications stated in the recruiting material, and it can be as short as necessary to accomplish that goal. The screening interview is a good opportunity to get some

initial impressions of the candidate: Did she call you back at the specified time? Does she communicate well?

2. **Initial in-person interview.** Try to narrow the field to four to seven candidates before holding an initial interview. This interview will probably last thirty to sixty minutes. For less demanding positions, you may find out everything you need to know about the candidate in that conversation. In other cases you will need to see the person again.

3. **Second interview.** Be very selective about who rates a second interview. At this point, other people with a stake in the process may participate, such as direct reports, potential peers, or other managers. This interview aims to bring out more of the "real" person.

Structured Versus Unstructured Interviews

In a structured interview, you ask all the candidates the same questions so you can compare answers. Structured interviews are used in order to be fair and objective, but they may not elicit as much information from the candidates. Unstructured interviews are individual conversations that do not necessarily cover all the same questions with every candidate. Instead, they follow promising lines of inquiry as they appear. You may learn more about the candidates this way, but it will be more difficult to compare their responses. And you may miss key information you need in order to make a decision.

It's probably a good idea to steer a middle path between these two approaches—be flexible in your line of inquiry, but be sure that all interviewees respond to a core set of questions. By preparing those core questions in advance, you can assure yourself and the decision-making team that all key points are covered, and that all candidates respond to them. The unstructured element of the interview opens the door to productive areas of inquiry that neither you nor your colleagues may have anticipated.

Be Prepared

Would you go into a meeting with a vendor to discuss a $500,000 to $1 million custom software package with no preparation? Certainly not. You'd give lots of thought to what you expected the software to do and the features you needed. You'd probably formulate a list of key issues to discuss. Your hiring decisions are probably costing you something in this same range. So should you walk into a job interview with notes and prior preparation, or should you simply wing it?

You will gather more of the information you need to make a good hiring decision if you take the time and trouble to prepare. To prepare, review the job description and make a list of the key responsibilities and tasks of the job, the training and experience needed, and personal attributes required to do the job well. For each of the areas you need to explore with the candidate, prepare several questions in advance. (Note: In Appendix A you'll find the Interview Preparation Form, which is a handy way to organize your questions. You can download a printable version of this form and other interactive tools from the Harvard Business Essentials Web site at: www.elearning.hbsp.org/businesstools.)

There are three phases to the interview: the opening, the body, and the close. Let's consider each in detail.

The Opening

Generally, this should take about 10 percent of the allotted time. Your goal in this phase is to make the candidate feel sufficiently comfortable so that he or she will open up. To create this sense of comfort, be on time and be friendly. Introduce yourself and tell the candidate something about yourself. Explain the structure of the interview with questions like these:

"I'm going to ask you about your experience."

"I'm interested in finding out about you as an individual."

"We're interested in finding out whether there is a good fit between your interests and abilities and our organizational needs."

"I will give you information about our organization."

"I'll be glad to take your questions at the end of the interview."

Use this interview phase to establish rapport with the candidate. Acknowledge some of the difficulties or awkwardness of being interviewed, such as meeting a lot of new people or being tired at the end of the day. A little humor is generally effective in dispelling the tension. Find information in the résumé that will help you build rapport, or compliment the person on some aspect of his experience. Acknowledge that you have something in common, such as having lived in the same city, a mutual acquaintance, or the same outside interest.

The Body

Plan to use 80 percent of your allotted time in this phase. Use that time to gather the information you need to evaluate the candidate and to "sell" your organization. During the body of the interview, you need to assess the candidate's qualifications, skills, knowledge, and experience and compare those to the job description. Pursue a direct line of questioning based on the résumé. Identify similarities and patterns of behavior consistent with your ideal profile. Ask for samples of work and references to review after the interview. Samples, if they are not confidential or proprietary, may include a sales brochure, product, customer survey, or training course designed by the candidate. These samples can tell you a great deal about a candidate's capabilities.

It is sometimes difficult to get a candidate to be specific about the accomplishments listed on the résumé. But don't allow difficulty to stand between you and the information you require. Ask directly for details, and probe for tangible measures of success. Table 2-1 provides some examples of typical résumé statements, and how you can respond in order to get more detail.

You are also assessing the candidate's personal qualities during this phase, such as leadership, problem-solving ability, communication, teamwork skills, and motivation. Use scenario-based questions to determine how people tend to handle situations, such as:

TABLE 2-1

Responses to Typical Résumé Statements

Résumé Statement	Possible Response
I successfully managed development of a new line of consumer kitchenware.	How was success measured: by revenues, time-to-market, other measures? Specifically, what was your role in the development effort?
I worked effectively with marketing and sales to increase annual unit sales by 25 percent over the past twelve months.	What was the nature of your contribution? How were unit sales increased: by more effective selling or by slashing prices?
I initiated the redesign of key department processes.	What processes? What do you mean by "initiated"? Why did you decide to do this? Why was this initiative important?

- **For a process manager candidate:** "Suppose that the loan processing department was taking two days more than its competitors to make its decisions and notify customers. How would you approach that type of problem?"

- **For a sales manager candidate:** "Let's say that one of the people in your sales district was well liked by customers and company personnel, had great potential, but wasn't pulling her weight after two years on the job. How would you deal with a situation like that?"

Responses to scenario questions like these will give you an idea about how the candidate approaches problems.

Also, ask candidates how they handled past situations similar to those they will likely encounter as one of your employees: "Tell me about a time when you had to (fire an employee/handle a key customer whose business you'd just lost/lead a process improvement team/ etc.)." Be on guard, though, as some people have developed canned responses to some of the more likely scenario-based questions.

Maintaining control of the interview is very important. The key to maintaining control is to ask most of the questions and do most of the listening. You should be listening 80 percent of the time—you will learn nothing while you're talking.

Be sure to take notes during the interview. They will help you recall significant facts about the candidate. But be unobtrusive about it, and tell the candidate up front that you will be taking notes. Remember that your interview notes will become part of the employment file. Avoid writing anything down that could be construed as inconsistent with equal opportunity employment laws.

More About Questions

There are good questions, there are aimless questions, and there are outright bad questions. Good questions have a purpose, are tied to your decision-making criteria, encourage communication, are job-related, and are nonthreatening. Good questions reflect favorably on you and demonstrate your interest and your preparation. Examples of some good questions:

- Self-appraisal questions that require the candidate to give some thought to his or her interpersonal skills and abilities. These allow the candidate, rather than you, to interpret the facts. (For example: "Why do you think you were selected to lead the task force?")

- Accomplishment questions that ask for evidence of the candidate's demonstrated qualities. They help you learn why and how something was accomplished, and reveal a candidate's level of involvement in past accomplishments. (For example: "Tell me about your contribution to that team effort.")

- Broad-brush questions that make the candidate think about a big topic, choose an answer, and organize his or her thoughts. (For example: "Tell me about your experience as a project manager with the fiber optics group.")

- Comparison questions that reveal a candidate's analytical and reasoning abilities. (For example: "How would you compare working with the fiber optics group to working with the polymer group?")

Examples of bad questions:

- Leading questions that direct the candidate to the answer you want. (For example: "Would you say you have the motivation required for this job?" Would you expect anyone to say "no" to this?)

- Irrelevant questions that waste everyone's time. (For example, "I see that you are a University of Minnesota alumnus. My daughter may apply there. What are its best programs?")

Questions to Avoid

United States laws and regulations are clear about which questions are illegal. If you are not familiar with these laws and regulations, consult your human resource specialist or legal counsel. Prohibited questions in the United States include the following:

How old are you?

Are you married?

What is your citizenship?

What is your sexual orientation?

How much do you weigh?

Are you disabled?

When did you graduate from high school?

Do you have children?

What country are you from?

Where were you born?

Have you ever been arrested?

Would your religion prevent you from working on weekends?

For a more complete discussion of legal and illegal interview questions, see "Legal Landmines in Hiring," in Appendix B.

The Close

Plan on 10 percent of your allotted interview time to wrap things up. The close is your opportunity to

- thank the candidate for coming in;

- explain how and when the person will hear about follow-up interviews or decisions;

- ask if the candidate has questions, especially those that might affect his or her decision to participate in the next step of the process (If you have reached the interview's time limit, invite the person to call you later with further questions.);

- ask whether there is anything that has not been covered or is unclear;

- promote your organization, targeting the features of your organization that are most likely to appeal to the candidate;

- shake hands and make eye contact;

- walk the person to the door or to the next destination.

Some candidates will have questions about salary or benefits at this stage. In some organizations, the human resource department addresses these questions. Others allow the interviewer to disclose the salary or salary range.

Once the candidate has departed, immediately write down any additional notes or observations while they are still fresh in your mind.

Evaluating the Candidates

Once you've interviewed all the candidates, you and others involved in the hiring decision must make an objective evaluation of each one. A decision-making matrix such as the one shown in Appendix A can be a helpful tool for comparing the candidates to one another. (Note: You can download a printable decision-making matrix and other interactive tools from the Harvard Business Essentials Web site at: www.elearning.hbsp.org/businesstools.) Complete this form after you interview each job candidate for a particular position, entering a score for each of the key areas. By tallying the total scores and reviewing your interview notes from the interviews, you will reduce the chance of making a nonobjective evaluation.

Common Evaluation Mistakes

Even though you may take a structured, methodical approach to evaluating your candidates, the evaluation process is still, in the end, subjective. You can neutralize some of that subjectivity by avoiding:

- Being overly impressed with maturity or experience, or overly unimpressed by youth and immaturity

- Confusing a quiet, reserved, or calm demeanor for lack of motivation

- Mistaking the person's ability to play "the interview game," or his or her ability to talk easily, for intelligence or competence

- Allowing personal biases to influence your assessment (for example, you might be tempted to judge someone harshly because she reminds you of someone you dislike)

- Looking for a friend or for a reflection of yourself in the candidate

- Assuming that graduates of certain institutions or employees of certain organizations are automatically better qualified

- Giving too much weight to familiarity with the jargon of your business

- Focusing only on one or two key strengths and overlooking the absence of others

- Failing to value the motivation to get ahead

Reference Checks

Reference checks verify claims made by the candidate during the interview process and fill in information gaps. They can also provide valuable outside perspectives on the candidate and his or her potential fit with the position. Check references when you are near the end of your recruiting process and close to making a decision. But be sure to obtain permission from the candidates first to avoid affecting someone's current employment—for example, the applicant's company may have no idea that he or she is interviewing for a job elsewhere.

In checking references you have two aims. The first is to verify what the applicant has told you about his or her work experience: where, how long, last position held, and particular assignments. The second aim is learn about the applicant's successes and failures, work habits, strengths and weaknesses, and so forth.

The business of reference checking is critically important since it helps ensure that the job candidate has truthfully represented his position, work experience, and accomplishments. The comments of a reference can also provide another slant on the candidate's persona. Unfortunately, particularly in the United States, many companies are wary of saying much of anything about a current or former employee for fear of being sued for libel or slander if the employee fails to get a job because of something they said. So getting straightforward comments from some references may be difficult.

Here are some tips for checking references:

- Use the telephone to check references. Since nothing is written down, a person who might be wary of being sued for saying something negative about the applicant is more likely to give you a candid response. Don't check references via letter; you probably won't get much information.

- Take a little time to build rapport with the references; that will make them more comfortable with sharing information with you.

- Briefly describe the job that the candidate is applying for and ask if this is something for which the person would be well suited.

- Ask about the candidate's style, character, strengths, and weaknesses.

- Ask tough questions and follow up with detailed probes.

- Avoid asking vague questions, such as: "Did Jack do a good job

managing his department?" Instead, ask more specific questions, such as: "What was Jack best at?" "What did his subordinates like best about him?" "What did they like least?" "Are
there any jobs that would be inappropriate for Jack?" "What
kind of organizational environment would suit Jack best?"

- Let one reference lead to another. If a reference gives you some
  information, ask "Do you know anyone who could tell me
  about Jack's experience in this area?" The more people you talk
  to, the clearer a picture you will get.

Many people find reference checking a distasteful chore, and
give the task limited attention. Checking references for candidates "is
about as appetizing as eating fish eyes," says Pierre Mornell. But the
stakes are so high that you must make the effort and be persistent in
digging out the information—even though people may be unwill-
ing to share it. In his book, *Hiring Smart!*, Mornell offers this fast and
legal hint for reference checking:

> *Call references at what you assume will be their lunchtime—you want
> to reach an assistant or voice mail. If it's voice mail, leave this simple
> message. If it's an assistant, be sure that he or she understands the last
> sentence of your message. You say "John (or Jane) Jones is a candidate
> for (the position) in our company. Your name has been given as a refer-
> ence. Please call me back if the candidate was outstanding.*[3]

The results, says Mornell, are both immediate and revealing. "If
the candidate is outstanding or excellent, I guarantee that eight out
of ten people will respond quickly and want to help." In contrast, if
very few or no references return your call, their silence speaks vol-
umes about the candidate without making any derogatory or li-
belous statements.

Making the Decision and Offer

Résumés, interviews, and reference checks all inform the decision-
making process. At some point, you must ask yourself, "Do we have

enough information to make a good decision?" If the answer is "yes," then it's time to move ahead with the hiring decision. Rank your top three candidates, and then ask this question about each: "Do we want this person to work for us?" Remember that the goal of the hiring process is not to simply choose the "most qualified" of the existing applicants, but to hire a person who can help the organization meet its objectives.

Once you've answered both questions affirmatively, make an offer to the candidate who is most able and most likely to help your company meet its goals. If you do not have sufficient information to make a good decision, then determine exactly what additional information you and your colleagues need, how you will obtain it, and what uncertainties you can reasonably expect to reduce. To reduce important uncertainties you may need to call a candidate back for yet another interview, or you may need to do more reference checking.

The Job Offer

Be sure that you understand your organization's policy on who makes the job offer. In some organizations, the immediate supervisor or manager makes the offer. In others, it's the job of the human resource department.

Job offers are usually made in person or by telephone. After extending a verbal offer, you should also send a written confirmation. In both cases, make the offer with enthusiasm and a personal touch, perhaps by referring to something positive that you recall from the interview. Even as you make the offer, continue to gather information from the candidate regarding his or her concerns, the timing of the decision, and other organizations he or she may be considering.

The Offer Letter

An offer letter is an official document, so be sure to seek advice from the appropriate channels before sending it. Do *not* imply that the offer is an employment contract. Include important facts in the letter, including:

- Starting date

- Job title

- Expected responsibilities

- Compensation

- Benefits summary

- Time limit for responding to the offer

Don't Forget Process Improvement

This chapter has described hiring as a process with a number of identifiable steps. In this sense hiring is similar to other business processes: billing, order fulfillment, manufacturing, customer service, and so forth.

Like other processes, hiring should be the focus of continual improvement. Every major hiring experience should be followed by a postmortem in which participants evaluate the effectiveness of each process step, pinpoint weaknesses and seek their root causes, and identify opportunities for improvement. The individuals involved in hiring should ask the following:

- How effective is our approach to defining job requirements? Are the right people in the company involved? Are we more concerned with how the job *has been* designed than with how it *should be* designed?

- Is our current mix of recruiting methods producing an attractive mix of candidates? If it isn't, what can we do to attract more and better-qualified candidates?

- Is our method of screening applicants efficient and effective? What are best practices in this area?

- Does our interview process produce the information we need to make good hiring decisions? Is there consistent quality across interviewers and interview sessions? Do some interviewers need more training?

- Is our candidate evaluation process objective, rigorous, and consistent? How could we make it better?

- When we make a job offer, is the offer clear and compelling? When we strike out with a job offer, do we find out why our offer was rejected?

When an effort is made to improve the hiring process, the quality of your hires will likewise improve.

Summing Up

This chapter has described hiring as a process with a number of key steps:

- **Defining job requirements.** You have to know very clearly what you're hiring for, and the package of skills, experience, attitude, and personal characteristics that you and other people involved in the hiring process require.

- **Recruiting.** This step involves casting your net strategically in order to create a pool of qualified candidates. Screening résumés is part of this step.

- **Interviewing.** The interview process aims to provide both the interviewer and the job candidate with an opportunity to obtain the information they need to make the best possible decision. The best interviews have a core of questions asked to all candidates, and these provide a common base of comparison and evaluation later.

- **Evaluating the candidates.** Once all candidates have been interviewed, the people involved in the hiring decision must conduct an objective evaluation of each. Here, a decision-making

matrix can help to organize the interview notes and recollec-
tions of many people.

- **Making a decision and offer.** The last step of the hiring process
  is making the decision and extending a job offer. Always aim
  for the individual who can contribute the most to your organization's success.

Keeping the Best

Why Retention Matters

Key Topics Covered in This Chapter

- *Why retention matters to companies and their managers*

- *Why people stay—and why they leave*

- *Differentiating between individuals and employee segments*

- *Tips on managing for retention*

HIRING AND RETENTION are two sides of the same coin. They complement each other, and if both are done well, they produce what every company desperately needs: first-class human assets. In this chapter we will shift our focus from the hiring process to strategies for keeping the good people you already have.

If you did everything described in the previous chapter, and filled all your positions with only talented, hard-working people, you'd most likely have a considerable advantage over your competitors, since few companies ever accomplish this goal. But your hiring success would create another challenge: keeping those star employees on board. After all, if your human assets were measurably superior, other companies would notice and try to lure them away with higher pay, more authority, and more appealing work situations—perhaps the same inducements you used to recruit them! You'd find yourself on the defensive, forced to look at your own employment practices, benefits, and compensation scheme to determine if these were undermining bonds of loyalty between your company and the great people you've hired.

Retention is a challenge faced by many of the world's most admired companies. Consider the experience of many companies in the United States from 1992 to 2000. U.S. businesses enjoyed tremendous economic prosperity during this period, and just about every able-bodied person who wanted a job was enlisted in the work force. In many employment categories—particularly high-skilled areas such as IT, software development, electrical engineering, accounting,

and finance—demand outstripped supply, touching off what has become known as the "war for talent." Many companies recognized
that a lack of human talent was a serious constraint on future growth
and pulled all the stops in order to retain their most valuable employees. Ernst & Young went so far as to establish an Office of Retention with direct reporting responsibility to the CEO. Others set
up work-life balance programs to alleviate stress on the home front.
Casual dress regimens, on-site child care, and foosball tables prolifer-
ated. More than a few companies allowed employees to bring their
dogs to work. Books and magazine articles on "how to keep your
employees happy and productive" were cranked out by the score.

The great war for talent in the United States appeared to end
with the recession that hit the country in late 2000. But recessions
don't last forever, and most people recognized that the war for talent
would heat up again once the economy got back on track. And in
some sectors of the economy, the war never really subsided.

This chapter focuses on employee retention. It explains why it is
so important to your business—and why it is so challenging. It offers
insights into why people stay with their current employers and what
factors influence them to leave, and it offers suggestions on what you,
as a manager, can do to retain your best people.

Retention Matters

Retention is the converse of turnover (turnover being the sum of
voluntary and involuntary separations). Industrywide and company-
specific measures that track turnover rates reveal that most companies
surveyed by the Center for Organizational Research had turnover
rates in the 15 to 50 percent range, though a sizable minority enjoyed
single-digit turnover.

Retention isn't simply a "feel good" issue. The retention of good
employees matters for three important bottom-line reasons: (1) the
growing importance of intellectual capital; (2) a causal link between
employee tenure and customer satisfaction; and (3) the high cost of
employee turnover. Let's examine each of these in turn.

The Importance of Intellectual Capital

During the Industrial Age, a firm's physical assets—such as machinery, plants, and even land—determined how strongly it could compete. In the current "Knowledge Era," intellectual capital is what defines a company's competitive edge. Intellectual capital is the unique knowledge and skills that a company's work force possesses. Today's successful businesses win with innovative new ideas and top-notch products and services—all of which originate in the knowledge and skills of employees.

Whenever employees leave, your company loses their knowledge and their (often expensively) acquired skills. When those employees go to a competitor, the loss is compounded. Not only has your company been deprived of an important part of its knowledge base, your competitors have gained it—without having to invest the time and dollars in training that your company may have invested.

Retention and Customer Satisfaction

Everyone understands that customer satisfaction is one of the most —if not *the* most—important factors in business survival and growth. This is another reason that retention is so critical. Simply stated: *Employees who are satisfied with their work and their company are more likely to create satisfied customers.* Although this may be intuitively obvious, a growing body of research supports this correlation.

Retention and the Service-Profit Chain

During the early 1990s Harvard Business School professors James Heskett, Earl Sasser, and several associates developed a model that recognizes the role of employee satisfaction, loyalty, and retention in profitability.

Seven fundamental propositions form the links of the service-profit chain:

1. Customer loyalty drives profitability and growth. A 5 percent increase in customer loyalty can boost profits by 25 to 85 percent.

2. Customer satisfaction drives customer loyalty. Xerox found that "very satisfied" customers were six times more likely to repurchase company equipment than were customers who were merely "satisfied."

3. Value drives customer satisfaction. An insurer's efforts to deliver maximum value include funding a team that provides special services at the sites of major catastrophes. The company has one of the highest margins in its industry.

4. Employee productivity drives value. Nucor Corporation's production teams are the most productive in the steel industry. It's no coincidence that Nucor has created more value per employee for its shareholders than any other steelmaker over the past twenty years.

5. Employee loyalty drives employee productivity. One auto dealer's annual cost of replacing a sales rep who had eight years of experience with one who had less than a year was $432,000 in lost sales.

6. Employee satisfaction drives employee loyalty. In one company study, 30 percent of all dissatisfied employees expressed an intention to leave, compared to only 10 percent of all satisfied employees. Moreover, low employee turnover was found to be closely linked to high customer satisfaction.

7. Internal quality drives employee satisfaction. Service workers are happiest when they are empowered to make things right for customers and when they have responsibilities that add depth to their work.

SOURCE: James L. Heskett, Thomas O. Jones, Gary Loveland, W. Earl Sasser Jr., and Leonard A. Schlesinger, "Putting the Service-Profit Chain to Work," *Harvard Business Review*, March–April 1994, 164–172.

The Cost of Turnover

The high price of turnover is the third major reason that retention matters. Employee turnover involves three types of costs, each of which saps bottom-line results:

- Direct expenses, including the out-of-pocket costs of recruiting, interviewing, and training replacements. (In a tight labor market, replacements may require a higher salary than the people who are defecting—not to mention the potential cost of signing bonuses.)

- Indirect costs, such as the effect on workload, morale, and customer satisfaction. Will other employees consider quitting? Will customers follow the employee who left?

- Opportunity costs, including lost knowledge and the work that doesn't get done while managers and other employees focus on filling the slot and bringing the replacement up to speed.

What do these add up to? Estimates vary widely, in part because the cost of losing and replacing an employee depends on the individual and the industry involved. But it is rarely low. For employees in general, the U.S. Department of Labor estimates a turnover cost of about one-third the new person's salary. Among managerial and professional employees, the percentage increases dramatically. Generally, estimates are in the range of one to two times the departing employee's annual salary. Those figures mask lots of variability, however, much of it related to the effectiveness of the departing employee. The cost of losing a highly effective employee is obviously much higher than the cost of losing an average performer—even though the salaries and benefits of the two may be very similar.

Turnover Isn't All Bad

There is another side to the cost-of-turnover coin, however. The turnover of an incompetent employee may not produce *any* cost since the departure of such employees may actually eliminate certain hidden costs. Consider, for example, the cost of having mediocre or incompetent people in key positions. What is the cost of the poor decisions made by such employees? Author/consultant Bradford Smart has estimated the cost of an inept middle manager at roughly $1.2 million per year. The price tag goes up as you consider incompetence at the senior management level. And what is the cost associated with the poor morale and defections they create? That's anyone's guess.

Periodic turnover also creates vacancies you can use to move deserving employees up the career ladder. The same vacancies represent opportunities to bring new people with new skills and different experiences into the organization.

So don't make the mistake of thinking that you must reduce turnover at all costs. In some cases, turnover has a positive impact on the business.

Why People Stay

People stay with a company for many different reasons, including job security, a work culture that recognizes the importance of work-life balance, recognition for a job well done, flexible hours, or a sense of belonging. These reasons can vary widely from country to country. However, in cultures in which it's assumed that people may freely change jobs, the major motivations for staying are:

- **Pride in the organization.** People want to work for well-managed companies headed by skilled, resourceful leaders.

- **A respected supervisor.** The employee-supervisor relationship is extremely important. People are more likely to stay if they have a supervisor whom they respect and who is supportive of them. This is the factor over which you, as a manager, have the greatest control and the most numerous opportunities to boost retention.

- **Fair compensation.** People also want to work for companies that offer fair compensation. This includes not only competitive wages and benefits but also intangible compensation in the form of opportunities to learn, grow, and achieve. Your control of wages may be limited, but you can compensate the people you want to retain with interesting assignments.

- **Affiliation.** The chance to work with respected and compatible colleagues is another element that many people consider essential.

- **Meaningful work.** Finally, people want to work for companies that let them do the kinds of work that appeal to their deepest interests. Satisfying and stimulating work makes all of us more productive.

The findings of the McKinsey & Company "2000 War for Talent Survey" of middle and senior managers generally supported these findings. Authors Ed Michaels, Helen Handfield-Jones, and Beth Axelrod make a case from these and other findings that companies can attract and retain talented people if they pay attention to what they term the "employee value proposition," or EVP. EVP is the workplace equivalent to the value proposition that every company offers its customers: a measure of perceived value for a particular cost. The three suggest that if companies want to be more successful at attracting and retaining talent, they should evaluate and strengthen their value propositions to employees:

> To create a compelling employee value proposition, a company must provide the core elements that managers look for—exciting work, a great company, attractive compensation, and opportunities to develop. A few more perks, casual dress, or more generous health plans won't make the difference between a weak EVP and a strong one. If you want to substantially strengthen your company's EVP, be prepared to change things as fundamental as the business strategy, the organization structure, the culture, and even the caliber of leaders.[1]

Though the data on which Michaels et al. base their conclusions focused on managers and executives, it's likely that other employees will respond similarly.

Why People Leave

People also leave organizations for many different reasons, but primarily because one or more of the above conditions was either absent at the beginning or has since been eliminated. For example:

- **The company's leadership shifts.** Either the quality of top management's decisions declines, or new leaders—whom employees don't yet trust or feel comfortable with—take the helm.

- **Conflict exists with immediate supervisors.** People may also leave when their relationship with their bosses becomes stressful or problematic, and they don't see any other options in their company. (See "Managers and Supervisors Are Key" for more on this topic.)

- **Close friends leave.** One or more colleagues whom an employee particularly likes and respects leaves the firm, thus taking away a meaningful affiliation link.

- **An unfavorable change of responsibilities has occurred.** A person's job responsibilities change so that the work no longer appeals to his or her deepest interests or provides meaning or stimulation.

- **Problems with work–life balance are present.** Employees whose workplace responsibilities separate them from friends and family for extended periods eventually lose interest in their jobs.

Managers and Supervisors Are Key

You can have terrific pay and benefits, employee-friendly policies, and all the other things that induce loyalty and retention, but a few rotten apples can spoil the barrel. Specifically, a bad manager can neutralize every retention scheme you put in place.

Gallup researchers Marcus Buckingham and Curt Coffman put it this way:

Managers trump companies. It's not that . . . employee-focused initiatives are unimportant. It's just that your immediate manager is more important. She defines and pervades your work environment. . . . [I]f your relationship with your manager is fractured, then no amount of in-chair massaging or company-sponsored dog walking

Continued

will persuade you to stay and perform. It is better to work for a great manager in an old-fashioned company than for a terrible manager in a company offering an enlightened, company-focused culture.[a]

Beth Axelrod, Helen Handfield-Jones, and Ed Michaels of McKinsey & Company reached a similar conclusion about bad managers, which they describe as "C performers." "[K]eeping C performers in leadership positions lowers the bar for every-one—a clear danger for any company that wants to create a performance-focused culture. C performers hire other C per-formers, and their continued presence discourages the people around them, makes the company a less attractive place for highly talented people, and calls in question the judgment of senior leaders."[b] (We have more on C performers and how to handle them in chapter 8.)

While many say that the company culture is what matters in retention, the culture of operating units is what really matters to the people who work in them. If the boss is a jerk or an incom-petent, the best people will leave.

[a] Marcus Buckingham and Curt Coffman, *First, Break All The Rules: What the World's Greatest Managers Do Differently* (New York: Simon & Schuster, 1999), 34.

[b] Beth Axelrod, Helen Handfield-Jones, and Ed Michaels, "A New Game for C Players," *Harvard Business Review,* January 2002, 83.

Market–Wise Retention

Retention of human capital is an important management function, but it should never become an end in itself. Your goal should not be to retain everyone or to do whatever it takes to reduce employee turnover, but to retain those people who truly add value and are dif-ficult and costly to replace—in other words, to practice market-wise retention. As previously mentioned, turnover among employees who demonstrate poor or mediocre performance can actually be a positive thing: the vacancies they create give you an opportunity to hire people with the potential to make greater contributions.

The first step toward market-wise retention is to identify the individuals and employee segments most critical to the success of your organization. So, within your unit, make a list of the individuals who:

- provide formal or informal leadership to others;

- consistently create excellent results;

- contribute practical and valuable new ideas;

- require little or no supervision to accomplish their tasks;

- facilitate the work of others;

- act as important information transfer "nodes" within the company;

- have unique knowledge or skills that would be costly and time-consuming to replace; or

- could do the company great harm if they defected to direct competitors.

Also give some thought to the employee *segments* that are most essential. Think about the employee segments in your operation that are essential to the operation but in short supply; create the most disruption when they defect; are most costly to recruit and train; and control the company's link to customers.

Once you've identified the individual employees and employee segments that have the highest value, be sure that they receive the bulk of retention resources and attention.

Compensation

Most people in the know give compensation a low rating as a retention strategy. Compensation matters in the sense that you cannot recruit or retain desirable employees if they view their compensation as unfair or noncompetitive. Even people who are more dedicated to their crafts or professions than to money see their compensation as an indication of the organization's appreciation of their contributions and abilities. If they feel undervalued, they will walk.

Nor is compensation a reliable motivator. Years ago, Frederick Herzberg, the tribal elder of motivation, found that the incentives employers most commonly use to motivate—including pay raises—produce temporary performance improvements at best.[2] The limited value of pay as a retention tool is corroborated by various studies. Clearly, other strategies have greater impact on retention.

Peter Cappelli, a human resources expert and professor at the Wharton School, offers these pieces of advice for market-wise compensation:

- Pay "hot skills" premiums to employees with crucial, rare expertise. This keeps them in place for critical periods—for example, the late design stages of a key product. Stop premiums when the skills become more available or less important to your business.

- Pay signing bonuses in stages—for example, pay out the new CEO's sign-on bonus over five years.[3]

You may or may not have much say about companywide pay and bonus policies, but you can use performance evaluation to determine who should receive the lion's share of pay and bonuses.

Job Redesign

Job redesign is another retention strategy. If you can identify the elements that create satisfaction and dissatisfaction within a particular job, you may be able to split off the dissatisfying tasks entirely and give them to other individuals who will appreciate the work. Outsourcing unwanted tasks is another solution, and something that every company practices to one extent or another. The big securities dealers on Wall Street, for example, don't ask their traders and clerical personnel to clean out the restrooms and vacuum the carpets before they go home at night. They outsource those tasks to commercial cleaning companies. Your company does the same.

So, if you experience unacceptable turnover in a key job that is difficult and costly to refill, put that job under a microscope and ask:

- Which aspects of this job create employee dissatisfaction? (Ask several employees directly.)

- If we separated objectionable tasks from the job, would we need to add something else to keep it a "whole" job? And what would that something else be?

- Assuming that someone must do the objectionable tasks, what alternatives exist for handling them?

- Which is more costly to the organization, job redesign (and its consequences) or the current rate of turnover in the key job?

General Strategies for Retention

So what can managers do to keep as many good employees as possible? Here's a short list that will cover most of the bases.

1. **Get people off to a good start.** This begins with hiring people who are suited to their jobs and making sure that they understand what they are getting into. A good start also begins with a new-employee orientation that makes people feel welcomed and part of the group.

2. **Create a great environment—with bosses whom people respect.** Managers often assume that company policies and corporate culture determine the working environment. They do, to an extent. But policies can be circumvented. In any case, the atmosphere in a department or unit is more important to individual employees than the culture of the corporation as a whole.

   Bad bosses are not conducive to a great environment. How many of your unit's managers or supervisors are repellent to their reports? How many have temper tantrums, berate their subordinates in public, blame others for their own failures, or never have the sense to say "Thanks, you're doing a good job"? If your managers or supervisors are repellent, count on every employee with marketable skills to leave.

In the end, it's better to replace bad managers and supervisors than to replace an endless stream of good employees.

3. **Share information.** Freely dispensing information—about the business, about financial performance, about strategies and plans—tells employees that you trust them, that they are important partners, and that you respect their ability to understand and contribute to the business as a whole.

4. **Give people as much autonomy as they can handle.** Many people enjoy working with a minimum of supervision. So give your employees as long a leash as they can handle. Doing so will make them happy and make your job as manager easier.

5. **Challenge people to stretch.** Most people—particularly the ones you want most to retain—enjoy a challenge and the feeling that you've entrusted them with bigger responsibilities than they had a right to expect. So put the people you want most to retain into jobs that will make them stretch—and give them the support they need to succeed.

6. **Be flexible.** Flexible work arrangements are highly successful in retaining employees. To be sure, not every manager has the authority to create whole new work arrangements. But nearly everybody can allow some on-the-spot flexibility, letting employees rearrange work to care for a sick child, for example, or to keep a doctor's appointment. Today's harried employees value that kind of flexibility.

7. **Design jobs to encourage retention.** Nothing is more soul-deadening for an intelligent employee than a job that is too repetitive, too isolated, insufficiently challenging, or downright unpleasant. So if you see unacceptably high turnover in a critical job category, take a good look at what you're asking people in that job to do every day. You may be able to cure the turnover problem through job redesign: adding variety to a repetitive job, engaging isolated employees in occasional team projects, upping the challenge, and so forth. If a job involves one or more repugnant tasks, consider eliminating or outsourcing those tasks.

Tips for Detecting Potential Defectors

Are some of your people considering leaving? B. Lynn Ware, founder of the retention consulting firm ITS, Inc., counsels clients to watch for early signs of dissatisfaction and disaffection, including the following:

- A change in behavior, such as coming in later or leaving earlier

- A decline in performance

- Sudden complaints from a person who hasn't been a complainer

- Wistful references to other companies (for example, "I heard of this guy who got a $30,000 signing bonus at XYZ Company.")

- Withdrawal behavior (for example, an employee who had always participated in meetings, or volunteered for projects, suddenly stays in the background or does just enough to get by)

- Talk about "burnout"

If you see one of these warning signals, get right on it. Arrange to meet with the employee as soon as possible. Use probing questions to identify the source of the problem. Indicate that you value him or her as an employee, and ask how you can work together to create a better work experience.

SOURCE: "Employee Retention: What Managers Can Do," *Harvard Management Update*, April 2000, 2.

8. **Identify potential defectors early.** Great work environments and great jobs are a matter of opinion; what challenges one person may terrify another. You won't know how well you're doing on either score unless you ask.

9. **Be a retention-oriented manager.** Never forget that part of your responsibility as a manager is to ensure proper staffing in your unit. Retaining good and excellent performers is part of

that job. So look at how you manage people and how you schedule workflow. Are you the kind of boss who manages in ways that encourage the best people to stay, or are you unknowingly driving them away?

The Role of Work–Life Balance

Work–life balance was one of the hottest business topics prior to the 2000–2003 economic downturn in the United States. And despite the shock of recession-driven layoffs, it is an issue that refuses to go away. The reason that it won't is because work–life balance is a core element of employee satisfaction, loyalty, and productivity. This means that if you provide a workplace in which employees can effectively balance the requirements of work and their personal lives, retention will be less of an issue. And if you develop a reputation in the labor market as a place that supports work–life balance, you'll have an edge in hiring good people. Work–life balance isn't just a "feel good" issue, or a perk that will cost your company money. It translates into better business performance.

Work–life balance is a major issue today because so many people are fed up with long days, paltry vacations, evenings spent in hotel rooms, and weekend e-mails from the boss. Many companies have gotten the message and have responded with programs that help their employees balance the two sides of their lives.

At first blush, you'd think that every concession toward work–life balance would represent a cost to the sponsoring company. But as Stewart Friedman, Perry Christensen, and Jessica DeGroot explained in a widely read *Harvard Business Review* article, work–life balance can be approached from a "win–win" perspective, and not as a zero-sum game. These researchers offer three principles for breaking through the zero-sum game:[4]

1. **Make sure that employees understand business priorities and encourage them to be equally clear about their personal priorities.** The work of the organization must get done, and work–life

balance should not be an excuse for letting it slide. Alternatively, work cannot be an excuse for letting important personal matters slide. Friedman, Christensen, and DeGroot counsel managers to be clear about company goals and performance expectations. At the same time, they encourage employees to be

Tips on Work-Life Balance

Taking our cue from the "three principles" of work-life balance described above, here are a few things you can do to make work-life balance a win–win situation:

- Give employees specific goals, but also greater autonomy over how they achieve them. Say, "You are responsible for conducting a customer survey and producing a complete report between now and mid-March. I'd like you to develop a plan for handling that."

- Give more attention to results than to how, where, and when the work gets done.

- Get to know your employees and coworkers on a more personal level. Do they have civic obligations that need tending? Do they have children or aging parents to support? Do they have other skills that might benefit the company? As workplace researchers found many decades ago, simply *showing an interest* in employees as individuals can have a positive impact on morale and motivation.

- Encourage people to find new and better ways of meeting their responsibilities. For example, sales managers and product development people may discover that a $5,000 investment in teleconferencing equipment could save the company $15,000 each year in travel expenses—and save each of them from hundreds of hours of unproductive travel time, and many nights away from home.

clear about their goals as family members and as individuals. Once everyone's cards are on the table, schedules and assignments can usually be arranged in ways that satisfy both sides.

2. **Recognize and support employees as "whole people" with important roles outside the workplace.** Managers can only deal with work-life conflict if they understand and show some interest in the nonworking lives of their employees. And showing a sincere interest creates trust and loyalty.

3. **Continually experiment with how work gets done.** Smart managers know that work processes must be periodically rethought and redesigned for greater efficiency and effectiveness. Work-life balance provides opportunities to experiment with these processes.

So, according to Friedman, Christensen, and DeGroot, work-life balance doesn't have to be a zero-sum game. Managed correctly, work-life balance can improve morale, increase productivity, *and* help you hire and retain the best employees. (See "Tips on Work-Life Balance.")

Telework

Many companies have found that *telework* is an effective tool for creating work-life balance. Telework describes work done by employees in locations other than their regular offices, facilitated by telecommunications and Internet capabilities. The International Telework Association & Council (ITAC) estimates that some 20 million U.S. employees were involved in some form of telework in 2001.

Proponents of telework point to measurable cost savings and benefits, including lower real-estate costs, greater employee productivity, greater employee loyalty and job satisfaction, and lower personnel turnover. And the teleworkers themselves report that it helps them balance work and personal responsibilities. AT&T, which has used telework heavily since the early 1990s, conducted a survey in 2000 of 1,238 managers and found that teleworkers put in more hours. Respondents indicated that they worked at least one hour more per day; were more productive; were more loyal; and found greater satisfaction in their work. Two-thirds of these managers reported that the company's telework policies made their job of retention and attraction notably easier.

AT&T also reported saving $25 million annually in real estate costs through full-time teleworkers.[5] These remarkable findings are not unique to AT&T. But before you rush out and advocate a telework program, your company or unit should think through a number of questions, including:

- Which jobs are appropriate for telework?

- What are the legal, regulatory, insurance, and technology issues? (Individual stockbrokers, for example, cannot work from an unsupervised office of a broker-dealer.)

- How will you supervise teleworkers and ensure accountability?

- Will employees worry that becoming a teleworker will negatively affect their chances for promotions and other recognition?

Despite claims on its behalf, telework is not appropriate for every organization. In an article for *Harvard Business Review*, Mahlon Apgar addressed this question, explaining that programs such as telework are most appropriate when companies are

- committed to new ways of operating;

- more informational than industrial;

- dynamic, nonhierarchical, technologically advanced;

- not command-driven;

- willing to invest in tools and training.[6]

Telework also requires adaptation on the part of managers and supervisors. After all, their subordinates will not be under their watchful eyes. Who's to know if they are working or watching *Seinfeld* reruns? The remedy, according to most experts, is for managers to focus on results instead of activities. That means setting clear goals for individual teleworkers, making sure that they understand those goals, and setting up a system for monitoring progress in short-term stages. Managers must also integrate teleworkers into the larger group; otherwise people may become isolated and out of touch.

Telework clearly presents new challenges for managers, but the benefits—especially in terms of work-life balance and retention—can be substantial.

Flexible Work Schedules

Flexible scheduling is another mechanism for helping employees achieve work-life balance and, by extension, keeping them with your organization. Flexible scheduling allows individual employees to work something other than the usual nine-to-five, forty-hour, five-day week. This creates opportunities for people to work even as they accommodate the needs of young children, infirm relatives, and so forth.

Many people favor flexible schedules. This is something that the accounting and consulting firm Deloitte & Touche learned through research and practice. As of June 2001, more than 1,100 of the firm's professionals had opted for some form of formal flexible work arrangements. Twenty of those were partners. According to Deloitte's employee surveys, 90 percent of professionals on flexible work arrangements indicated satisfaction with their arrangements.[7] Here are some typical flex-schedule arrangements used in business today:

- **Reduced–time schedules.** For example, an employee works from ten o'clock to five o'clock in order to accommodate her need to drive her children to school in the morning.

- **Seasonal schedules.** For example, a tax specialist works sixty-hour weeks from January through April to accommodate the tax-filing crunch, then works thirty-hour weeks for the balance of the year.

- **Compressed schedules.** For example, to accommodate his weekend acting vocation, a computer technician puts in forty hours Monday through Thursday, leaving Fridays free for rehearsals.

Summing Up

This chapter has described major issues relating to employee retention and highlighted ways in which managers can make a difference. In particular:

- Retention matters because high turnover creates high replacement costs and is clearly associated with low levels of customer satisfaction, customer loyalty, and lost revenues.

- People stay with their employers when they see the organization as a source of pride and affiliation, when they respect their supervisors, when they are fairly compensated, and when they perceive their work as meaningful.

- People seek greener pastures when leadership changes unfavorably, when they are in conflict with their immediate superiors, when close friends depart, and when their responsibilities change in ways that they do not favor.

- Managers should be less concerned with turnover than with retaining people who truly add value to the organization and its customers.

- Programs that enhance work-life balance generally help to increase employee satisfaction and reduce turnover.

4

Delegating with Confidence

Avoid Being Overworked and Overwhelmed

Key Topics Covered in This Chapter

- *The benefits of delegating*

- *Signs that you should do more delegating or more effective delegating*

- *Guidelines for effective delegating*

- *Approaches to delegation*

- *Preparing to delegate*

- *Making the assignment*

- *Monitoring performance*

- *Learning through after-action review*

MANY MANAGERS FEEL overwhelmed with too many problems and too much to do. Are you one of them? Do you find yourself running out of time while your subordinates are running out of work? If you do, you should examine your approach to delegating work.

The job of management is to get results through people and other resources. Among other things, that means delegating many tasks to others. *Delegation* is the assignment of a specific task or project by one person to another, and the assignee's commitment to complete the task or project. When you delegate, you not only transfer work to another person; you also transfer accountability for completing that work to stated standards.

Delegation is one of the most important skills demonstrated by successful managers, and one often neglected by "overworked" managers. Effective delegators spend less time "doing" and more time planning work assignments, organizing resources for delegatees, and coaching people who need help. This chapter explains the timeless principles of delegating, and practical ideas for applying them today.[1]

Benefits of Delegating

Effective delegation can have real benefits for you, your people, and your organization. Let's start with you. When you delegate, you reduce your workload and stress level by removing tasks from your to-do list that others are qualified to handle. This will give you more time to focus on activities that require your unique skills and authority: planning, business analysis, controlling operations, obtaining resources, and dealing with key people problems.

Delegating improves the level of trust between you and your staff. To get trust, you must first give trust, and delegating is one way to do so. The message in delegation is, "I trust you to get the job done." It also helps everyone learn how to achieve goals through cooperative effort.

Lastly, delegating is an effective way of "testing" a staff member's capabilities prior to offering a promotion. Assign a series of tasks to an employee and you'll soon have a very good estimate of that person's strengths and weaknesses.

Good employees likewise benefit from the delegation of tasks and projects. Every assignment is an opportunity to learn how to accept responsibility, to plan work, and to enlist the collaboration of others. In effect, delegating gives employees experience with managerial work. And developing people is part of your job.

Delegation makes some managers uneasy. They fear losing control of staff and projects, and worry that they're abdicating their responsibilities. Sometimes they just believe that it's more efficient to do the job themselves: "By the time I explained the job to Henry, I could do it by myself." And maybe they could. In the long term, however, every manager must share some control and teach others how to do the work. Other excuses for insufficient delegation include:

"I don't have confidence in my staff." These managers should start delegating small tasks; this will allow them to build confidence gradually.

"I like to have things done my way." This should not be an impediment. Managers can get things done their way by communicating preferences and standards. That's more efficient than trying to do everything by themselves.

"My staff will resent the additional work." Maybe so. But good employees appreciate opportunities to take responsibility for important work. And these are the ones you want to keep and develop.

Delegation and Empowerment

The term "empowerment" has been bandied about liberally over the past five or ten years. Is this term synonymous with delegation? If not, how is it different?

Delegation implies that the manager retains authority, control, and responsibility. To do otherwise would be abdication. The manager says, "This is what I'd like you to do." Even if he or she describes the required ends without specifying the means, the manager will probably review the employee's plan, and monitor performance as it unfolds. In the absence of authority, control, and responsibility, delegation is abandonment. Empowerment, on the other hand, shifts power and responsibility to the recipient. The empowered individual or team has the authority to determine the means and takes responsibility for results. Self-discipline and accountability are substitutes for the manager's control.

"People expect me to be the problem solver and decision maker." That's true to an extent, but problem solvers and decisions makers are needed at all levels. Make it clear to your staff that your role is to support them in making decisions for themselves. Also, make it clear that some delegated tasks represent opportunities to do new and interesting work.

Warning Signs

Here are some "warning signs" that a manager's delegating skills require sharpening. Do any apply to you?

- Your in-box is always full.

- You are regularly working overtime on tasks that "only you can do."

- Delegated assignments are often incomplete and deadlines are missed.

- Direct reports feel that they lack the authority or resources to complete assignments.

- You second-guess staff decisions and personally rework staff assignments.

- Direct reports feel unprepared to carry out assigned tasks.

- You frequently intervene in projects assigned to others.

- Morale is low and staff turnover is rising.

- People are not taking responsibility for the tasks you delegate.

Guidelines for Effective Delegating

It is very important to establish the right tone and environment for effective delegating. You can do this if you follow these guidelines:

- Be very clear on what you want done, and on when and how results will be measured. Ambiguity on your part will lead to a disappointing experience.

- Encourage staff to tell you about their special interests at work and time availability for new projects.

- Build a sense of shared responsibility for the unit's overall goals.

- Avoid dumping only tedious or difficult jobs on your subordinates. Instead, delegate tasks that spark interest and can be enjoyable.

- Provide career opportunities for others by delegating functions that have high visibility within the company.

- Delegate to people whose judgment and competence you trust. This, of course, requires that you know your subordinates and their capabilities very well.

- Recognize that delegation is a learning experience for your staff, so offer training or coaching as needed.

- Develop trust in less-skilled staff members by delegating very structured assignments. Then provide the support they need to develop increased competence.

- Whenever possible, delegate an entire project or function, not just a small piece; this will increase motivation and commitment.

- Follow up, monitor, and provide feedback.

- Maintain open lines of communication. Say, "Let me know if you run into problems you cannot handle."

Approaches to Delegation

Delegation can be carried out in several ways. It is usually best to delegate responsibility for an entire task, project, or function to one person. Dividing it among several people will create a condition in which no one "owns" the job. Even if the delegatee subdelegates parts of the job to others, the locus of responsibility will remain clear.

Delegating by task is the easiest approach and a good place to start if you're new to this. It involves assigning specific tasks or subtasks to staff members. These might include writing a report, conducting research, or planning a meeting.

Delegating by project represents a higher level. A project involves a group of tasks associated with the achievement of a specific objective. Delegating by project increases the scope of the delegated assignment and generally requires a staff member who can handle a wide range of responsibilities. Examples of project delegations might include developing a new employee handbook, conducting a customer survey, or training other employees on a new piece of computer software.

Managers with large numbers of direct reports may choose to delegate assignments by function. A *function* refers to groups of tasks and projects that are all related to one ongoing activity such as sales, marketing, or training. In this approach, each function is delegated to one staff member who provides the manager with regular updates on activities within that function.

Preparing to Delegate

As you prepare to delegate, first determine which tasks you want to delegate. When that's done, consider the skills and capabilities required to complete the assignment successfully. Finally, you need to match the assignment with the most appropriate staff member.

What (and What Not) to Delegate

Is your workload crushing you? If it is, assess that workload. Determine which parts of it others can handle. Be open to delegating these, even if they are jobs you enjoy doing and don't want to give up. Some of those chores could provide variety and motivational challenges to the right individuals.

Some assignable jobs require specific training or experience. And if a task is too important to assign to others, think about a sharing of responsibility. For instance, if you have a brochure development project, identify one person with excellent writing skills to write the text; team this person with another person who has graphics, layout, and production skills. Here's another example:

One of Colin's responsibilities during the first half of this year was to design, administer, and document an annual employee survey. This was a big job, but not so big that Colin couldn't handle it himself—as he had in previous years.

But times had changed. Now that he was the department manager, Colin had very little time to spare. Yes, he could still do this job himself, but that would involve many weekends in the office and take time away from other pressing responsibilities.

In the end, Colin formed a task force around the survey. He provided leadership and oversight, and two new employees with good analytical skills were assigned the time-consuming parts of the job. When the final survey report was circulated within the company, it bore the names of Colin and his two helpers.

Of course, not all tasks can or should be delegated. As a manager, you should retain responsibility for the following tasks:

- Planning, directing, and motivating your people

- Employee performance evaluation

- Complex customer negotiations

- Tasks requiring your specific technical skills

- Hiring, firing, and career development

Other nonassignable tasks will depend on your circumstances.

Task Analysis

Once you've identified tasks or projects suitable for delegation, determine the work involved and skills required. Task analysis involves answering these three questions:

1. What thinking skills are needed for this job? (For example, problem-solving ability, logical thinking, decision making, planning, creative design.)

2. What activities must be performed and what equipment is needed? (For example, filing, using a word processor, organizing, training, developing.)

3. What interpersonal skills are needed to complete the assignment? (For example, speaking with suppliers, negotiating for resources, consulting with experts.)

The Right Person for the Job

Once you have identified the assignment and the required skills, ask yourself, "Which of my subordinates is the right person for the job?" As you ponder this question, be sure to consider the following:

- Any previously expressed desires by staffers for growth and development that could be addressed with this assignment. Ask yourself who has shown initiative and asked for a new challenge.

- The staff member's availability. Don't pile work on people who are already loaded to the limit—even if these people are conscientious and reliable.

- The level of assistance a staff member will need from you to complete the assignment.

- How long the staff member has been on the job. Avoid loading new employees with added assignments until they are comfortable with their core jobs.

- The number of previous assignments you have delegated to that person. Try to delegate tasks among all staff members to avoid any feelings of favoritism.

- The possibility of dividing the task between two or more people to make the best use of skills.

You'll be in a better position to select the right people if you routinely keep track of special skill sets that you may need to call upon for special projects. For example, someone who can simplify abstract concepts might make a good trainer, while good organizational abilities would be important for someone overseeing operations.

Making the Assignment

Once you've matched the right person with the task, you need to communicate the proposition and deliver sufficient authority to do the job. This should always be done in a face-to-face meeting in which you describe the assignment and secure the employee's acceptance of the task. Open communication and trust are critical factors in this interaction. To achieve both, do the following:

- Clearly describe the task, project, or function.

- Define its purpose and how it fits into the big picture.

- Review the scope of the employee's responsibilities.

- Identify other personnel who will be involved, if applicable, and describe their roles.

- Discuss feasible deadlines for completion.

- Establish agreed-upon standards of performance, measures of success, and levels of accountability.

- Set firm metrics for such things as quality, time, and cost.

- Be clear about the employee's accountability in meeting the standards you have agreed upon.

- Define the resources and support that will be available.

- Identify any materials and physical resources needed to complete the assignment and confirm their availability.

- If necessary, allocate additional staff to assist in meeting the assigned goals.

- Ask the employee what support she thinks she may need from you throughout the assignment.

- If special training or coaching is needed, discuss how it will be given.

- Agree on a date to review progress.

In granting authority to a staff member, it is important to establish clear guidelines and expectations from the start. The amount of authority you choose to give an individual depends upon his capabilities and your confidence in him. You will want to assess the staff member's past performance as a decision maker. You'll also want to determine the minimum amount of authority needed to complete the assignment successfully.

After you have determined the level of authority you will delegate, be sure to communicate your decision to everyone involved in the assignment or affected by it.

"How can I avoid having staff members feel like I'm dumping work on them?" Some managers make the mistake of pushing every chore onto the one or two who either (a) have demonstrated that they can get things done, or (b) accept added work—unlike others—without having a tantrum. These reliable individuals may be flattered by their boss's confidence in them—at least for a while. But too much of this can create a backlash, especially when those who take on the added work don't feel that they are being compensated for it. "Why does she always ask me to handle these chores? I'm not the only person in this department." Resentment can lead to malingering or defection.

You can avoid this problem by balancing the assignment of tasks seen as tedious or difficult with tasks and projects that spark staff interest, are enjoyable, and gain them recognition by others. Split tasks or projects seen as dirty work among more than one staff member as well as yourself to promote a sense of shared responsibility for jobs seen as boring or unpleasant. Seek input from your staff as to the types of assignments they find interesting and challenging.

Control, Monitoring, and Feedback

The biggest challenge for the delegating manager is to ensure that the subordinate does not fail. The best way to do that is to maintain an adequate level of control by providing target completion dates and regular monitoring of progress. When you say, "I want this done by next Friday," you are maintaining control of the work, which is your duty as manager. When you add that "I'd like to meet with you on Wednesday afternoon, just to see how you're progressing and to discuss any problems," you are monitoring the delegated assignment. Monitoring provides opportunities to give coaching and feedback, another key responsibility of every manager.

Depending on the number and complexity of assignments you've delegated, you may use an assignment log to track all projects, tasks, or functions within your department. Other managers use large wall calendars to keep track of delegated assignments and to give a visual sense of progress. Still others require periodic written status reports to keep up-to-date on the assignments they have delegated.

In monitoring, be alert to early signs of trouble. When your subordinate hits an impenetrable barrier or begins to fall behind, intervention may be necessary. Of course, you don't want to solve every problem that you've delegated to others—and which they have accepted. Doing so would defeat your purpose. So use coaching, encouragement, and added resources as you see fit to help them help themselves. Provide this support without being intrusive, especially for subordinates who are committed to learning how to handle things by themselves, and without dictating the "right way." Remember that accomplishing the task is more important than your idea of *how* it should be accomplished.

After–Action Review

Use completed assignments as opportunities for learning—for both you and your subordinate. The two of you should evaluate what went right, what went wrong, and how things might have been done differently or better. In addition,

- ask for the employee's opinion about how this delegation worked for him or her;

- recognize the employee's achievements and provide positive reinforcement for tasks done well;

- use the experience to support the employee's growth through ongoing coaching or additional training as needed.

You should also ensure that your employee is recognized for his or her good work, not only by you, but by peers, your manager, and customers, as appropriate.

Tips for Delegating Effectively

- Recognize the capabilities of your staff.

- Focus on results—let go of any urge to dictate how tasks should be accomplished.

- Use delegation to develop the skills of your staff or to position people favorably with senior management.

- Always delegate to the lowest possible level.

- Explain assignments clearly and provide the resources needed for successful completion.

- Provide feedback to your staff and support them through their mistakes.

Summing Up

- If you are overwhelmed with work and your subordinates are not, you need to do more delegating. If the tasks you delegate are done poorly or late, you need to become a more effective delegator.

- Effective delegators have several things in common. Among them are: being clear in what they want done, delegating both tedious and stimulating tasks, and careful monitoring.

- It is usually best to delegate responsibility for an entire job to one person. That invests ownership of the job in a single person.

- Don't delegate tasks that are clearly your responsibility—that's not delegation, it's abdication.

- Use a face-to-face meeting when you delegate—and always give sufficient authority and resources to get the job done.

- Monitor and be ready to intervene if the delegatee gets off track.

- Use an after-action review to learn from the delegating experience.

Managing Your Time

Making the Most Out of Your Day

Key Topics Covered in This Chapter

- *Analyzing how you are spending your time*

- *Using key goals to identify which tasks should have priority*

- *Techniques for scheduling priority tasks*

- *Strategies for combating time-wasters*

THREE LONG meetings. At least a dozen phone calls—some total time-wasters. Lunch with the boss scrapped at the last minute ("Let's reschedule for next Tuesday"). Two reports to write. Work on the upcoming presentation to senior management. Simmering conflict between two rival employees to deal with. And it's already time to start next year's budgeting process.

Does this sound like a day from your calendar? If it does, then your day is like that of most other managers—filled with meetings, fragmented activities, interruptions, and spontaneous brushfires to extinguish. Handling these would not be a problem except for one hard reality: There are only twenty-four hours in a day. Indeed, finding time to get all their work done is one of the biggest challenges faced by managers.

This chapter will help you make the most of your time. You'll learn to identify the jobs that are most important—and least important—and you'll discover how you can focus your time on the most critical tasks and avoid time-wasters.

Time management is the process of controlling your life through your use of the 168 hours that you—and everyone else—has in each week. Managing that time will force you to be explicit about what you value in your professional and personal life, and help you direct your efforts accordingly. Mastering time management will help you balance the many pressures on your time and achieve your goals. That balance will help you avoid burnout and stress, and make you more effective.

Understanding How You Spend Your Time

Where does your time go? Like your household budget, you cannot plan and control your time assets unless you understand your current spending habits. How much of your time is spent on paperwork? In meetings? On the telephone? In travel? Get an accurate picture of how you are spending your time and you'll know whether it is being spent effectively or it is wasted on activities that do not further your goals.

To understand your time-spending patterns, try logging your activities for at least a day or two, preferably for an entire a week. Be as vigilant as possible in recording the length of time spent on each activity. When you have completed your log, tally your activities into categories:

- Telephone calls

- Scheduled appointments

- Drop-in visits

- Meetings

- Administrative work

- Report writing and analysis

- Travel

- Breaks

- Meals

- Personal chores done at work

Once you have logged your activities into categories, examine the time log to identify patterns of time usage. Perhaps you spend a lot of time Monday mornings on the telephone, or you tend to have unexpected visitors after lunch. Perhaps meetings cluster late in the week. Then ask, "Does this time usage match my key responsibilities?" Spending most of the day on telephone calls may be fine if you're in sales, but not if you're in accounting.

How Managers Spend Their Days

In his classic article on the work of managers, Henry Mintzberg underscored the frenetic pace of modern managerial life. "Study after study has shown that managers work at an unrelenting pace, that their activities are characterized by brevity, variety, and discontinuity, and that they are strongly oriented to action and dislike reflective activities." They spend almost no time sitting quietly in contemplation of the future. Instead, they are on and off the phone every few minutes, running into and out of meetings, and dealing with problems that seem to appear out of nowhere.

Like other managers, the time available to CEOs is highly fragmented. Mintzberg found that the typical CEO allocates his or her time among various stakeholders as follows:

Directors	7%
Peers	16%
Clients, suppliers, associates	20%
Independents and others	8%
Subordinates	48%

SOURCE: Henry Mintzberg, "The Manager's Job: Folklore and Fact," *Harvard Business Review*, March–April 1990, 164, 169.

Then look for the payoff. You don't want to spend 50 percent of your time on activities that have minimal payoff in terms of your responsibilities. Perhaps many of these activities can be delegated. Think about whether each activity you pursued supported your goals and priorities or whether it was a time-waster. Then, develop ways to avoid the time-wasters.

Let Your Goals Guide Your Way

Goals are critical to effective time management; they point the way to how you should be spending your time. Focus on your goals and you will know what is most important to accomplish on a daily and weekly basis. Goals will guide your time usage by helping you identify the specific tasks you need to pursue and those you should *not* pursue. We recommend the following three steps to using goals to manage time:

Step 1. Break each goal into a manageable set of tasks. Review each goal, then list all of the tasks required to achieve it. Put the tasks in the correct sequential order.

Step 2. Estimate how much of your time each task will require. Knowing how much time will be required isn't always clear. But if you have completed a similar task before, you can often use that as a basis for a time estimate. If an activity is new to you, consult with colleagues, your manager, or others who may be able to help you with a time estimate. Then add a 10–20 percent cushion to allow for unanticipated problems. You should also establish a deadline for the completion of each task or activity. For more complex activities, set up milestones along the way to track your progress.

Step 3. Prioritize. Once you are satisfied that your list of tasks is complete, assign A, B, or C priorities to each one. The priorities you assign should reflect the importance of the goal that each task supports:

A priorities are tasks with high value and primary concern

B priorities are tasks with medium value and seondary importance

C priorities are tasks with little value and little importance

As you examine these tasks, you will notice that some need to be completed in a sequence, with each being more or less finished before the next task can begin. For example, a major report developed for senior management might have this sequence:

Gather data → Outline report → Write report → Circulate for comment → Submit report

Other activities are not dependent on completion of any other particular tasks, or may be done at any time before or after a particular stage is reached. Make a note of these relationships and keep them in mind as you create your schedule.

Scheduling Your Time

Once you've identified and prioritized all the tasks on your plate, you need to deal with them in a systematic way. A *schedule* is the best approach to treating time systematically. A schedule is a written commitment to accomplish tasks within a specific time frame. A schedule allows you to visualize time resources and how you've committed them. It allows you to see at a glance time periods in which you are under- or overcommitted. You can also see whether priority tasks are being crowded out by less important tasks.

There are plenty of scheduling tools:

- To-do lists

- Appointment calendars

- Daily and weekly planners

- Scheduling software and hardware (for example, PC-based calendars and personal digital assistants)

Many companies have calendar-planning tools that allow you to maintain your schedule and, if they are server-based, to view the calendars of your colleagues. Use these if they are available. But keep in mind that scheduling is personal; if the tools available at your firm do not fit your personal style, seek others that do.

Building Your Schedule

To build your schedule, take your top-priority tasks and insert them into appropriate time slots over the coming days, weeks, or months.

Available-to-Promise

Not sure if you have the capacity to take on additional responsibilities or projects? Here's a tool that can help you.

Manufacturers rely on master scheduling to match their supply of parts and production capacity with their demand for completed orders. Within the discipline of master scheduling is a tool called *available-to-promise*. This tool, which is usually set up on an electronic spreadsheet, reveals at a glance the volume of production capacity available in any given time period to accept additional orders. This same tool can be adapted to an individual's work schedule.

Consider this example. Astrid, a freelance writer, is currently working with five clients on as many books and articles. She has set up an available-to-promise tool in Excel, indicating her total work capacity (in days) for each of the next six months. Her estimate of the number of days required to satisfy each client when they need to be served is also indicated in the tool. The tool calculates total work demand for each month (total demand), and subtracts that number from each month's total number of working days (total capacity). The result is the number of days Astrid has available in every month to take on new business. In this example, Astrid plans to work twenty-six days in July, and has already committed twenty-four of those days to various clients, leaving two left "to promise" to whomever requires her services.

PROJECT	JUL	AUG	SEP	OCT	NOV	DEC
Client A	1		6			
Client B		10				
Client C	4	3				
Client D	7		4	12		
Client E	12	10	7	10		
Total Demand	24	23	17	22	0	0
Total Capacity	26	25	19	25	24	20
ATP	2	2	2	3	24	20

Tips for Time Efficiency

- Open mail while you're booting up your PC or waiting for someone who's scheduled to meet with you.

- Consolidate similar activities, such as returning phone calls, appointments, paperwork, and meetings, to one block of time. For example, make all your phone calls at one scheduled time during the day. Then identify tasks to work on when you have unexpected free time.

Keep in mind that your days undoubtedly have periods of high and low energy. For example, afternoons are periods of low energy for many. Important work or activities that need creativity and intelligence should be scheduled for times when you are most alert and energetic. Routine tasks should be carried out during the periods of low energy.

Schedule only part of your day, leaving time to deal with crises and the unexpected. Combine tasks, where possible. As the week progresses, move uncompleted priority tasks to the days still left in the week. When your schedule changes, be sure to record what really occurred. If you begin to see a trend (for example, always underestimating the time needed for tasks) rework future portions of your schedule to reflect what you have learned.

Once you have created your schedule, keep it accessible. A wall or desk calendar should always be in view; a computer-based calendar should always be open on your desktop. Check your progress throughout the day to see if you are on track.

Working with a To-Do List

A to-do list is one of the simplest and most commonly used scheduling tools. It captures all of the tasks you need to complete on a given day. Many people use to-do lists in combination with a weekly or monthly schedule, and many planners and computer calendars have to-do lists built in. An effective to-do list includes the following:

- Meetings you are scheduled to attend

- Decisions you need to make

- Calls you need to make or expect to receive

- Memos, letters, and e-mails you must write

- Unfinished business from the previous day

One of the virtues of a to-do list is that it allows you to break down the tasks on your schedule into specific activities. For example, where your schedule might direct you to "return phone calls" on Tuesday, your daily to-do list would likely detail each person you need to call, as in the following list:

Do These Today

Return phone calls, 9–10 A.M.

- Herb—performance appraisal meeting

- Juanita—salary review

- David K.—his late shipment

Work on budget, 10 A.M.–noon

Team meeting, 1–3 P.M.

Finalize decision on London trip

Be realistic about how many things you can do in a day. A rule of thumb is to include half the number of things you think you should be able to do. Cross off each item as you complete it.

Three Enemies of Time Management—and How to Defeat Them

The ability of managers to allocate their time effectively is imperiled by a number of factors. Some, such as unanticipated crises, are beyond their control. Many time-management problems, however, have their origins in individual behavior and habits, both of which can be corrected. This section considers three of these self-imposed time-management enemies and how you can correct them.

Overreaching

Some people—including many dedicated people—make the mistake of overloading their schedules. Perhaps you're one of them. They take on new responsibilities and *then* try to figure out how they'll get the work done. Consider this example:

> *Harvey is a hard worker and is highly motivated to do good work. He is also willing to do whatever is necessary to help his team accomplish its goals. When the team leader says, "Someone needs to develop a proposal for the next stage of our project," most people hunch down in their seats or start looking at their notebooks. "Can someone take this on?" the leader asks again. Seeing that no one will volunteer, Harvey will step up to the task. And when he gets the work done, it's always done well. The problem is that Harvey has trouble getting things done on time.*

People like Harvey are terrific employees, but they have one problem: They don't know how to say "No." They take on more responsibilities than they can handle—tasks that should be shared with others. Consequently, their schedules are hopelessly overloaded and they end up working nights and weekends—and still never get caught up.

Are you like Harvey? If you are, you should understand that trying to do too much has a negative impact on all areas of your life. You can avoid overloading yourself if you

- know your key responsibilities, and focus on your top priority goals and tasks;

- learn to delegate;

- resist the urge to step in and take over because others are not doing their job or not doing it to your standards;

- don't assume that everything has to be done; some things aren't important;

- learn to say no when added responsibilities threaten your effectiveness.

Saying no is not easy if you have an accommodating personality or like to be seen as a team player. But if you don't know how to say no, you'll end up like Harvey and never get your work done.

Saying no is a lot easier when you can articulate *why* you're doing it. The *why* of saying no becomes clear once you consider the consequence of saying yes—namely, destroying your ability to get priority jobs done on time. The big challenge, of course, is learning to say no to your boss when saying yes is so much easier. Saying yes to the boss will make you look good in the short-term, but if taking on every task undermines your ability to handle priority jobs, you will end up looking like a loser.

Here's a strategy for dealing with your boss when he asks you to add new projects to your responsibilities: List the projects you are currently working on and ask your boss to decide how these many projects—yours and the ones he is piling on—should be prioritized.

Assuming Subordinates' Problems

Some of the time squeeze experienced by managers may be self-imposed through a failure to delegate. See chapter 4 for ideas on how you can become a better delegator. But some individuals make themselves victims of reverse delegation—they allow subordinates to delegate problems to them, their managers. They end up taking on problems that their subordinates should be handling.

Do you find yourself spending an inordinate amount of time dealing with your subordinates' problems? If you do, you're not alone. This problem was addressed by William Oncken, Jr., and Donald Wass in their classic *Harvard Business Review* article, "Management Time: Who's Got the Monkey?"[1] "Why is it that managers are typically running out of time while their subordinates are typically running out of work?" they ask. The answer: Managers inadvertently take the monkey (the problem) off the subordinate's back and place it onto their own. Before long, they are weighted down with problems that their people should have handled.

Subordinates are only too eager to shift their problems onto their boss's back—after all, doing so lightens the load for them. And many managers, in their eagerness to support their people, are easy marks.

This is not to say that managers shouldn't help subordinates. It only means that they should help subordinates solve their own problems. As Oncken and Wass have a hypothetical boss telling one of his people: "When this meeting is over, the problem will leave this office exactly the way it came in—on your back."[2] The subordinate, according to these authors, should be allowed to seek counsel from the manager on the problem, but only to report his or her progress in handling it. That's good advice. Follow it, and may of your time problems will go away.

Controllable Time-Wasters

A time-waster is anything that keeps you from doing things that have more value and importance to you. Time-wasters are different for everyone. For some, a chat with a colleague might be a time-waster; for others, it's a chance to share ideas that may produce something new and valuable. Common time-wasters include:

- Coworkers who take their coffee breaks in your office

- Visitors who have no particular purpose

- Unwanted telephone calls

- Unnecessary paperwork

- Procrastination

- Poorly organized or unnecessary meetings

- Avoidable travel

What are your time-wasters? Identify them, and then develop strategies for dealing with them. For example, if travel is eating up a big chunk of your time each month, make an objective assessment of its value. The next time you take a business trip to attend a meeting or visit a branch office—or anything else—keep a log of the hours spent in valueless activities: getting to the airport, waiting around in the terminal, getting to your destination, returning home, and so forth. Then estimate what those hours are costing your company. Add this cost to the cost of transportation, lodging, and meals, and compare the sum to the value produced by your trip. Is there a net benefit or a net loss? Then consider the value you could have produced if you hadn't taken the trip.

Some executives feel that travel is essential. This may be true in many cases, but certainly not all. Many of the values created through travel can be generated just as well—and at much lower cost—through travel alternatives, such as conference calls and video-conferencing.

You can apply the same logic to other major time-grabbers and potential time-wasters, such as meetings. If you're like most managers, you are spending between 30 percent and 50 percent of your time in meetings. How many of those meetings are really necessary? How many truly require your presence? Could a subordinate be delegated to attend? How many of the necessary meetings are using your time efficiently?

Brainstorm strategies for reducing or eliminating each time-waster. If you do a good job of this you will free up enormous amounts of time—time you can use for things that really matter.

A Tip for Avoiding Time-Wasters

Office settings are full of distractions. There's today's *Wall Street Journal* to read. E-mails from colleagues and friends. Conversations with coworkers around the coffee machine. And, of course, there's the Internet. Each of these stands between you and the things that really need doing.

Here's one simple but helpful device for cutting through distractions—one that salespeople and managers have used for a long time with good effect. Simply attach this note to your telephone console, your desk, or computer monitor:

> IS WHAT I'M DOING RIGHT NOW
> MOVING ME TOWARD MY GOALS?

That little message can often shift your focus back to the things that matter.

Summing Up

- Keep a log over several days to determine how you are spending your time. Organize your log into categories: meetings, telephone calls, travel, and so forth. Then identify patterns and payoffs.

- Use your goals to guide your time allocations. This means setting priorities.

- Once you've identified your priorities, schedule your task using a scheduling tool, such as a day planner or to-do lists.

- Leave room in your schedule for unanticipated events. If those events don't happen, use that time for other priorities.

- Many managers create their own time-management problems. One is overreaching, or volunteering to do more than they can possibly handle. Another is reverse delegation—or assuming responsibility for problems that subordinates should be handling. Yet another is falling prey to a variety of time-wasters such as procrastination, avoidable travel, and attending poorly organized or unnecessary meetings.

Part Two

Reaching the
Next Level

6

Managing Teams

Forming a Team That Makes the Difference

Key Topics Covered in This Chapter

- *When and why to use teams*

- *Characteristics of an effective team*

- *How to design a productive team*

- *Operating as a team*

- *Leading a team effectively*

- *Handling team problems*

- *Evaluating and rewarding team performance*

INDIVIDUALS are the source of most innovative ideas, but teams of people working together are generally an organization's best instruments for turning ideas into marketable products and services. What is true about ideas is equally true about business processes. Do you have an ineffective customer service process? A properly constituted team is more likely to find and implement a solution than is any individual, including you.

Companies have greatly expanded their use of teams to attack a wide variety of objectives: new product development, process reengineering, the delivery of professional services, adopting new technologies, revitalizing business units in decline, creating e-commerce infrastructures. Teams can do wonders, but they can also be impediments to real progress if they are not properly designed, staffed, and operated.

If you are a new manager, or a seasoned one with little experience in team-based work, being part of a team can throw you off stride. If you're the team leader, you'll quickly discover that you cannot act like you're the boss. So how should you act? If you're a team member, you must find a collaborative way to contribute and support your colleagues. How can you do that? This chapter will answer those questions and get you off to a good start. It describes the essentials of team-based work and how you can use teams to good advantage.

Teams—and When to Use Them

What is a team? A CEO refers to the people around him as "My team." Even front-line supervisors talk about the "teams" they manage. Are these really teams or simply individuals with common reporting arrangements? A *team* is not just a collection of individuals; it is a small number of individuals with complementary skills committed to a common purpose with collective accountability.

Teams are particularly useful when organizations confront situations in which:

- Completion of a task requires a particular combination of knowledge, expertise, or perspective that cannot be found in an individual

- The work of individuals must be highly interdependent

- The task or project will result in a defined deliverable

- The task at hand will not be ongoing, but will terminate

Are you facing any of these situations? If you are, a team may be just the right solution. If not, normal work procedures may be quicker and easier. Consider this example:

> Both management and employees of Gizmo Products Company recognized that the time had come to upgrade its Web site. It had an old-fashioned look, customers found it difficult to navigate, and its underlying architecture could not accommodate the frequent changes and upgrades required by this rapidly changing company.
>
> The CEO's first thought was to hire a consulting group to handle the job. But he quickly learned that employees in just about every function had a stake in the design and implementation of the new site: sales and marketing, customer service, IT, fulfillment, each of the product groups, and even finance. Each could point to requirements they wanted reflected on the site.
>
> Seeing how interest in the new site cut across functions, the CEO met with her managers and asked them to establish a self-directed

work team *representing each important constituency to handle the job. That team would be given authority to identify and hire the right e-commerce consultant, define the goals and specification of the new site, and work toward its implementation.*

The advantages of teams like the one just described flow from the power of the assembled skills, creativity, and experiences of team members, and from communication processes that allow for ongoing problem-solving. Conversely, if the task at hand is relatively simple and no variety of skills is required, a traditional manager-led working group may be more appropriate.

Characteristics of Effective Teams

If analysis of your situation confirms that a team approach is the best way to approach your goal, you'll be eager to select team members and get them into gear. Resist the temptation to leap into team-building for just a bit. Take some time to consider what teams need to be effective.

Management scholars and consultants have studied teams and team-based performance fairly intensely for the past ten or twelve years. As a result, there is a great deal of consensus on the characteristics of effective teams. This chapter draws on the best of management literature to explain the characteristics every team must have to be successful:

- Competence—everyone brings something that the team needs

- A clear and compelling goal

- Commitment to the common goal

- Every member contributes; every member benefits

- A supportive environment

- Alignment

Competence

You're probably familiar with the expression, "A chain is only as strong as its weakest link." That certainly applies to teams. An effective team is composed of people who each bring critical competencies to the effort. Each is a link in a chain of competencies that, together, has the talent, knowledge, organizational clout, experience, and technical know-how to get the job done. If any competencies are weak, they must be strengthened—something most teams learn to do as they move forward. If any essential competencies are absent, they must be added.

Some companies make the mistake of basing team membership on formal titles or on organizational position. Someone will suggest that, "You'll really make Susan angry (or jealous) if you don't put her on your team," or "Simon is the national sales manager, so be sure to include him on the team." Unfortunately, neither Susan's potential angst nor Simon's title are reasons to put them on a team. If you are a team leader, your assignment is to achieve a particular goal: to design the new product line within ten months, or to reduce annual production costs by $1 million per year. Susan's discomfiture is not your primary consideration. Likewise, Simon may have extremely important technical and organizational competencies to contribute, but if his duties as national sales manager mean that he'll be traveling most of the time, those competencies won't do your team much good. What you need are individuals who can, and will, bring critical competencies to the effort.

A Clear, Common Goal

Have you ever been part of a team or project group that didn't have a clear idea of its purpose? Where different people had different ideas about their ultimate objective? If you have, you probably understand why these groups are rarely successful. One person has one idea about the team's purpose; another has a similar, but slightly different idea. It's nearly impossible to be successful when team members cannot articulate a clear and common goal. And it's absolutely impossible when the executives who sponsor and charter teams are unclear or uncertain about what they want done.

A Compelling Purpose

Being clear about the team's goal is important, but insufficient. The goal must also be compelling. People must see it as urgent, very important, and worthy of effort. Lacking a compelling purpose, some members will not subordinate their personal goals to the goal of the team. They will not identify with the team or its purpose.

Commitment to the Common Goal

A shared understanding of the goal is extremely important, but really effective teams go a step further. They are composed of members who are committed to the goal. There is a big difference between understanding and commitment. Understanding ensures that people know the direction in which they should work. Commitment motivates them to do the work and to keep working when the going gets tough.

The essence of a team is a shared commitment to goal achievement. That means that each team member must see the goal as very important and worthy of effort. In almost every case, commitment emerges from a sense of goal ownership and mutual accountability. Here are a few things you can do to enhance commitment:

- **Keep teams small.** There is an inverse relationship between the size of a team and the commitment of its members.

- **Co-locate team members.** People need to see and interact with other team members on a regular basis. This is best accomplished if they are situated in close physical proximity. Video-conferencing and e-mail are poor substitutes for physical co-location and the cohesion that normally develops through frequent and direct contact. Consider the use of a "team room" dedicated to team activities.

- **Recognize effort and accomplishment.** Make sure that the team and its members receive credit for its success. Don't let the boss or the team leader collect all the accolades.

- **Remember that commitment generally develops and deepens as the team proceeds with its work.** So if it isn't there at the beginning, be patient.

Don't confuse shared commitment with social compatibility. It's less important that people get along with each other than that they are willing to work together to get things done. Having a purpose that all see as important can overcome social incompatibilities.

Every Member Contributes—Every Member Benefits

Have you ever been on a rowing team? If you have, you know that every member of the team must pull his or her oar with the same intensity and at the same pace as everyone else. There is no room for slackers. Work teams are very similar. Performance depends on everyone contributing—pulling for the goal. Individual members who simply show up at meetings to render their opinions but do no work drag down performance and demoralize more active teammates. If team membership is to have value, it must be earned through real work. That means that "free riders" cannot be tolerated.

This is not to say that every member must put in the same amount of time on team activities. A senior manager, for example, may be a regular team member even though much of his or her attention must be directed to other duties. This person's contribution may be to secure resources or to build support for the team within the organization.

The team leader must also do real work—including a share of the less pleasant tasks. He or she cannot be a team member *and* behave like a traditional boss, delegating all the work to others. Thus, there is a certain element of role ambiguity for the team leader, who must wear a leadership cap some of the time and a team member's cap the rest.

And just as each member must contribute to the team's work, each should receive clear benefits. Benefits can take many forms: the psychic reward of doing interesting and meaningful work; a learning experience that will pay future career dividends; or extra money in the paycheck. In the absence of clear benefits, individuals will not contribute at a high level—at least not for long; the benefits they derive from their regular jobs will absorb their attention and make team duties a secondary priority.

A Supportive Environment

No team operates in a vacuum. A team is a small organization embedded within a larger environment of operating units and functional departments. It depends on these organizational kin to one degree or another for resources, information, and assistance. The extent to which they are supportive, indifferent, or hostile to the team and it goals is bound to have a impact on team effectiveness. In particular, the team-builder needs to consider environmental factors:

- **Leadership support.** Support at the top is essential. That support ensures a source of resources and makes it possible to recruit the right people. Leadership support also provides protection from powerful managers and departments that for one reason or another would be inclined to torpedo the team effort.

- **A nonhierarchical structure.** Team-based work is more likely to be successful if the organization does not conform to a rigid hierarchical structure.

- **Appropriate reward systems.** Companies that are new to team-based work need to examine their reward systems before launching teams. This means finding a different balance in rewards for individual and team-based success.

- **Experience with team–based work.** Teams benefit when their company and individual members have plenty of experience with team-based work. Experience provides insights into what works and what does not, how best to organize around a goal, and how to alter the team at different points in its life cycle.

Alignment

Alignment refers to the coordination of plans, effort, and rewards with the highest goals of the organization. In an aligned organization, everyone understands both the goals of the enterprise and the goals of his or her operating unit. In an aligned organization everyone is working in the right direction—and the rewards system encourages them to do so.

Teams also need alignment. A team shouldn't even exist unless it represents the best way to help the organization achieve its goals. That means that team goals should be aligned with organizational goals. It means that individual team members should have goals that are aligned—through the team—with those higher organizational goals. And everyone's efforts should be aligned through the rewards system.

Designing the Team

The best assurance of having a successful team begins in its design—which should be addressed before any of its members are recruited or its activities are triggered. You wouldn't begin construction of a house without first thinking through important details: How big should the house be? Who are the right people to build it? Can we attach it to the city water and sewer system? How will we pay for it? A team should be approached with the same sense of planning and design. Doing so will avoid problems later. Once you've determined that a team effort is called for, consider the following key design elements:

- Specifying the team's goals, authority and duration

- Identifying roles and responsibilities

- Determining rewards

- Selecting team members

Specifying Goals, Authority, and Duration

As the team is forming, it needs goals around which it can focus its efforts. These should be specific, realistic yet challenging, and some should be achievable in a reasonably short period of time. Team goals should also be consistent with the vision and values of the larger organization.

Though some teams are charged only with the job of making recommendations to management, others must be empowered to make and implement decisions. Team leaders cannot be expected to run back to management every time an operational decision is needed. Team leaders and members must also be aware of the limits of their authority.

Finally, teams must have a time frame within which to pursue their goals. Some teams exist on an open-ended schedule. For example, a manufacturing plant may have a permanent process-control team for every line. Others teams are chartered with specific time frames in mind. An example would be a team charged with creating an e-commerce Web site by the end of the current calendar year. In either case, there should be specific schedules for reaching goals or producing deliverables.

Roles and Responsibilities

An essential ingredient to team development is clear identification of roles and responsibilities. Who will be on the team, and what will be their duties? Here are some typical roles and responsibilities:

- **Team sponsor.** This is usually the executive who authorizes the team and supports its activities. The sponsor plays only an indirect role in the team's work.

- **Team leader.** The leader fosters development of the team, secures team resources, and arranges (if appropriate) for special team rewards. Team leadership may be invested in a single person or in a council of no more than three.

- **Team members.** The members do the bulk of the actual work. As a result, they must collectively have all the skills and experience needed to do the job. (More on member selection below.)

- **Facilitator.** Some teams benefit from having someone, often a trainer or consultant, who can help people work together more effectively.

These role assignments may be rotated periodically. Some may even be shared.

Determining Rewards

There should be a fair value exchange among team members. Reward structures for teams are influenced—if not constrained—by the compensation plan of the larger organization. Where teams are allowed to have special rewards, designers face a dilemma. Where they should place the greater emphasis—on individual contributions or on team performance—is the challenge. Putting too much emphasis on individual rewards can negatively affect teamwork. On the other hand, if rewards are based on team performance exclusively, one creates the problem of "free riding"—allowing noncontributors to share in

Tips for Team Compensation

When crafting team-based rewards, keep these tips in mind:

- Remember that rewards are not the most important element of team performance management.

- Express incentives in terms of team goals.

- The amount of incentive pay must be meaningful.

- Match the incentive to the value of the task.

SOURCE: Loren Gary, "How to Compensate Teams," *Harvard Management Update*, November 1997, 3.

the rewards generated by people who did all the work. Team-based rewards can also motivate people to do things that are best for the team but not best for the organization.

Since the literature does not reveal any "right way" of rewarding team members, many companies adopt a mix of individual and team-based goals, including spot awards to recognize exceptional individual contributions, and gain-sharing that gives participants opportunities to share in the value created through team efforts.

Selecting Members

This can be the trickiest and most important part of team design. Failing to get the right people on the team is the surest way to jeopardize success. When selecting team members, seek out individuals who can contribute the appropriate mix of skills.

While the ideal mix of people will vary with the team's mission, all teams require a blend of technical/functional expertise that includes problem-solving and decision-making talents, interpersonal skills, and team skills. With respect to team skills, look for people who know how to

- speak up in groups;

- say "no" to requests when their time is fully utilized;

- deliver and receive constructive feedback, both positive and negative;

- make requests to authority figures, such as stating what they need in terms of organizational support;

- negotiate;

- take responsibility for their own actions.

How many members should you have on a team? The optimal number depends on the team's goals and the work it must do to achieve them. But more is not necessarily better. In general, small teams (five to nine members) tend to be most effective when tasks

Creating a Team Charter

It is a good idea to articulate the purpose of the team, duration, roles, and other elements of team operations within a written charter. That charter should specify:

- the team's executive sponsor;

- a concise description of team goals (deliverables);

- timelines;

- leadership roles;

- measures of success; and

- resources available to the team.

Everyone on the team—and relevant managers within the company—should be conversant with the charter.

are complex and require specific skills. Larger teams (up to twenty-five people) can be effective if their tasks are fairly simple. The key problem with larger teams—in addition to the dilution of member commitment—is coordination. If you think that finding a suitable meeting time for five people is difficult, try finding agreement among twenty-five!

Team size need not be fixed. For example, different skills may be needed at different times in the life of the project. Thus, it may be necessary to increase or reduce membership.

Operating as a Team

A good design can help a team get off to a good start—but it cannot ensure its success. Success is a function of team members working *together* toward stated goals. Working together is the greatest challenge. But there are also plenty of housekeeping chores that must be taken care of. Prioritizing is one. When there are many goals, the team must establish priorities. Which must be attacked first? How will limited people-hours and resources be allocated?

Scheduling is another operational function. Scheduling helps a team accomplish its tasks within time constraints. It answers these questions:

- What has to be done?

- How long will a particular activity take to complete?

- In what order must each activity happen?

- Who is responsible for each activity?

Software such as Microsoft Project Manager can make scheduling a team with many tasks easier and more complete.

There is also the issue of how decisions will be made. The team must determine *who* will make the decisions (the team leader, the team, individuals in the team) and *how* they will be made (consensus, majority). *Who* and *how* are closely related. Here are four possible approaches:

1. **Majority rules.** Team members bring input to the meeting, discuss, and then vote. The decision that receives over 50 percent of the votes is adopted.

2. **Consensus.** Every member of the team must agree to adopt a decision. The team develops new alternatives if consensus is not reached.

3. **A small group decides.** A group of individuals with relevant experience and skills is selected to make decisions.

4. **The leader decides.** The team leader gathers input from team members, then makes the decision.

There are strengths and weaknesses in each of these approaches. For example, if team members are highly involved in the decision-making process, they will be more likely to support the decisions actually made. As a result, the consensus and majority rules approaches can help build team commitment. These approaches, however, take time

—perhaps time that the team does not have. If time is an issue, consider using different approaches for different types of decisions. Use one of the "team decides" approaches to make the decisions that are the most important to team members, and use a more streamlined approach for the rest.

As you might suppose, the sponsor and team leader play a role in determining how decisions will be made. The leader, for instance, may unilaterally maintain control over key budget decisions.

The Leader's Role

Every team needs a leader to act as a source of energy, a primary contact between the team and the rest of organization, and as a team spokesperson. In some cases the sponsor may assign the leadership role. In others, the leader is selected by team members. If you are a manager, it's likely that you'll find yourself playing this leadership role at one time or another.

The team leader must do what other leaders have always done: keep the higher goal visible and keep people on track toward it; obtain needed resources; motivate people; and get the team "unstuck" when it runs into problems.

Handling Problems

Teams can get "stuck" for a variety of reasons. Some members' sense of direction or commitment may weaken. Others may put their individual interests above those of the team and its goals. Critical skill gaps may emerge. Or feuding between members may undermine group cohesion.

Fortunately, there are many things a leader can do to get a team "unstuck." For example, a leader can get the team in a discussion that revisits its purpose, approach, and performance goals, using the charter as a centerpiece. He or she can settle conflicts between team members—and can even oust noncontributors and troublesome individuals. For dealing with other team problems, see the "Team Troubleshooting Guide" in table 6-1.

TABLE 6 - 1

Team Troubleshooting Guide

Problem	Characteristic Behavior	Try This
Unhealthy conflict	• Personal attacks and sarcasm • Arguments • Absence of support for others • Aggressive gestures	• Interrupt personal attacks and sarcasm; confront them directly • Ask members to focus on behavior instead of attacking character • Create norms about contentious discussion
Trouble reaching consensus	• Holding rigidly to positions • Same arguments with no new information	• Look for smaller areas of agreement • Ask what needs to happen in order to reach agreement • Discuss the consequences of no consensus
Team fails to communicate	• Members interrupt or talk over others • Some remain silent • Problems are hinted at but never formally addressed	• Create group norms for discussion • Actively solicit views • Consider use of an outside facilitator
Low participation	• Assignments not completed • Poor attendance • Low energy at meetings	• Confirm that the leader's expectations for participation are generally shared • Ask why there is such low involvement • Assess the fit of members with their tasks
Lack of progress	• Meetings seem a waste of time • Action items not completed on time • Continuing to revisit closed issues	• Restate goals and assess what remains to be done • Ask member to identify causes of late work; brainstorm solutions • Move members from closed issues to next steps
Inept leadership	• Leader does not solicit member contributions • Leader doesn't delegate • No vision • Myopic leadership represents only one of many constituencies	• Meet with leader to discuss perceived leadership deficiencies • Volunteer to share the load • Push for a group consensus on the vision • Bring unresolvable leadership problem to the team sponsor

Source: Adapted from Harvard Business School Publishing "Teams Guide."

When the Leader Is the Problem

By way of warning, the team leader can be the source of problems in some cases. Why is that? Since many team leaders are managers, they are subject to one of two errors. The first error is continuing to act like a traditional boss, telling the team what to do and how to do it. The second error is thinking that they have "empowered" the team and can take a hands-off approach. This doesn't work either.

Based on his research, Harvard professor Richard Hackman contends that team leaders must maintain an appropriate balance between being a boss and empowering team members. In practice this means that leaders have to spell out the team's objectives to prevent it from spinning its wheels. But at the same time they give team members decision-making authority over the means to those objectives. Team members can act as a team only if they have real authority.

SOURCE: "Why Some Teams Succeed (and So Many Don't)," *Harvard Management Update*, January 2000, 5.

Evaluating Team Performance

Like every other activity, team performance should be regularly evaluated. Traditional performance evaluation is most often oriented toward results or outputs: the number of new products put into production; the number of customer calls answered per day; and so forth. Team evaluation likewise should evaluate results. But it should go one step further, to evaluating the way in which teams achieve those results. The collaborative process used to achieve results is an important measure of team performance. Given that, the performance factors listed below as examples are divided into two equally important categories: results and process.

Results factors:

- Achievement of team goals

- Customer satisfaction

- Quantity of work completed

- Job knowledge and skills acquired

Process factors:

- Support of team process and commitment to the team

- Level of participation and leadership

- Oral and written communication within and on behalf of the team

- Collaboration

- Conflict resolution

- Planning and goal setting

- Win–win decision making

- Problem solving and application of analytical skills

- Adherence to agreed–upon processes and procedures

- Application of project management skills (for example, budgeting and scheduling)

- Building and sustaining interpersonal relationships

Team Evaluation Methods

There are many approaches for measuring your team's success, and they vary widely in complexity, cost, and time required. You should consider a more elaborate method for a team whose mission is extensive and will have a significant impact on organizational performance; for teams with narrower missions, simpler methods will usually do the job. The methods include benchmarking against other teams in similar organizations, evaluating team progress against original goals and schedules, observation by an outside consultant, and even debriefing sessions at which people try to identify what did and did not go well.

Team Member Evaluations

Evaluation isn't just for the team as a whole; it should extend to its individual members. If team participation is an important part of an employee's job, that person should be evaluated on his or her contributions. (Note: Many of the concepts described in chapter 7, "Appraisal and Coaching: Improving Results with Feedback," can be applied to team member evaluation.)

Keep in mind that the individual team member actually performs a number of roles: as an individual contributor, as a member of the team, and as a member of the larger organization. Thus, in reviewing performance, it is helpful to combine at least a couple of the following methods:

- **Peer ratings.** Team members assess each other's contributions.

- **Customer satisfaction ratings.** Internal and external customers rate the performance of the team and its individual members.

- **Self-appraisal.** Each team member rates his or her own performance.

- **Team leader review.** You, as the team leader or the supervisor, evaluate each individual's performance.

Becoming an Effective Team Leader

We've already explored the role of leader in team situations, but it's fitting to end this chapter with a closer look at that role and how you, as a manager, can become more effective in it.

Traditional managers play many roles: decision maker, delegator, director, and scheduler of others' work. You are probably accustomed to these roles. When you are a team leader, on the other hand, you must act more like a coach. On a cross-functional team, you will not be the "expert," and so you must rely more on the expertise of others. Thus, you may find it useful to consciously shift your focus from directing to facilitating. In addition, you will be operating with less direct authority than you enjoy as a manager. That means that you must empower others to solve problems and create plans.

So lacking some of the usual trappings and tools of a manager, how can you be effective as a team leader? Here are several suggestions:

- Be an initiator. Begin actions and processes that promote team development and performance.

- Be a model to others. Use your own behavior to set expectations for the team.

- Be a good coach. Act as counselor, mentor, and tutor to help team members improve performance.

- Be a facilitator of communication and collaboration between the team and other groups.

- Be a mediator of conflict between team members.

Do each of these things and the chances of your team's success will be much improved. And, like everything else, the more you do them, the better your team leadership capabilities will become.

Summing Up

- Teams are particularly useful when organizations confront tasks that require particular knowledge or skills, when work is highly interdependent, when there is a defined deliverable, and when the task has a terminal point.

- Competence, commitment, common goals, contributions by all members, an enabling structure, a supportive environment, and alignment are characteristics of effective teams.

- The biggest challenge to compensating teams is finding the proper balance between team and individual rewards.

- As with rewards, evaluations of team performance must look at both team results and the performance of individual members.

- Selecting members is the most important part of team design. Look for individuals who represent the right blend of technical/functional expertise, problem-solving and decision-making talents, interpersonal skills, and team skills.

- Team leaders usually lack the authority of traditional managers. Thus, their effectiveness depends on their ability to initiate activity, model behavior, facilitate communications and collaboration, and mediate conflict.

7

Appraisal and Coaching

Improving Results with Feedback

Key Topics Covered in This Chapter

- *Performance appraisal*

- *Eight steps for doing it right*

- *Coaching for better performance*

HOW WELL are your people doing their jobs? Are some falling short of the mark? If so, do you understand why? Do they? Are they even aware that their work isn't meeting your expectations?

Many companies use regular performance appraisal to evaluate how people are doing. It is one part—but an important part—of a larger system of performance management that includes rewards, training, coaching, and career development. The first half of this chapter will show you how to handle performance appraisal and offers eight steps for doing it right. The balance of the chapter explains a related activity—how to improve performance through coaching. These two activities provide opportunities for both the manager and subordinate to provide feedback to one another—feedback on what is going well, what is not going well, what help would benefit the employee, and how their working relationship could be improved. This feedback is an essential element of management.[1]

Performance Appraisal

Performance appraisal is a formal method for assessing how well people are doing with respect to their assigned goals. Its ultimate purpose is to communicate personal goals, to encourage good performance, to provide feedback, and to correct poor performance.

Performance appraisal is generally conducted annually, with follow-ups as needed. Like the physical exam administered by your doctor, this annual checkup gives a manager and the company opportunities to spot performance problems before they become chronic. It also helps employees and managers focus on the goals and performance expectations that impact salary, merit increases, and promotions. Appraisal sessions are both a confirmation and a formalization of the ongoing feedback that should be part of every manager-subordinate relationship.

Performance appraisals are not widely popular. Star performers may like them because they know that they'll get positive strokes from their bosses. "Well, Ms. Abercrombie, as usual you've met or exceeded all of your goals. I just wish that we had ten more people like you." Most others employees approach appraisals with apprehension, fearing that they'll get the same report card they received from their eighth-grade teacher: "Dear Mrs. Jones: Jimmy is very bright, but he's not working up to his potential." People don't like being told that they are short of the mark.

Busy managers are not particularly fond of performance appraisals either, and generally for two reasons. First, few managers enjoy telling people to their faces that they're not doing their jobs as well as they should. Second, giving performance appraisals to each of many direct reports consumes time—for preparation, administration, documentation, and follow-up. And time is every manager's scarcest asset.

Indeed, performance appraisals are sometimes uncomfortable and definitely take time. But when they are approached with the right frame of mind and done well, they are well worth the effort. When you consider that a manager's fundamental responsibility is to get results *through people*, a systematic approach to assessing the human assets at one's disposal is a must. In addition to providing insights into employee performance, appraisal sessions give the manager opportunities to

- communicate goals to direct reports;

- increase productivity by providing timely feedback;

- help the organization make valid decisions with respect to pay, development, and promotions;

- protect the organization against lawsuits by employees who have been terminated, demoted, or denied a merit increase.

Eight Steps to Effective Appraisal

There is no "one right way" to conduct performance appraisal. Every company has a set of suggested procedures, and every subordinate presents a different challenge to the appraising manager. Still, effective practice generally involves the following eight steps, addressed in this order.

STEP 1: BE PREPARED Like every activity, performance appraisal benefits from preparation—by both employee and managers. Little can be accomplished if either manager or employee—or both—strolls into an appraisal meeting without having reflected on what has happened during the preceding months.

Let's consider the employee first. It is important to involve an employee in every stage of the appraisal process so that both sides of the story are on the table. One of the best ways of doing this is to have the employee complete a self-appraisal. In many cases, the human resource department provides a checklist for this purpose. That checklist states the employee's goals and the job behaviors and functions associated with them. (Note: Those goals should have been established with the employee at the very beginning of the appraisal period.)

In self-appraisal, the employee evaluates his or her performance against goals. If your human resource department doesn't provide a checklist, here are a few questions you should ask the employee to address in a self-appraisal:

- To what extent did you achieve your goals?

- Which if any goals have you exceeded?

- Are there particular goals with which you are currently struggling?

- What is inhibiting your progress toward these goals: lack of training, resources, direction from management, etc?

Self-appraisal has two key benefits. First, it gets the person involved. That involvement sets a tone of partnership for the appraisal process and makes the employee more open to subsequent feedback by the manager. Second, it gives the manager a different perspective on the subordinate's work and any related problems.

STEP 2: CONDUCT THE PERFORMANCE APPRAISAL MEETING
Many people are anxious about performance appraisal meetings. So create a tone of partnership from the very beginning. Start by setting the person at ease; don't let the person feel that he or she is in the prisoner's dock. Then review the purpose of the appraisal and its positive benefits for both parties. This will psychologically prepare you and the employee and will act as a warm-up for dialogue.

Then ask the employee to talk about his or her self-appraisal. This will help you understand the employee's point of view and prevent you from controlling too much of the conversation. Listen very carefully to what the person is saying. Don't interrupt until the person has had his or her say. Demonstrate that you are listening by repeating what you've heard: "If I understand you correctly, you feel that you are meeting all goals with respect to the weekly sales reports, but that you're struggling to contact all the key customers you've been assigned. Do I have that right?"

Once the employee has laid all of the cards on the table, move on to your appraisal.

STEP 3: IDENTIFY PERFORMANCE GAPS As you disclose your appraisal, give priority to how the employee's accomplishments compare to agreed-upon goals. For example, if Joan says that her greatest achievement was organizing and chairing a meeting between key customers and your R&D personnel, ask yourself, "Was this one of her goals?" If it was, how close did that performance come to meeting the metrics of that goal? How did she do relative to her other goals? Look for gaps between actual and expected performance. Your big problem here may be that some performance is difficult to quantify. For example, if a hotel manager has given his desk personnel the goal of creating a welcoming environment for guests, how would he measure their performance?

If your appraisal has found a "gap" between the employee's goal and actual performance, make this the focus of your discussion and feedback. As a starting point, identify a larger organizational goal to explain how the employee's goal supports it. People can and do change when they understand the consequences of their behavior and work. For example, you might say:

> *Our department's goal is to resolve all customer warranty problems within one week. That's our contribution to the company's higher goal of creating customer satisfaction and loyalty—both of which guarantee our future employment and bonuses. We can't accomplish that if any team member fails to handle his or her share of customer complaints. Do you see how what we are doing fits in?*

Make sure the employee affirms your statement. Then move the conversation toward identifying the root cause of substandard performance. "If you're falling short of your goal, why do you think that is?" Listen carefully to the response; give your employee the first opportunity to identify the root cause. If you don't hear a thoughtful reply, probe with other questions: "Could the problem be that you need more training?" "Are there too many distractions in the office?"

STEP 4: FIND THE ROOT CAUSES OF PERFORMANCE GAPS
Identifying the root causes of performance gaps will, in most cases, create an atmosphere of objectivity in which both you and your subordinate can contribute in positive ways. You won't be attacking the subordinate, and he won't be defending himself from your criticism. Instead, you'll be working together to address "the problem," which in most cases is *outside* the subordinate (e.g., lack of proper training, too few resources, the workplace environment). The following suggestions can help you offer more useful feedback:

- Encourage the employee to articulate points of disagreement.

- Avoid generalizations such as, "You just don't seem involved with your work," in favor of specific comments that relate to the job, such as, "I have noticed that you haven't offered any suggestions at our service improvement meetings. Why is that?"

- Be selective. You don't need to recite every shortcoming or failing. Stick to the issues that really matter.

- Give authentic praise as well as meaningful criticism.

- Orient feedback toward problem-solving and action.

(Note: For a handy checklist for planning a feedback session, see Appendix A. You can download free copies of the same checklist and other tools used in the Harvard Business Essentials series from the series' Web site: www.elearning.hbsp.org/businesstools.)

STEP 5: PLAN TO CLOSE PERFORMANCE GAPS Once you've identified performance gaps and discussed their root causes, make sure that the employee acknowledges them and recognizes their importance. Once that is done, begin a dialogue about their resolution.

Give the employee the first opportunity to develop a plan to close any gaps. Say something like, "What would you propose as a solution?" Putting the ball in the employee's court will make him or her more responsible for the solution and, hopefully, more committed to it. As the employee describes her plan to close any gaps, challenge assumptions and offer ideas for strengthening that plan. If the employee cannot put a credible plan together, you'll have to take a more active approach. In either case, seek agreement and commitment from the employee to the plan. A good plan includes

- specific goals;

- a timeline;

- action steps;

- expected outcomes;

- training or practice required, if applicable.

The development plan should become part of the employee's record.

If you cannot settle the matter of closing performance gaps during your appraisal meeting, establish a time and place for a follow-up meeting, and explain its purpose: "Over the next week I'd like you to think about the things we've discussed today. I'll do the same. We'll then meet again and develop a plan for getting the help you need to handle these problems."

Before concluding the meeting, conduct a brief review of what was said and what agreements were made.

STEP 6: REEXAMINE PERFORMANCE GOALS Since an entire year may have passed since their last performance appraisals, reexamine the goals toward which your subordinates are expected to work. This is especially important when the organization is in a state of change, and when a subordinate is on a rapid trajectory of workplace mastery.

Involve the employee in the goal-changing process to be sure that (1) he or she has the capacity to assume new goals, and (2) the employee understands the details and the importance of these goals.

In all cases be very clear about the new goals and how performance against them will be measured. Also, depending on employee skills, this is the time to create a development plan (coaching, training, etc.) for giving the employee the capability required to meet the new goals.

STEP 7: GET IT ON THE RECORD It's very important to document your meeting, its key points, and its outcomes. That means that you'll need to take rough notes during the meeting and complete them immediately afterward, when you memory is still fresh. Make a record of

- the date;

- key points and phrases used by the employee (not necessarily verbatim), including his or her self-appraisal;

- key points and phrases used by you;

- points of disagreement, if any;

- a summary of the development plan;

- agreed-upon next steps;

- performance goals for the coming year.

Chances are that your company will require that copies of this record be provided to the employee and added to the employee's

> ## *Tips for Effective Appraisal*
>
> - Make the employee feel that he or she is part of the process.
>
> - Provide honest feedback to the employees.
>
> - Cover the full spectrum of the employee's job responsibilities in terms of what was done right and what was done wrong.
>
> - Make it balanced: neither a love fest nor total criticism.
>
> - Identify what should be done in terms of employee development.

human resource file and to your files. In most cases, both the manager and the employee are asked to sign the performance appraisal report, and the employee has a legal right to append his or her own comments to the report.

STEP 8: FOLLOW UP You should plan on following up every appraisal meeting. The high performers and satisfactory performers will obviously need less follow-up. However, if you've given them new, more demanding goals, you'll want to monitor their progress and determine if they need added training, coaching, or support.

Employees with performance gaps who have committed to development plans should be more carefully monitored. That monitoring could take the form of a follow-up meeting every few weeks or months. Here, your goal will be to check for progress against development plans. These meetings represent opportunities for coaching and encouragement from you.

Coaching

Coaching, like performance appraisal, is part of a larger performance management system. It quite naturally flows from performance appraisal, since, as a manager, you're bound to encounter subordinates

Managing Versus Coaching

Though managers must often act as coaches, management and coaching are quite different activities, and the difference makes coaching difficult for many managers.

Managing focuses on:	Coaching focuses on:
• Telling	• Exploring
• Directing	• Facilitating
• Authority	• Partnership
• Immediate needs	• Long-term improvement
• A specific outcome	• Many possible outcomes

who need extra help in doing their work and meeting their goals. Performance appraisal will also reveal that others are ready to step up to greater responsibilities and more challenging goals; all they need is an extra boost. Chances are that your company has formal and on-the-job training to help both types of employees. But it also looks to you to provide one-on-one coaching.

Coaching is a two-way activity in which the parties share knowledge and experience in order to maximize a subordinate's potential and help him or her achieve agreed-upon goals. It is a shared effort in which the person being coached actively and willingly participates. Good managers find coaching opportunities not only in performance appraisal, but also in the course of everyday business.

Why Coach?

You and a subordinate may agree to form a coaching relationship when both believe that working together will lead to improved performance. Coaching can help subordinates to:

• Rekindle motivation

• Get back on track if they are having performance problems

• Maximize their strengths, such as building on their analytical skills

- Overcome personal obstacles, such as reducing a fear of dealing directly with a difficult customer

- Achieve new skills and competencies, such as learning how to make a better stand-up presentation

- Prepare themselves for new responsibilities, such as developing leadership skills

- Manage themselves more effectively, such as improving time management

Good coaching produces greater job satisfaction and higher motivation. It may also improve your working relationship with subordinates, making your job as manager much easier. Just remember that effective coaching requires mutual agreement. The other person must *want* to do better and must *welcome* your help.

Begin with Observation

The first step in effective coaching is to understand the situation, the person, and the person's current skills. The best way to gain that understanding is through direct observation. Your goal should be to identify strengths and weaknesses, and to understand the impact that the person's behavior has on coworkers and on his ability to achieve his goals. As you observe, keep these points in mind:

- Learn what the person is doing or not doing well. Be as precise as you can be and try to get to the cause of problems. Consider this example:

  After observing several team meetings, a manager noted something about Harriet. She interrupted others frequently. This behavior appeared to prevent others from expressing their views. A less observant manager might have said, "Harriet isn't a good team player." But that general statement would not have isolated Harriet's specific problem—a problem amenable to coaching.

- Avoid premature judgments. One or two observations may give an incomplete impression. So continue observing, particularly if you have any doubts about your perceptions.

- Test your theories. Where appropriate, discuss the situation with trusted peers or colleagues. Add their observations to your own.

- Avoid unrealistic expectations. Don't apply your own perform-ance yardstick to others. You've probably progressed in your ca-reer by setting high expectations and achieving an outstanding track record. Assuming that others have identical motivations or identical strengths may be unrealistic and unfair.

- Listen carefully. A person may be asking for your help, but you may not be hearing him. Ask yourself, "Have I passed up chances to listen?" People don't always know what kind of help they need or exactly how to ask for it. When you see an oppor-tunity, take the time to listen actively to direct reports.

Discuss Your Observations with the Employee

Once you've determined where coaching can help, enter into dia-logue with the employee. But stick to observed behaviors. For exam-ple, begin by saying, "This is what I observed." Also cite the impact of the person's behavior on group goals and on coworkers. For example, you might suggest that "If I were in one of your coworker's shoes, I might think that you were trying to dominate the meeting. I'd have that impression because of how you interrupt others."

When describing behavior and its impact, be truthful and frank, yet supportive. Leave motives out of the discussion; doing otherwise will only make the person feel that he or she is under personal attack. Those motives would be pure speculation on your part in any case. Here's an example of an assumed motive: "Your inability to get re-ports done on time tells me that you don't like this type of work."

Be an Active Listener

As a coach you must be highly tuned in to the other person. You do this through active listening. Active listening encourages communi-cation and puts other people at ease. An active listener pays attention to the speaker by

- maintaining eye contact;

- smiling at appropriate moment;

- avoiding distractions;

- taking notes only if necessary;

- being sensitive to body language;

- listening first and evaluating later;

- never interrupting except to ask for clarification;

- indicating that he's listening by repeating what was said, such as, "So if I hear you right, you're having trouble with . . ."

Ask the Right Questions

Asking the right questions will help you understand the other person and determine his or her perspective. There are open-ended and closed questions. Each yields a different response.

Open-ended questions invite participation and idea sharing. Use them to:

- Explore alternatives: "What would happen if . . ."

- Uncover attitudes or needs: "How do you feel about our progress to date?"

- Establish priorities and allow elaboration: "What do you think the major issues are with this project?"

  Closed questions lead to yes or no answers. Use them to:

- Focus the response: "Is the project on schedule?"

- Confirm what the other person has said: "So, your big problem is scheduling your time?"

When you want to find out more about the other person's motivations and feelings, use open-ended questions. Through this line of questioning you may be able to uncover the other person's views and deeper thoughts on the problem. This, in turn, will help you formulate better advice.

Begin Coaching

Once you understand the person and the situation, you can begin your coaching sessions. Effective coaches offer their ideas in such a way that the person receiving them can hear them, respond to them, and consider their value. It is important to advocate your opinions in a clear and balanced way.

- Describe the individual's situation in a neutral way—without value judgments.

- State your opinion.

- Make the thoughts behind your opinion explicit.

- Share your own experiences if they might help.

- Encourage the other person to provide his or her perspective.

Your collaborations will be most successful if you use both inquiry and advocacy in your communications. Overreliance on inquiry can result in the participants' withholding important information and positions. Conversely, if you emphasize advocacy too heavily, you create a controlling atmosphere that can undermine the coaching partnership.

Give and Receive Feedback

Giving and receiving feedback is a critical part of coaching—and supervision in general. This give-and-take goes on throughout the coaching process as you identify issues to work on, develop action plans together, and assess the results. Here are a few tips for giving feedback:

- Focus on behavior, not character, attitudes, or personality. This will prevent the person from sensing that she is being personally attacked.

- Describe the other person's behavior and its impact on projects and/or coworkers, but avoid judgmental language that will put that person on the defensive. For example, instead of saying, "You're rude and domineering," say, "You interrupted Fred several times during each of our last three meetings." Notice how the behavior, and not the person, was attacked in that last statement.

- Avoid generalizations. Instead of saying, "You did a really good job," offer something more specific, such as, "The transparencies you used for your presentation were effective in getting the message across."

- Be sincere. Give feedback with the clear intent of helping the person improve.

- Be realistic. Focus on factors that the other person can control.

- Give feedback early and often in the coaching process. Frequent feedback that is delivered soon after the fact is more effective than infrequent feedback.

Feedback is a two-way street. That means that you must be open to feedback on how effective *you* are as a manager and coach. Coaches who are able to request and process feedback about themselves learn more about the effectiveness of their management styles and create greater trust. To improve your ability to receive feedback, ask for specific information. For example, "What did I say that made you think I wasn't interested in your proposal?" or "How were my suggestions helpful to you?"

When you ask for clarification, do so in a way that doesn't put the other person on the defensive. Instead of saying, "What do you mean, I seemed hostile to your idea?" say, "Could you give me an example?" Also,

- be willing to receive both negative and positive feedback; and

- encourage the other person to avoid emotion-laden terms. For example, "You said that I am often inflexible. Give me an example of things I do that make you believe that."

And be sure to thank the person for his or her feedback, both positive and negative. Doing so will improve trust and be a model of productive behavior to the person you are coaching.

Develop an Action Plan

Some coaching situations benefit from an action plan. A situation in which a subordinate must bring performance up to standard within a certain time or risk dismissal is one clear example. Another would be when you have an excellent subordinate you wish to prepare for a higher-level job within a few months. In each case, a plan assures systematic attention to performance improvement.

An action plan should be written by the person being coached and should describe the specific changes in behavior or new skills the person must work on. Like any effective plan, it should include a timetable and measures of success. Your role in creating the plan should include

- ensuring that the goals are realistic;

- helping the subordinate to prioritize the tasks needed to achieve his goals;

- highlighting potential obstacles and brainstorming potential solutions;

- determining what additional coaching support or training will be required.

Work together on these agreements. Your involvement will demonstrate your interest in the subordinate's success and your commitment to the action plan.

Always Follow Up

Effective coaching includes follow-up that checks progress. Follow-up helps individuals continue to improve. Your follow-up might include asking what is going well and what is not. Follow-up sessions are also opportunities for praising progress, and looking for opportunities for continued coaching and feedback. If the action plan needs modification, the follow-up meeting is the place to do it.

If you're a new manager, or new at coaching, your first efforts may feel uncomfortable and may not be entirely effective. Just remember that you will get better with practice.

Summing Up

- Performance appraisal is a formal method for assessing how well people are doing with respect to their assigned goals. You and your company will need these assessments when you make decisions on pay and promotion.

- The eight steps of effective appraisal are preparation, the appraisal meeting, identifying gaps between actual and expected performance, finding the root causes of the gaps, planning how the gaps will be closed, reevaluating goals, documenting your meeting, and follow-up.

- Coaching is a two-way activity in which the parties share knowledge and experience in order to maximize a subordinate's potential and help that person achieve agreed-upon goals.

- Coaching begins with observation, moves on to a discussion of observed problems with the employee, involves two-way feedback and an action plan, and ends with follow-up by the manager.

Handling Problem Employees

Motivating or Letting Go

Key Topics Covered in This Chapter

- *Using motivation and feedback to change employee behavior or performance*

- *The best ways to handle "C" performers*

- *The do's and don'ts of dismissing employees*

PROBLEM EMPLOYEES. Their performance is unsatisfactory. They eat up your time and create dissatisfaction for you and their colleagues.

Some problem employees can be helped through coaching or training that corrects performance shortfalls. Others can do the job but, for one reason or another, are not motivated to do it. These individuals can often be helped by the savvy manager. Some problem employees, however, simply cannot or will not perform to expected standards, despite intervention, and must either be moved to more appropriate jobs or dismissed.

Coaching was treated in the previous chapter; this one concentrates on motivating problem employees, how to deal with "C" employees, and how to handle dismissals when necessary.

Principles of Motivation

Motivation is everyone's preferred choice as a way to change the behavior or performance of problem employees. The principles of effective motivation were spelled out in the 1960s by Frederick Herzberg. He found that "extrinsic" incentives such as bigger paychecks and plush offices don't necessarily make people work harder or smarter. Even when they do, their positive effects are short-lived. Why? Because most of us are motivated by "intrinsic" rewards: interesting, challenging work, and the opportunity to achieve and grow into greater responsibility. These intrinsic factors answer people's deep-seated need for growth and achievement. Thus, the real key to motivating employees isn't praise, threats of punishment, or even cash. The secret is finding ways to activate their internal generators. And for most people, that means making their jobs more interesting. He offered this advice about making jobs more interesting:[1]

- Remove some controls while retaining accountability for results.

- Give a person a complete natural unit of work (module, divisions, area, and so on) instead of a narrow, highly specified piece of a job ("Screw bolt A into hole B").

- Make periodic reports directly available to workers themselves rather than only to supervisors.

- Introduce new and more difficult tasks.

- Assign specific or specialized tasks to individuals, enabling them to become experts.

Herzberg's prescription remains valid today, and you can use it to enhance the motivation of all your subordinates. Nevertheless, poorly performing employees merit special attention. Motivating them is more difficult.

Do you have subordinates who simply are not motivated to do what's required? Here are the usual signs: They show little commitment to the job and appear bored. Employee entitlements interest them more than the unit's goals. Counseling sessions always end the same way: They agree to change but do not follow through. Organizational psychologist Nigel Nicholson has explained that most managers make one of two mistakes in trying to motivate employees with these characteristics:

- They try to "tell and sell." Tell-and-sell managers try to convince the poor performer of the logic of their viewpoint. "You see, Frank, if we all work together, everyone's job will be easier and we'll get the job done."

- They assume that the employee is of bad character: slothful, self-centered, not a team player.

The problem with the tell-and-sell approach, according to Nicholson, is that it puts the manager in the role of an evangelist bent on converting the nonbeliever. And people don't like being preached to. The same manager would probably do better if he acted like a psychologist seeking the cause of the person's unmotivated behavior. The problem with the second—assuming low character—is that it fails to improve the situation, and in many cases is likely to be wrong.[2] Neither of these approaches gets to the bottom of an employee's performance problem or corrects it.

The Feedback Approach

Another approach to dealing with performance or behavior problems is communication—specifically, giving and receiving direct feedback. Feedback gives each party an opportunity to tell his or her side, and to hear the same from the other. Here are ten tips for using the feedback approach:

1. Make sure that the work expectations and performance objectives are clear. The only way to verify the existence of a performance problem is to state the expected level of performance and measure the employee's actual performance against it.

2. Have all the details before you meet with the employee. Review job description, memos, and documented conversations with the employee that relate to the specific behavior. Don't try to wing it!

3. Give the person advance notice and specify the issue of concern. For example, for a person who is chronically late for work you might say, "I'd like to speak with you tomorrow about work hours." Let the person know whether the solutions are open to discussion or whether you have specific requests that you need addressed. For example, "Please come prepared to discuss your starting time."

4. When your meeting date finally arrives, start off in an upbeat manner. Doing so will set the tone required for a productive session.

5. Describe the problematic behavior and its impact on you and others. For example, "You've been coming to work a half-hour late several days each week for the past month. That is making it difficult for your coworkers to get their work done. And it's setting a bad example for everyone else."

6. Refer to the context of the problem. "This is not the first time we've had to talk about this. We discussed this problem, according to my records, six weeks ago, and again last December. And yet the problem continues."

7. State the concrete effect on you and others of the behavior. For example, "I recognize that you make up the missed time by either staying late or working through lunch, but that's not a solution. Because we operate in work teams, having one person unavailable can mess up the work that three or four others are doing."

8. Listen actively to the employee's response. Don't get distracted with thinking about what you'll say next. Be open to what the person says.

9. Make a suggestion or request, and then check for understanding. For example, "What I'd suggest is that you rearrange things at home so that you can be punctual. That will make our work around here much easier and make everyone on your team happier." Then check for the receiver's understanding of your suggestion. For example, "Do you understand why I'm insisting on your being on time?"

10. Check for agreement/commitment on next steps. For example, "So you agree that you'll be here at 9 A.M. every morning." Keep a record of what was said and any agreement made. Check to determine if the employee is complying with the agreement.

When giving feedback, focus on improving performance—don't use feedback simply to criticize. Make sure that feedback is future-focused; pick issues that can be reworked in the future. For example, if a behavior or action was a one-time event, you might let it go. Also, don't limit feedback to poor performance. It is equally important to give affirming, reinforcing feedback that enables people to learn from what they did right. For example, "I hate coming down on you about being late to work, because the work you do when you're here is exemplary. The trouble is that you need to start that exemplary work at 9 A.M."

Handling "C" Performers

Every organization has a distribution of performers, and not every employee is promotable. At the top are the "A" performers, whose contributions are exceptional. "B" performers do very good work, while "C" performers do work that is just barely acceptable. In their study of managerial talent in two large companies, Beth Axelrod, Helen Handfield-Jones, and Ed Michaels of McKinsey & Company found that the contributions to profit growth of these groups were miles apart. On average, A managers grew profits 80 percent in one company and 130 percent in the other. C managers in these same companies achieved no profit growth whatsoever. This raised a question about where skill and career development resources should be focused. Certainly, well-managed investments in the development of A and B performers make perfect sense. But what about C performers? Should you invest in their improvement or simply move them out of the way?

Some companies regularly prune the ranks of their C-performing managers while others try to bring them up a notch. But most do nothing to deal with them. The cost of this indifference is high, both in terms of defections by good employees and lack of profit growth. As the authors write:

Consider that every C performer fills a role and therefore blocks the advancement and development of other more talented people in an organization. At the same time, C performers usually aren't good role models, coaches, or mentors for others. Eighty percent of respondents in our survey said working for a low performer prevented them from learning, kept them from making greater contributions to the organization, and made them want to leave the company. Imagine, then, the collective impact on the talent pool and morale of a company if just 20 of its managers are underperformers and if each of them manages ten people.[3]

So, what should be done? These authors suggest a three-step approach:

1. Identify your C performers.

2. Agree on explicit action plans for each C performer. Some C players can improve their performance substantially if given the direction and appropriate developmental support.

3. Hold managers accountable for the improvement or removal of C performers.

Many C performers are not worth keeping, at least not in their current positions. Those who cannot improve after coaching should be moved into lower-level jobs where they have the potential to be A performers. Failure in those positions should be followed by termination.

Nevertheless, investments in C performers may be worthwhile. The only way to know for sure is to make an estimate of how organizational performance would improve if you could shift a C-level person to the next highest level. What would be the cost of doing this relative to the benefits? Is the cost less than the benefits? If the cost exceeds the benefits, then the recourse is to either move the individual to a job he or she can do better, or to ask the person to leave the organization.

When All Else Fails: Handling a Dismissal

Disclaimer: At several points, this section refers to legal concerns involved in making and communicating the decision to dismiss an employee. It is not intended as legal advice. Consult with legal counsel who can advise you on the specifics of your situation.

In some cases, no amount of coaching, extra training, feedback sessions, or haranguing can get an employee's performance up to an acceptable level. Dismissal is often the only feasible course of action in these cases—one of the most difficult and painful tasks in any manager's life.[4] Dismissals can be emotionally difficult and, if poorly handled, they can permanently damage individual reputations, negatively affect a company's reputation, and lead to lawsuits. They may also destroy trust and morale throughout the organization. Friends and supporters of the former employee may feel angry. Those who felt frustrated by the dismissed person's poor performance, however, may feel relieved.

To dismiss an employee is to terminate an individual's employment. Except in cases of layoffs, an individual's dismissal should be a consequence of problems with his or her performance or behavior—for instance, as a consequence of performance or behavior that is hopelessly problematic, or when an employee violates the law or a company policy (for example, by stealing or by sexually harassing another employee).

The laws and company policies governing dismissals are complex. Various forms of employee status—such as exempt versus nonexempt, or union versus nonunion—add to this complexity. A general awareness of these implications can guide you when dismissing an employee. However, it's vital that you follow your firm's policies exactly and seek legal advice from your internal or external corporate counsel. Sloppy handling of a dismissal can result in a wrongful-dismissal suit, so let your company's legal department guide you every step of the way.

Most managers feel some confusion or uncertainty over how to decide whether to dismiss a worker or how to actually implement a dismissal if matters should come to that. This is natural. For example, they wonder:

- When is it legal to dismiss someone?

- How and when should I break the news to an affected employee?

- How should I handle the action in terms of legal and company policy?

- How can I preserve morale and trust among remaining team members who may question the dismissal decision or who may be friends of the affected employee?

- What's the best way to realign work roles in the department after the person leaves?

Grounds for a Dismissal

What constitutes a solid legal reason for dismissing an employee? In some cases, you stand on firm legal ground when you dismiss a worker. In other cases, the situation is murky—and you need to proceed carefully. In the United States, the following are offenses for which immediate dismissal is almost always justifiable:

- Possessing an unapproved weapon at work

- Flagrantly violating the most serious company rules, such as giving away trade secrets to competitors

- Being dishonest about significant workplace issues, such as lying about one's travel expenses

- Endangering coworkers' health and safety

- Sexually harassing coworkers or otherwise threatening them in ways that prevent them from doing their work

- Engaging in criminal activity

- Using alcohol or drugs at work

- Gambling on the job

Laws vary from state to state and from nation to nation. So consult legal counsel to make sure you understand the regulations unique to your situation. In U.S. businesses, the following workplace wrongs merit dismissal if they persist or go uncorrected after being brought to the employee's attention:

- Performing poorly on the job

- Refusing to follow instructions

- Having a persistently negative or destructive attitude

- Being insubordinate

- Abusing sick leave and other privileges

- Being chronically late or absent

Whatever your reason for dismissal, it's vital to document the employee's behavior and the steps you've taken to correct it. Being able to point to a history of problem behavior in documented employee performance reviews, personnel files, memos, and private notes can be invaluable if a dismissed employee claims that his or her dismissal was unjustified.

When You Cannot Dismiss an Employee

There are certain behaviors for which a company *cannot* legally dismiss an employee. These vary from nation to nation, but examples may include employee behaviors such as:

- Filing a workers' compensation claim

- "Blowing the whistle" on illegal behavior on the company's part

- Reporting or complaining about company violations of occupational safety and health laws

- Exercising the right to belong or not to belong to a union

- Taking time off from work to perform a civic duty, such as serve on a jury or voting

- Taking a day off from work that was available under federal or state law

Again, ask your legal counsel to advise you regarding these regulations. The rules are complicated, so don't try to interpret them on your own.

A Special Note About Discrimination

Various countries have established laws against dismissing employees based on race, gender, sexual orientation, marital status, physical or mental disability, age, and reproductive status (that is, whether they're pregnant or plan to become pregnant). In some cases, staying on the right side of these laws can be tricky, which explains why discrimination is the most cited reason for wrongful discharge claims. So pay scrupulous attention to how employment discrimination is defined in your situation before deciding whether to dismiss someone. Consulting an experienced lawyer who specializes in employment law is the best way to ensure that you don't unwittingly discriminate against a worker by dismissing him or her.

Handling a Dismissal

At some point in your career, you will have to dismiss an employee. To do it right and in a professional manner, make sure that you've done your homework with respect to legal issues, written documentation of the employee's performance or behavior, and the steps you've taken to help. You want to feel confident that dismissing the person is the right thing to do—for him or her, for your team, and for your company.

Once you've done your homework, schedule a meeting with the employee to break the news. Some experts advise against dismissing an employee on a Friday afternoon. A dismissal just before a weekend may cause the person to stew over the weekend and possibly ponder a lawsuit or think about returning to the office with disruptive intentions. So consider scheduling a meeting on a Monday afternoon. That way he or she will have all week to start looking for another job. Whichever day you choose, you'll want to make sure that that day is the person's final day on the job. Most experts advise against allowing a person to remain on the premises for any length of time. Doing so creates discomfort in the workplace and gives a disgruntled individual opportunities to take proprietary files, sabotage computers, and send out nasty e-mails to other employees.

Meet with the employee in a place that keeps both of you out of sight, such as a windowless conference room or office, or some other space that gives you complete privacy. Also, arrange for a path to and from the meeting to avoid areas that are likely to be populated by curious coworkers. Keeping the meeting private shows respect for the affected employee. No one wants to know that his or her coworkers are overhearing or seeing what is bound to feel like a humiliating experience.

To handle the dismissal as effectively as possible, enlist someone from human resources to be present at the meeting. That person can

- serve as an impassive voice if you or the employee become overly emotional during the meeting;

- act as a buffer in case of an emotional or physical outburst from the employee;

- answer the inevitable questions regarding pensions, insurance, and severance pay;

- serve as a witness to the conversation in the case of a future dispute.

Get the meeting over with as quickly as possible—in ten minutes or less. Don't allow it to drag on. The more concisely you convey the news to the employee, the less prone you'll be to say something that might expose your company to liability. Be dispassionate, direct, and focused. Convey a sense of serious purpose and resoluteness. To avoid planting the seeds for legal problems, resist the temptation to apologize or to reconsider your decision in light of protests from the employee. The person must know that your decision is final and not subject to negotiation.

So what should you say? Explain in general terms that the job has not worked out. If you choose to explain in more detail, do so in an objective, neutral tone that doesn't make the employee feel personally attacked. Examples might include the following: "We talked

What Not to Say During a Dismissal Meeting

The specific language you use while dismissing an employee can play a major role in whether the person decides to sue. Use the following "don'ts" as guidelines during a dismissal:

- Don't side with the worker or foster an "us against them" mind-set to ease your own discomfort. For example, don't say, "Personally, I don't think that letting you go is the right decision."

- Don't tell a dismissed employee that the dismissal is part of a layoff when it is not. This "white lie" could come back to haunt you in the form of a discrimination suit if you hire someone new to fill the vacated position.

- Don't say anything like, "We're after a more dynamic, aggressive work force," or "You just don't fit into the team," or "We need people with fewer family commitments who can see clients after normal work hours," or "We need to project a high-energy image." These kinds of statements could give the impression that the employee is being dismissed for discriminatory reasons, such as being too old, foreign, married, and so forth.

- Don't use humor or try to make light of the situation. You'll only make the meeting even more painfully awkward. Worse, you may make the person feel laughed at or humiliated—and therefore more motivated to sue for wrongful dismissal.

- Don't threaten an employee who implies that he or she may challenge the dismissal; for example, by implying that you'll withhold the person's final paycheck unless he or she agrees not to sue. These forms of persuasion are considered illegal coercion and may come back to haunt you in court.

about your not meeting the performance goals for your role six times over the past year. These goals still haven't been met." Or, "You've received coaching and counseling to help you deal with your critical attitude toward colleagues, but your behavior hasn't changed."

Citing objective reasons in a neutral tone will lessen the chances that the person will sue or defame you or the company.

Strike a balance between being concise and direct, and being empathetic. That is, do acknowledge that losing a job is likely to have a profound impact on the person's life; for example, "I know this is hard for you." After delivering the news, give the person time to vent his or her anger, confusion, or bitterness for a few moments. Empathy and a chance to process emotions can help people bear difficult news.

Deliver the news in a way that preserves the person's dignity. This includes making arrangements for the employee to remove his or her personal effects from the office during off-hours or over the weekend (with monitoring from someone in the company). Employees who are made to feel humiliated before colleagues or disrespected and personally attacked during a dismissal will be more likely to feel angry and thus desire retribution.

Finally, describe whatever severance package, outsourcing assistance, or unused vacation pay is available.

After the Dismissal

Once you have made it through the difficult conversation in which you had to dismiss a problem employee, you will likely feel relieved that the task is over. However, you still have a lot of work to do. In the immediate and longer-term aftermath of a dismissal, you need to

- ensure that the company and the employee honor any employment contracts—such as noncompete and nondisclosure agreements, a promise to provide service letters, or collective-bargaining agreements;

- avoid saying anything about the former employee (whether informally or formally through job references) that might be construed as damaging to his or her professional reputation;

- document the terms of the employee's dismissal.

You or your company's human resource department can address this last point through what's called a separation letter addressed to the employee and delivered to him or her during an exit interview. The letter should clarify when the worker's employment ended. Depending on the circumstances of the situation, it may also describe:

- Severance benefits, including what kinds and when they will be provided

- Final pay, including any bonuses due and accrued benefits, such as vacation time

- Health-insurance coverage or conversion (for example, COBRA in the United States)

- Outplacement help

- Treatment of vested stock options

- Any noncompete or nondisclosure agreements

- Any terms stipulated in a collective bargaining agreement

- Any agreements you've made about providing the person with a service letter or references

- Any release the worker has agreed to, such as a promise not to sue the company in exchange for special benefits, such as additional money

In the United States, if the dismissed employee is in what's known as a protected class—such as a minority, disabled, female, or older worker—and he or she has agreed to sign a release, laws regarding the acceptance of the separation letter become more complicated.

In this case, you or your company should consult legal counsel regarding exactly how to word the separation letter.

Make No Negative Statements

Once the dismissed employee has left the company, take care not to do or say anything—even in an offhand way—that anyone could perceive as damaging to the former employee's reputation or chances of finding another job. Such a statement could come back to haunt you in the form of a defamation suit or through resentment among the former employee's fellow workers. The best policy is simply not to say anything negative about a former employee.

What About References?

At some point, potential employers of the dismissed individual may phone you or your company as part of their reference checking process. If the former employee asks you for a reference and you feel you have little or nothing good to say about the person, stick to the bare essentials. Indeed, your company may have a clear policy specifying what information you can provide in a reference. Check with your human resource and legal departments to familiarize yourself with your company's reference policies.

Getting on with Your Work

After a dismissal, you need to address team members' concerns, redistribute the former employee's work among remaining team members, and ensure that the former employee's skills are still represented in the group.

You'll need to notify workers as soon as possible after someone has been dismissed. Pretending that nothing has happened will only fuel gossip or concerns among remaining group members that they'll be dismissed next. The best approach is to hold a team meeting in which you concisely explain what has happened. For example, you might say, "Toby was dismissed after many months of unsuccessful effort to improve his work performance." Do not go into detail or elaborate on your decision. Also, be sure not to criticize the former employee. Then reassure team members that the dismissal had nothing to do with their own performance or behavior. Acknowledge that this is a difficult time for the entire department and that you understand that some people will be feeling uncomfortable about it. Then explain what your plans are for seeking a replacement and whether the team's focus will change because of the employee's departure.

But don't let your communication end there. After the initial group meeting, schedule time with each person to listen to his or her concerns and help them process their feelings about the change.

Frequently Asked Questions

What documentation am I required to give the dismissed employee?

Consult legal counsel to confirm what documentation you should provide. In general, documentation should be as brief as possible, but may include details of continued benefits, severance, effective dates of termination and pay, and possibly a nondisclosure or noncompete agreement. The documentation should not contain explanations of the reasons for the dismissal.

If I have to dismiss someone, can I get someone else to deliver the news, or can I do it by e-mail?

The short answer is: Deliver this type of message in person; it is part of your job. As painful as delivering hard news is, it's much better to do it yourself, and in person. That's because people form relationships with their managers much more so than with their companies. By delivering hard news in person, you honor that relationship and the other person's humanity, and you help him or her achieve closure on the relationship.

Should I explain the rationale behind a dismissal?

A dismissal should never come as a surprise to the affected employee. If it does, the manager involved has not sufficiently communicated job expectations with the worker. If the employee wants to know why you're dismissing him or her, it's appropriate to say something like, "Here's the goal we agreed on six months ago. We discussed ways you would try to reach that goal. But you have not performed as we agreed." By providing a brief, honest response, you help the person achieve closure.

Should I usher people out immediately after their exit interview, or should I give them time to say goodbye to coworkers?

It's appropriate to escort the person out of the building as soon as possible after termination of his or her employment with the company, especially if the person is being fired for a major indiscretion, such as sexual harassment, theft, or the use of drugs. He or she may return later for the scheduled exit interview. Opinion is divided over this issue when the dismissed person simply wasn't doing a good job. In these cases, escorting the person from the building may be draconian. Still, he or she shouldn't be allowed to linger for days.

What should I do about e-mail and phone messages for employees who have been dismissed?

If you're going to cancel the affected employee's e-mail accounts and voice mail immediately after a dismissal, make arrangements to forward any incoming messages to the employee for a designated amount of time. Of course, with dismissed employees, you don't want suppliers or customers to maintain contact with a possibly bitter or vindictive former worker. On the other hand, it can be upsetting to these outside constituencies to be unable to reach a person they're used to working with—and to get no explanation from your company for what has happened. Clearly, you need to make careful decisions regarding what kinds of communication channels you want to keep open, for how long, and in what respect. Balance concerns about what an abrupt communication cutoff may do to the company against any risks involved in forwarding messages to former workers for a time.

Summing Up

- The key to motivating most people is to offer them intrinsic rewards: interesting, challenging work, and the opportunity to achieve and grow into greater responsibility.

- In addition to providing intrinsic rewards, a manager should provide good feedback about an employee's problems, and how they can be solved.

- "C" performers should be helped to higher performance levels or moved to a position in which they can excel.

- If you're considering a dismissal, familiarize yourself with employment laws in your location. Slipping up during a dismissal could result in a lawsuit.

- If you must dismiss an employee, do it in a short, resolute, and professional manner. Conduct your meeting in a place and manner that does not show disrespect to the employee.

- Follow up a dismissal with documentation. Allow the person to say goodbye to workplace associates, but don't allow his or her presence to drag on. Communicate with other employees about the matter.

Dealing with Crises

Don't Wait Until They Hit

Key Topics Covered in This Chapter

- *Avoiding crises through planning*

- *Preparing to manage crises you can't avoid*

- *How to recognize crises and contain them*

- *Resolving crises in the most effective way*

- *Learning from past crises*

- *Frequently asked questions about managing crises*

PICK UP ANY major newspaper and turn to the business section. Chances are that you will find one or more stories about companies in trouble. An impending bankruptcy. Loss of key data in a computer breakdown. A product liability lawsuit. The possible perils are limitless. Consider this one:

> The auditor looked dour as he walked into Beth's office. Then he showed her the balance sheets for the pension fund. "Something is wrong here," he said.
>
> She could see that he was right. "Could it be embezzlement?" she asked.
>
> "That is the most likely explanation," the auditor opined. "In fact, it's probably the only explanation."
>
> Embezzlement! The press would be all over this. The union would demand an investigation. The police would be involved. There would be no way of dealing with this quietly, within the company. As CEO, Beth would have to go public soon, but how should she handle it? Should she buy time by saying that she had no comment? And what would she say when they asked her who had taken the money? And how had the culprit gotten it so easily? How was the company going to recover the money? One way or another, a private crime was about to become a public issue.

This CEO's problem is not unique. Crises affect all businesses sooner or later. Some are preventable. Others can be anticipated. Still others strike out of the blue. No matter what their origins, the things we do and the decisions we make can make the situation a lot worse—or better.

This chapter offers practical ideas for preventing crises, anticipating them, and managing them when they occur. It also includes answers to frequently asked questions about handling crises.[1]

What Is a Crisis?

Simply put, a crisis is a change—either sudden or evolving—that results in an urgent problem that management must address. Crises have many sources. It would be impossible to list them all, but understanding some major categories can help you identify the crises you and your organization need to avoid (if possible), prepare for, and handle in the most effective way.

Natural events of catastrophic magnitude—earthquakes, tornadoes, blizzards, floods, and fires—can strike unexpectedly, crushing buildings, destroying infrastructures, and interrupting communications. Health- and environment-related disasters, though not necessarily caused by the company, are directly related to it. The company is responsible—or perceived responsible—for dealing with them. Consider the following examples:

- Product tampering by an outsider can harm consumers and damage the image of your product and company.

- Serious product problems or defects, such as defective tires or food contamination, can result in huge financial liabilities and damage your company's reputation.

- Environmental pollution unknowingly caused by your company in years past can come back to haunt you.

- Technological breakdowns can result in huge damage if backup systems are not in place.

- Hackers can take down your e-commerce site during the busiest season of the year.

Whatever their sources, crises pose a continual threat to business success and survival. Therefore, every company—and every manager—must be prepared to deal with them. That preparation should begin long before crises occur.

This chapter presents a six-stage approach to crisis management. These stages are adapted from those offered by Norman Augustine, former CEO of Lockheed Martin, to readers of his article on this subject in the *Harvard Business Review*.[2] Those stages are:

Stage 1: Avoiding the crisis

Stage 2: Preparing to manage the crisis

Stage 3: Recognizing the crisis

Stage 4: Containing the crisis

Stage 5: Resolving the crisis

Stage 6: Learning from the crisis

Avoiding the Crisis

Crises that are handled poorly get lots of negative media attention. But we don't often hear about crises that were prevented by people who were thinking ahead and preventing them from occurring. A famous exception was the Y2K bug. On New Year's Day 2000, virtually every computer in the world made the calendar switch to the new millennium without a hitch. The only thing that people listening for trouble heard was the quiet sound of a crisis prevented. For years, businesses had worked to solve Y2K problems before they happened. And their efforts paid off.

Managers at many levels prevent minor crises every day:

- A sales manager notices that a client's name is misspelled on every page of a major sales proposal. He has all the copies destroyed, makes the adjustments, and has new proposals printed at an all-night copy center, saving the company from the potential loss of a major account.

- A financial manager, foreseeing a cash-flow shortage, takes steps to collect receivables ahead of schedule, puts a hold on all discretionary spending, and makes sure a credit line is available at the company's bank should the expected cash crunch occur.

- When informed that a key employee has been interviewing with other companies, her boss takes steps to identify a potential replacement.

Each of these managers actively avoided a crisis. Doing so was part of their jobs. You must do the same.

Perhaps the best way to avoid crises is to conduct a systematic audit of all the things that could go wrong within your sphere of responsibility. A crisis audit involves the following steps:

- Make crisis planning part of your normal planning. Whether you run an entire business or a single department, you still have to plan strategically for the future, and that planning should include crisis planning. So incorporate a crisis audit into your planning process.

- Collect ideas widely. People's perspectives about potential crises often differ greatly. By talking to people within your department, division, company, and circle of customers and suppliers, you may harvest some surprising information. For example, a sales rep may tell you, "We are very likely to lose our biggest account next year."

- Identify internal weaknesses. Understaffing would be an internal weakness if one resignation would cause an important project to collapse. Poorly trained quality assurance personnel would be another. Their substandard work will eventually allow defective or dangerous products to reach customers.

- Identify external threats. An external threat may take the form of an emerging new technology—one that will render your products obsolete. An impending regulatory change may be another.

As you conduct your crisis audit, pay particular attention to these areas: health and environmental issues; potential technical breakdowns;

economic and market volatility; and relationships with customers and suppliers. Ask yourself these questions about these areas: What are the worst things that could go wrong? What are the most likely crises that could occur?

Once you have audited your situation, you will be positioned to take positive steps to prevent crises. For example, if you've discovered that your IT system and all of its files could be lost to a fire or natural disaster, you can take steps to create a backup system.

Preparing to Manage the Crisis

Some of the potential crises identified in your audit can be avoided through preventive action, but others, such as natural disaster and criminal behavior by employees, will always remain a threat. If you cannot absolutely avoid these, you can at least develop plans for dealing with them. For example, if a natural disaster is on your audit list, you would develop a plan for evacuating employees, notifying second-shift personnel to stay home, and so forth. If public transit workers are threatening a strike, you might develop a car-pooling plan to help employees get to work.

Brainstorm the Possibilities

Brainstorming sessions with employees in various functions is one of the most productive approaches to contingency planning, since no single individual can foresee the dozens of things that will change if the potential crisis becomes a reality. Also give some thought to the possible side effects of your crisis plan—good and bad. Consider these examples:

> *When a chain of auto-repair shops wanted to boost sagging sales, management offered mechanics sales incentives. The more work they brought in, the bigger bonuses they'd make. Unfortunately, some of the mechanics began recommending unnecessary repairs. Customers complained that they were being ripped off, and the chain's reputation suffered. Similarly, a factory offered incentives for every defective product caught*

by employees, but this policy encouraged some workers to deliberately damage products in order to receive the awards. And when a pizza company promised to deliver its pizza "in thirty minutes or it's free," speeding drivers caused car accidents.

You don't have to cover every eventuality, but thinking things through carefully can help prevent problems.

Form a Crisis-Management Team

A team of people that is organized and prepared for a crisis will always perform better than will an ad hoc group thrown together during an emergency. So consider forming crisis-management teams around key threats. For example, a team organized around possible fire or storm damage to the workplace would map out the many things that would have to be done and who would do them. These would include

- how decisions would be made about evacuating the building;

- a plan to contact all employees outside of business hours;

- the circumstances under which employees would be asked to stay home;

- dealing with government agencies and the media;

- finding temporary work quarters while the building was being repaired or replaced.

Thus, each crisis-management team would create topical plans within a more general plan. The mere creation of these plans will prepare team members to deal with these situations should they ever develop.

Recognizing the Crisis

Some crises are evident. You pull into the parking lot to find firemen pumping water through the windows of your office building. Other crises are less evident. Consider this example:

Not many years ago, the CEO of a major corporation was alerted that the president of one of its subsidiaries—a film company—was suspected of embezzling money and forging checks. The CEO ignored the problem, refusing to believe that this individual would ever commit such crimes. But the issue didn't go away, and evidence mounted that something was amiss. By the time the CEO decided to fire the president, the charming thief had gotten board members lined up on his side. The board insisted on keeping him. The situation worsened, and soon new reports were tarnishing the name of the film company, the corporation, and all involved—including the CEO. It was an ugly, painful situation, and one that could have been avoided had it been recognized as a potential crisis and dealt with promptly.

Similar situations have been reported in other organizations. One restaurant chain, for example, was rife with problems of discrimination against minority employees. These problems were common knowledge inside the company, yet its leadership did nothing about it until the company was hit by a major lawsuit. Within twenty-four hours the story was in every major paper in the nation.

Many executives and managers are reluctant to face unpleasant situations. They either do not believe the bad news or would rather not deal with it. Unfortunately, unpleasant situations may be signs of an impending crisis.

Not every problem is a crisis in the making, and managers would dissipate their energy if they treated them as such. So how can you recognize a crisis when you see one? Here are a few suggestions:

- Pay attention when your instincts tell you "There's something wrong here!"

- Confront disturbing facts before they come knocking on your door. Don't ignore them, rationalize them, or minimize their importance. Instead, investigate.

- Consider the consequences if disturbing facts are found to be true (financial losses, physical injury, company reputation, etc.).

- Be guided by your values. What is important? What is the right thing to do? For example, if a subcontractor is illegally disposing of toxic waste from your company, harming the environment, and possibly endangering lives, and you suspect the company is turning a blind eye to it, do what your values urge you to do: Confront the situation. Don't sweep it under the rug.

Containing the Crisis

When a crisis does strike, the first thing you must do is contain the damage. That means making decisions quickly and being on the scene. Your physical presence is important. It lets everyone know that you care about what is happening. And you must communicate critical information to key people. Consider this example:

> *A supermarket chain was accused by a major TV network of selling spoiled meat. The value of the company's stock plummeted when the story was released. But the company's management team responded quickly. They gathered the facts, listened to stockholders, and paid close attention to store employees.*
>
> *Once they had the facts, the team put a plan into action. They immediately stopped the practice of selling less-than-fresh meat, and put large windows in the meat-preparation areas so that the pubic could watch meat being packaged. They expanded employee training, gave public tours of their facilities, and offered discounts to draw people back into the stores. The company eventually earned an excellent rating from health authorities, and sales returned to normal.*

Be Decisive

Decisiveness is a requisite of effective crisis management. Emergencies do not afford the luxury of time and the careful deliberation that characterize normal decision making. The manager who moves quickly can stabilize the situation and earn the confidence of peers and subordinates. Consider the following example:

When a torrential evening storm flooded a section of an office building, the computers, carpeting, paper records, and the workspaces of ten employees were badly damaged. The manager was on the scene, directing clean-up efforts, even as employees were arriving. She had operations back to normal in just a few days. But then workers began having breathing problems and complaining of headaches. Though the carpet had been cleaned, everyone suspected that it was infested with mold. Instead of having the carpet cleaned once again, or waiting for budgetary approval, this manager had all the carpet in the area removed and replaced.

This manager demonstrated two essential qualities necessary in a crisis—decisiveness and concern. First, her presence on the scene showed that she, and the company, cared. Her decisiveness in replacing the mold-infested carpeting demonstrated that the health of employees was more important than any other consideration.

Decisiveness is not always easy. Factual information is usually thin. And there is no time for fact gathering or exploration of alternatives. In the absence of these, you must combine the facts you have with your sense of the right thing to do.

Communicate

Communication in times of crisis is the strongest tool at the manager's disposal. Communication must extend from the crisis-management team to all stakeholders.

As you communicate, pick your words with care. What you say and how you say it will shape perceptions and guide action—for better or worse. But stick to the facts. You are not obligated to speculate. The facts are your best antidote for the rumors and misinformation that quickly surround these situations. Avoid these typical, but inappropriate messages:

"No comment."

"We haven't read the complaint."

"A mistake was made."

Resolving the Crisis

Crisis resolution requires fast, confident decision making. But how do you make good decisions when events are moving quickly? During times of confusion? When it's hard to sort out what's important and what isn't? The answer is: Identify the real problem and get the relevant facts.

Relevant facts aren't easy to find in a crisis situation. There is usually a flurry of information, most of it inaccurate, speculative, or nothing more than rumor. It's your task to discover the truth and face it by asking the right people, listening to the most reliable voices, and going to the right places. A leader in a crisis responds by

- facing the crisis;

- turning fear into positive action;

- being alert to new developments and new information;

Tips on Crisis Control

- Avoid blaming others. The impulse to blame others is almost irresistible. But creating a scapegoat is counterproductive. Focus on handling the crisis and leave the recriminations for later.

- Don't promise anything that you can't deliver. It is wiser to underpromise and then deliver more than to overpromise and come up short.

- Don't worry about the rules. Rules, policies, structures, procedures, and budgets are created to maintain order and provide a productive process in the normal course of business. These rules were not created with a crisis in mind. So do whatever has to be done to defeat the crisis, and don't worry about the "rules"!

- maintaining focus on the priorities—ensuring that people are safe first, and then assessing the next most critical needs;

- assessing and responding to what is in his or her control and ignoring what is not.

Learning from the Crisis

Every crisis has bad news and good news. The bad news is that your company was clobbered by the crisis. The good news—and sometimes the only good news—is that the experience can help you avoid a future crisis. But you must make the most of that fleeting opportunity.

Engineers use earthquakes and the damage they cause to develop stronger roads, bridges, and buildings. You can do something similar by conducting a postcrisis audit to learn and even profit from the earthquake that has hit your organization. The following pointers can guide you.

Conduct a crisis review as soon as possible after the event, while people's memories are fresh. Then analyze the crisis from beginning to end. Pinpoint actions, assumptions, and outside factors that precipitated the crisis. Then ask yourself these questions:

- Knowing what we knew then, could the crisis have been prevented? How?

- At what point did we realize we were in a crisis? Could we have recognized the signs earlier?

- What warning signals were ignored? Which signals did we pay attention to?

- In our response to the crisis, did we take the appropriate actions? What could we have done better?

Get input from many people. You need to get everyone's story, but pay attention in particular to those with expertise in the areas of greatest importance. Once you have clear answers to these questions, build them into your plans for future crisis avoidance and crisis management.

Frequently Asked Questions

Since it's not possible to cover all the details of crisis management in a short chapter, we conclude with answers to some frequently asked questions. Perhaps one or more of these are pertinent to your situation.

What if my boss wants to cover up a problem?

First, talk to your boss about the consequences. If that doesn't work, get a new job or blow the whistle, or both. If your boss covers up a problem, then you will either become part of the coverup, or appear to be part of it. You could even become the scapegoat.

Should I disclose possible problems to my boss or my colleagues if I am not certain that they are real problems or if there is a possibility that they might be avoided altogether?

In general, it is best to disclose even potential problems. No one wants to be seen as crying wolf, but keeping silent when you sense serious problems is the greater error.

What if I discover that a capable and loyal employee has violated the law, thinking that doing so would be in the company's interest?

When it comes to violating the law, intentions don't matter. The violation should be disclosed immediately to the legal department if not to the legal authorities.

How can I deal with rumors that are damaging morale?

The strongest antidote to rumors is the truth. Management should be very candid and get information to all parties in a timely fashion. This can be done with Web sites, telephone call-ins, taped messages, memos, group meetings, and so on.

How can I carry out my normal responsibilities and fight a crisis at the same time?

You probably can't. In times of true crisis, resolution of the crisis should be your top priority. If possible, delegate responsibility of day-to-day operations to a capable subordinate.

If I am required to talk to the media, should I speak off the record?

In general, it is a poor practice to speak off the record. If you don't want to see your statements in print, you probably shouldn't be making them. On rare occasions, it may be helpful to provide background information, but this should be done only in extraordinary circumstances.

If I'm in charge of a geographically diverse team, should I return to headquarters, where I have good communications and staff support, or should I go to the crisis location?

The best answer obviously depends on the circumstances. However, it is generally best to be at the center of the storm.

Should I say publicly how bad the outcome of a crisis might be?

An effective leader cannot be a pessimist. By the same token, a good leader must be a realist. Most people, including most employees, would rather know the full range of "reasonable possibilities" than to be surprised by a very negative outcome. By adopting a strategy of total candor, the possibility always exists for positive news—something that is welcomed in time of crisis.

Should I publicly admit error?

If an error was made, the answer would generally be yes. There are, of course, legal implications to doing so that must be weighed. In the long term, however, it is best to recognize errors—if for no other reason than they usually come out in the end.

Should the public spokesperson in times of crisis be the head of public relations?

If the crisis affects the corporation as a whole, the CEO should be the spokesperson. Only the most senior individual is recognized as having authority to speak on behalf of the entire organization. For crises confined to a part of the corporation, the head of public relations is generally the appropriate spokesperson.

Summing Up

- You can avoid some crises entirely by anticipating their possibility and by taking preventive measures.

- Because some crises are beyond your control, develop plans for handling them if they come to pass.

- Recognize a crisis when you see it by having an open mind.

- To contain a crisis, be decisive and quick. Communicate the facts to all stakeholders.

- Resolving a crisis requires prompt and confident decisions based on facts.

- Once the emergency has ended, conduct a postmortem to learn from the experience.

Developing Your Career

And Theirs

Key Topics Covered in This Chapter

- *Identifying your core business interests, work reward values, and skills*

- *Finding career opportunities within your organization*

- *Using career ladders and mentors*

- *Developing the careers of your subordinates*

T HE WORLD is changing fast, and the world of work is changing with it. Many years ago, "computer" was a job classification. People with mathematical skills and great capacities for detail would do the math required to fill actuarial tables, artillery trajectory tables, and the like. Those jobs have been eliminated, their work being relegated to machines with the very same name.

Managerial jobs have also been affected by change. Today, authoritarian command and control is giving way to collaboration between managers and employees. Decision-making authority is being pushed down to lower levels. Many tasks are now handled by teams. And companies are expecting everyone—including managers—to produce more with fewer resources. Each of these changes has had an effect on managers, their jobs, and their careers. How have they affected yours over the past five years?

Even in the absence of these general developments, your career would change because *you* are changing. You are acquiring skill, experience, and judgment. Each should make you more valuable to your employer, if not to other companies. The passage of time also produces greater self-understanding; you are probably getting a better sense of your values, strengths, and professional aspirations. The question is, should changes in your career be left to chance, or should they be managed toward some goal? If you chose the latter, then career development can help you.

Career development is the process of assessing where you are in your work life, deciding where you want to be, and then making the changes necessary to get there. It's a process that you can manage.

Managing one's career requires that you view your professional development as a path or a direction, rather than a point or a job.

This chapter will give you practical ideas for managing your career—whether it is just beginning, or well along the road.

Not Just Up

It's easy to think of career development as upward progress on a ladder that begins with entry-level jobs and culminates higher up in the organization, as shown in figure 10-1. This is a reality for most people. But thinking that the only way to develop is to move vertically is highly restrictive, boxing people into jobs and careers that may be less than optimal for them. Consider this example:

Sheila is an associate sales rep on the career ladder shown in figure 10-1. She is doing well, and her manager would like to see her move up another rung of the ladder. But though her outgoing personality has made her a successful salesperson, she is misplaced in sales. Her real passion, as she is learning year by year, is in tinkering, innovation, and getting to know what customers really want.

FIGURE 10-1

Climbing the Ladder

Career-*Ladder* Thinking

Vice President of Sales (1)

Sales Manager (1 of 2)

Customer-Account Manager (1 of 15)

Associate Sales Rep (1 of 25)

Junior Sales Rep (1 of 50)

"Up" is the *only* way to advance.

Source: Harvard ManageMentor®.

FIGURE 1 0 - 2

Career-*Lattice* Thinking

Source: Harvard ManageMentor®.

Sheila may find more fulfillment and make a greater contribution if she redirected her career to product development. In making such a shift she could leverage what she has already learned about customer needs into an area more suited to her true interests and talents.

Sheila's case suggests that people—especially people in the early stages of their careers—should stop thinking about a career ladder and start thinking in terms of a career "lattice." Lattice thinking (figure 10-2) encourages people to follow their passions, values, and personal strengths. The lattice analogy frees people from the straitjacket of thinking that the only way to advance and develop one's capabilities is to move up a narrow path within a single function. It allows them to follow their passions, values, and strengths.

First, Know Yourself

Following one's passions, values, and personal strengths is the foundation of successful career development. That foundation ensures that people develop in ways that make them more valuable and more satisfied with their lives at work. The only way to create this foundation is to know yourself.

What are your most passionate business interests? What are your deepest work values? Can you identify your strongest skills? Answers to these questions aren't always easy, especially for people still in the early stages of their careers. But answering them is the most important step in managing one's career. It helps you to identify the following:

- The types of work you like to do

- The activities that give you the most satisfaction

- The environments in which you prefer to work

- The sorts of people you like to work with

- The abilities you possess that you'd like to develop

You have three sources of information for knowing yourself: you; colleagues, friends, and family; and formal tools of assessment. To use yourself as an information source, look deep within yourself to identify key themes. Ask yourself what you cherish most about yourself. What is most special about you? What are your unique gifts? Imagine that you are stepping into retirement, and looking back over your entire work career. Then finish these sentences:

I am most proud of _____ .

I wish I had done more of _____ .

What do these statements suggest about your interests, values, and skills?

The people who know you best are often excellent sources of information about your work interests, values, and abilities. Indeed, if you imagine yourself as the CEO of your own professional growth, you can think of these people as your "board of directors."

Use each of the following activities to build self-knowledge with the help of your personal board:

Consult your colleagues. Ask them, "What's my reputation in the company? What am I best known for?"

Then query your friends. Pick five or six people who know you well. Prepare a questionnaire with the following questions and ask each of them to fill it out:

What four words best describe me?

If your best friend asked you to tell her more about me, what would you say?

What appears to motivate me?

What would be the ideal job for me?

What seems to make me most fulfilled and excited?

What work should I stay away from, and why?

What about myself do I have trouble seeing?

What aspects of myself do I need to change to be more successful?

What aspects of myself should I not change?

Knowing When It's Time for a Change

There's another important part of knowing yourself: recognizing when it's time to explore new work opportunities. The signals can differ for each person. However, here's a list of possible indications that you've outgrown your current role and are ready for a change:

• A feeling of dread when Monday morning rolls around

• Envy of what others are doing for work

• Restlessness or boredom

• A recurring sense of repetition in your work

• A growing interest in nonwork areas of your life

• Inability to see a future that you want to move toward

Collect all the responses and look for common themes. These themes will provide clues to your interests, values, and skills. Also, be sure to thank your board members for their honesty and thoughtful attention. They'll appreciate knowing that you're using the information and insight they've provided.

There are, of course, more formal assessment tools that can help you clarify your deepest interests, values, and skills. These are available through private career counselors, who can administer the tests and interpret them for you. Your company's human resource department may be able to provide the same service.

Your Core Business Interests

We said that in knowing yourself you should focus on your business interests, work values, and skills. Of these, core business interests are the most important qualities to recognize in managing your career, for several reasons. Interests are more stable than values and skills. Tests have shown that core business interests change little, if at all, over time. By contrast, your work values and skills may shift over the years, depending on your current priorities and your experience and training.

Interests are also the best indicators of work satisfaction. Having the right skills for certain work doesn't necessarily mean that you're going to find satisfaction in that work. If you don't feel a deep interest in the work, you'll soon burn out or get bored—no matter how good you are at it.

What are core business interests? They're long-held, emotionally driven passions. They derive from your personality, and they influence the kinds of activities that make you happy. Based on interviews with some 650 professionals in many industries over a ten-year period, psychologists Timothy Butler and James Waldroop developed a conceptual framework that outlines eight "embedded life interests" through which people generally find personal expression:[1]

1. Application of technology

2. Quantitative analysis

3. Theory development and conceptual thinking

4. Creative production

5. Counseling and mentoring

6. Managing people and relationships

7. Enterprise control

8. Influence through language and ideas

These embedded life interests—which often overlap—can be very useful in evaluating your "fit" with certain types of work.

Note: Butler and Waldroop's eight categories form the basis for their assessment tool, the Business Career Interest Inventory, and their online career-management program, CareerLeader.

Application of Technology

People with a life interest in the application of technology are intrigued by how things work; they seek better ways to use technology to solve business problems. As Butler and Waldroop write, "people with [this] life interest often enjoy work that involves planning and analyzing production and operations systems and redesigning business processes."[2] They cite the example of a money manager who acts as his company's unofficial computer consultant because he loves the challenge of this type of work more than he does his regular job.

Quantitative Analysis

"Some people aren't just good at running the numbers, they excel at it. They see it as the best, and sometimes the only, way to figure out business solutions. Similarly, they see mathematical work as fun. . . . Not all 'quant jocks' are in jobs that reflect that deeply embedded life interest," write Butler and Waldroop. In fact, more than a few find themselves in other kinds of work for the wrong reason: because they were told that following their true passion would narrow their career prospects.

If you are intrigued by cash-flow analysis, methods of forecasting sales, and other number-based activities, quantitative analysis may be your core business interest.

Theory Development and Conceptual Thinking

For some people, nothing brings more enjoyment than thinking and talking about abstract ideas, according to Butler and Waldroop. If you are excited by creating business models, explaining the competition in your industry, or analyzing the competitive position of your business units, this may be your core business interest.

Creative Production

People with this embedded interest are imaginative, out-of-the-box thinkers. They are comfortable and engaged during brainstorming sessions. Write Butler and Waldroop, "[M]any entrepreneurs, R&D scientists, and engineers have this life interest. Many of them have an interest in the arts. . . . Many people with this interest gravitate toward creative industries such as entertainment."[3]

Does this describe you?

Counseling and Mentoring

Individuals bitten by this bug like to teach. In business, teaching takes the forms of coaching and mentoring. Many like feeling useful to others; some genuinely take satisfaction from the success of those they counsel.

Your interactions with direct reports is a good clue to respect to this interest. Do you enjoy coaching your people? Have you gone out of your way to act as a mentor to a younger colleague?

Managing People and Relationships

Individuals with this life interest enjoy dealing with people on a day-to-day basis. They derive satisfaction from workplace relationships, but they focus much more on outcomes than do people in the counseling-mentoring category.

Do you like to motivate, organize, and direct others? If you do, this might be your core business interest.

Enterprise Control

These are people who like to be in charge, whether it's their high school class or a division of a corporation. They are happiest when they have decision-making authority over their little piece of the universe. Does this describe you? Do you ask for as much responsibility as you can get your hands on?

Influence Through Language and Ideas

People with this embedded interest enjoy storytelling, negotiating, and persuading. They are most fulfilled through writing, speaking, or both, and are often drawn to careers in public relations, journalism, and advertising. If you're the type who routinely volunteers to write up project proposals, new product presentations, and the like, this may be your embedded interest.

Your Work Values

People mean many different things when they speak of values. For example, many of us speak of family values, national values, or spiritual values. Work values are the values you place on the rewards that you may receive in return for performing your job. They are the values that motivate you and make you excited about your work. Examples include a tangible opportunity for wealth, an intellectual challenge, affiliation with people you admire or respect, or a satisfying work-life balance.

Understanding your values increases the likelihood that you'll choose satisfying work. There are other benefits to understanding your values. You can "shop" more efficiently for the right developmental opportunities. Just as you can evaluate a potential computer purchase much more quickly if you keep a few must-have features in mind, you can judge a work opportunity more wisely if you remember your most crucial rewards. You will also be in a better position to match your reward values to an organization's or department's culture.

Work rewards manifest themselves in an organization's or department's culture—the way people do things, what they expect, what they think is most important, and so forth. A large company's different departments (for example, engineering, sales, or human resources) might have markedly different cultures. By knowing your values, you can pick the culture that will provide those rewards.

Clarifying Your Work Values

There are many different ways to clarify your values. One is to ask reflective questions of yourself, such as, "What motivates me?" "What would I be willing to give up to pursue more satisfying work?" As you reflect on your values, however, remember that we are tempted to list values that we *think* we should have—like altruism—and to avoid listing values we think we shouldn't have—like desire for prestige or financial gain. Be as honest as you possibly can when doing this exercise; genuine answers will make it much easier for you to evaluate and choose the best possible work opportunities for you.

Note: You'll find a handy Rewards Worksheet in Appendix A. Use it to guide your work value self-appraisal. You can also find this worksheet and other interactive tools on the Harvard Business Essentials Web site at http://elearning.hbsp.org/businesstools.

A Practical Technique

Here's a useful technique for sorting out your true work values. Write all the work values you can think of on index cards, one value per card. These might include:

- An environment of openness, camaraderie, and friendliness

- Access to experts in the industry

- Good health and childcare benefits

- Stock options, pension plans, and profit sharing

- Scheduling options such as flex-time, telecommuting, and sabbaticals

On each card, write a short statement about what that value means to you. Then arrange the cards on a table in order of importance. If two or more values seem equally important to you, place them side by side. If you decide that a value has no real importance to you after all, set that card aside.

Now note the order of your cards. These reflect your preferences. Don't worry about which values seem to be "rising to the surface" at this point, or whether you're having trouble deciding which of two seemingly equally important values should come first. Just make a mental or written note that summarizes what you see happening at this stage.

Set the stack of cards aside. After a week or two, revisit the exercise to see if anything has shifted. Repeat the process until you feel confident that your hierarchy of cards accurately reflects your work values. Think of your top three or four values as your "shopping list" when considering job choices or career development opportunities.

Your Skills

You've identified your core business interests and clarified your work values in order to manage your career development. You also need to assess your business skills. Together, these three qualities make up the foundation of the self-knowledge you'll need to select the most suitable professional-development opportunities.

But what are business skills, exactly? Skills fall into a number of categories, and there are different ways to describe them. Here are some examples:

- Using your hands—to assemble things, operate machinery, repair things

- Using words—for reading, writing, speaking, teaching

- Using your senses—to observe, inspect, diagnose

- Using numbers—to count, compute, record

- Using analytical thinking or logic—to research, analyze, prioritize

- Using creativity—to invent, design

- Using artistic abilities—to fashion or shape things, decorate

- Using leadership—to initiate new projects, organize, direct, make decisions

Assessing Your Skills

What are your strongest skills? As you explore developmental opportunities at your organization, you'll need to know which are your strongest skills and which you'd like to strengthen or acquire. Remember, too, that some skills are transferable and others are not. Transferable skills are those that have value regardless of the business context in which you're using them; for example, writing, managing people, organizing data, and selling real estate.

Why is it important to know if your skills are transferable? Because transferable skills widen the selection of potential work opportunities available to you. If you have accounting or financial skills, for example, a transition from an electronics manufacturing company to steel fabricating company would not be a big problem. If your career path is blocked where you work today, you can move elsewhere without having to retrain or go back to school.

But what if your skills are nontransferable? Nontransferable skills are "firm-specific." They only have value to your current employer (or to a very small universe of other employers). An example would be the ability to operate a highly specific piece of equipment—one that no other firm has. If you had a nontransferable skill like this one your mobility would be very limited. On the other hand, your employer would not easily be able to hire someone to replace you.

As you assess your skills, give some thought to the issue of transferability. It will have a major impact on your mobility. At the same time, keep these points in mind:

- Skills are a "threshold" variable in your ability to do a job successfully. You need enough of a certain skill (being able to lift fifty-pound packages, for example), but in many cases, having a lot more of that same skill (being able to lift five-hundred-pound bags) won't make you any more successful.

- It's easy to alter your skills. Compared to your core business interests and work values, your skill set can change relatively easily. That is, you can strengthen existing skills or acquire new ones through practice, training, and new experiences.

- Everyone has weaknesses. Some people assume that they have to be good at everything. The fact is, we all have both strengths *and* weaknesses. Success comes from playing to your strengths and doing what you can to reduce weaknesses.

- Weigh the benefits of developing new skills against their costs. New skill development can be costly in terms of time, effort, and sometimes money. So when you're evaluating a potential new opportunity at work, consider the cost of developing the skills that the opportunity requires.

Note: You'll find a Skills Assessment worksheet in Appendix A. Use it to guide your self-appraisal. You can also find this worksheet and other interactive tools on the Harvard Business Essentials Web site at http://elearning.hbsp.org/businesstools.

Once you've assessed your skills, the next step is to combine that assessment with what you've already learned about your core business interests and work values. Together, these give you a complete picture of your professional standing, aspirations, and outlook.

Use this knowledge as you seek out and evaluate opportunities to develop your career. As you do so, remember this: Interests and values matter the most. Make sure that any opportunity you pursue matches your core business interests and work values. If it does, you may well decide to obtain the skills that will help you perform in that new position.

The "Test and Learn" Alternative

The assessment approach (interests, values, skills) described in this chapter can get you into trouble if your assessment of your true working identity is wrong; it might encourage you to make a big change that is ill-suited. As an alternative, career specialist Herminia Ibarra suggests a "test and learn" approach in which you put several working identities into practice, refining them until they're sufficiently grounded in experience to inspire a more decisive step. The tactics she recommends are:

- **Experiment.** Sample new professional roles without compromising your current job. You can do this through freelance assignments, sabbaticals, or moonlighting.

- **Shift connections.** Make new connections by working for people you admire and can learn from. Find people who can help you grow.

- **Make sense of events.** Your working identity is always in the making. Weave the events in your work life into a coherent story about the person you are becoming.

As Ibarra tells her readers, "Your working identity is an amalgam of the kind of work you do, the relationships and organizations that form part of your work life, and the story you tell about why you do what you do and how you arrived at that point. Reshaping that identity, therefore, is a matter of making adjustments to all three of those aspects over time."

The adjustments she describes happen tentatively and incrementally, making them seem haphazard. The process of testing, discovering, and adapting she advocates, however, is part of a logical process, and one that can be learned by almost anyone seeking professional renewal.

SOURCE: Herminia Ibarra, "How to Stay Stuck in the Wrong Career," *Harvard Business Review*, December 2002, 44.

Finding Development Opportunities at Your Company

Once you've identified your true working identity, finding the right position on the path to career development is the next step. In most cases, that position will be within your own company. And if it's a well-run organization, it will have an explicit process for moving you into areas of greater learning, responsibility, and professional growth. The best companies in this regard have formal career development programs based on training, progressive work assignments, and mentoring relationships. These companies recognize that career development helps to retain the most promotable people and to fill vacancies caused by retirements, defections, and growth. It creates a strong cadre of people who will one day lead the company as technical professionals, managers, and senior executives.

Here are some tips for finding opportunities for matching your work identity and aspirations within your company:

- If your company has career counselors, talk to them.

- Look for opportunities to sample different jobs by filling in for colleagues who are on leave or on extended vacation.

- Check the job postings in your human resources department.

- Network! Get to know people in your organization who can help you learn about and pursue career opportunities. Ask yourself: "Who knows the most about what's going on in the organization?" Then meet them and talk about your search.

- Cultivate relationships with influential managers and executives.

Career Ladders

Human resource people often refer to *career ladders* when they talk about career development. A career ladder is a logical series of stages that move a talented and dedicated employee through progressively more challenging and responsible positions. For example, in the publishing business, a person with senior editorial aspirations might be progressively moved through various positions in production or marketing, to editorial assistant, to editor. Each step is intended to broaden his or her skills and understanding of the business.

Formal training is generally an important element at different rungs of the career ladder. Some firms systematically analyze the person's current level of skills and experience and match those against the skills and experiences needed at the next step up the ladder. Gaps between what they have and what they need are then addressed through a plan that involves some combination of formal training, special assignments, and regular mentoring by a respected superior, as described in figure 10-3.

A career ladder will help you avoid a career "plateau" and the feeling of being stuck. If you want to improve and move ahead, you should always feels that you are learning and being challenged with a manageable new set of responsibilities.

Does your company have explicit career ladders? Ask yourself these questions about career ladders in your company or operating unit:

- What career ladders are available to me right now?

- Am I in a position to take advantage of them?

- Have I identified and made some provisions for the skills and experiences I will need to climb to the next level?

- What can I do to get "unstuck" from a career plateau?

FIGURE 10-3

Filling Skill and Experience Gaps

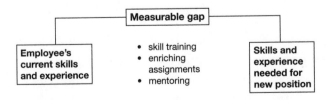

Find a Mentor

Most cultures applaud the self-made person. But the fact is that few successful people are entirely self-made. Most can point to a relative, a boss—a mentor—who helped them make the most of life's lessons and guided their professional development. A study by Harvard Business School professor Linda Hill concluded that at least half of all executives had bosses who mentored them during their careers. That percentage may be increasing, since more and more job applicants are inquiring about mentoring opportunities within the organizations that seek to recruit them.

Mentors are important facilitators of career development. Some companies arrange mentoring relationships for promising managers. If yours does not, you need to find a mentor who can help you. What type of person makes a good mentor? Here are some qualities to look for:

- Someone who has the credentials to empathize with your special challenges; for example, a female executive mentor for a woman employee in a largely male organization

- A person with a nurturing attitude

- A person who exemplifies the best of the company's culture

- A person with high standards

- Someone with rock-solid standing in the organization

Career Development for Your People

What's good for you is also good for the people who work for you—including career development. One of your jobs as a manager is to develop the capabilities of subordinates. In developing this "human capital," you will be increasing the value of the organization. And you'll be doing yourself a big favor. After all, you cannot move up to a higher-level job unless you've developed someone capable of filling your shoes.

Tips for Career Development

Provide a career ladder for every person you hope to retain. For promotable individuals, identify gaps between the skills and experience they now have and those they'll need to step into new roles. Then fill those gaps with training and appropriate assignments.

Don't allow good people to be stuck on career plateaus. If you do, you may lose them. And make sure that everyone who needs one has a suitable mentor—and that includes you.

To help subordinates develop their careers, encourage them to follow the same approach that we recommend for you: discover their embedded life interests, identify their work values, and assess their skills. Help them with this or direct them to a career counselor.

Once they have developed a realistic work identity, make sure that every employee with "the right stuff" has a career ladder to higher levels of achievement. Help each subordinate move up the ladder through appropriate prescriptions of training and progressive job assignments. Provide coaching as needed.

Finally, try to link every promising subordinate to an effective mentor. In most cases, that will not be you. The boss–subordinate relationship can get in the way of good mentoring. Look to others to fill mentor roles, using the criteria listed previously.

Summing Up

- Developing your own career begins with self-knowledge— one's passions, values, and strengths.

- Core business interests are more stable than values and skills. These interests are long-held, emotionally driven passions. They derive from an individual's personality and influence what kinds of activities make people happy.

- A well-run organization has an explicit process for moving people into areas of greater learning, responsibility, and professional growth.

- Mentors can have a substantial influence on the careers of managers.

- What's good for the careers of managers applies equally to their subordinates. Managers have a responsibility to develop the capabilities of the people who work for them.

- Link every promising subordinate with a mentor.

Becoming a Leader

The Final Challenge

Key Topics Covered in This Chapter

- *The characteristics of effective leaders*

- *Balancing tensions*

- *How to create a vision that others will follow*

- *Being a change agent*

- *Challenging complacency*

- *Leading without formal authority*

BEING A LEADER is not the same as being a manager, and vice versa. Managers create order out of complexity; they keep the trains running on schedule. Leaders, in contrast, deal with ambiguity, change, and opportunity; they push the train tracks where they've never gone before. This distinction is not entirely accurate, as leaders must also manage. To be effective, leadership cannot just be about inspiration and grand visions, but must also be about getting results.

Managers must also lead within their own spheres of responsibility. They must create a vision that others will follow, align people and resources with their vision, use communication skills to muster support, gather resources, motivate others to do their best, and harness the power of creative conflict. These are among the topics treated in this chapter.

The Challenge of Contemporary Leadership

In the past, leaders generally knew that they were invested with formal authority. They were the kings, the generals, the CEOs. Within clear constraints, their directives carried the weight of societal or organizational authority. That is much less true today. Because today's organizations are flatter and less hierarchical, many people called to lead find that their formal authority is not particularly useful; to get people moving in the right direction they must rely on personal influence, diplomacy, and skill in communicating; conflict resolution; and the carrot of motivation.

Today's formal and informal leaders also must be alert and enterprising. Owing to the rapid pace of change, they must be able to recognize opportunities and threats, and be capable of mustering organizational responses to them. More than anything, they must be able to maintain positive energy in the face of risk, ambiguity, and change. And they must balance the tensions that exist in every organization.

Characteristics of Effective Leaders

Leadership used to be viewed in terms of a set of innate traits: intelligence, self-confidence, vision, verbal eloquence, and a mystical blend of courage, charisma, and decisiveness. Epic poems and premodern histories celebrated these traits—and the individuals who possessed them. Here's just one sample, a description of England's King Richard I from Beha ed-Din Ibn Shedad's *Life of Saladin*:

> *This king, Richard Coeur-de-lion, was of terrible strength, proven valour and indomitable character. . . . In dignity and power he was inferior to the king of France, but he was richer and braver.*

It's difficult to think of any modern leader being described in those terms. In contrast, here are some traits of effective business leaders. How many do you have? How many can you develop?

- Caring—They empathize with other people's needs, concerns, and goals.

- Comfortable with ambiguity—They can operate in environments of uncertainty, where guideposts are few.

- Persistent—They maintain a positive, focused attitude in pursuing a goal, despite obstacles and failures.

- Excellent in communications—They know how to listen closely, make presentations, and speak in public.

- Effective negotiator—Good leaders are always negotiating, both with outsiders and their own people.

- Politically astute—They have a solid sense of their organization's power structure, listen especially carefully to the concerns of its most powerful groups, and know where to turn for the support and resources they need.

- Humorous—When the situation warrants it, they know how to relieve tension with a little mirth.

- Level-headed—In the midst of turmoil and confusion they maintain an inner calmness.

- Engaging—They are effective in gaining the commitment of others to organizational goals.

- Challenging—They convince others that they should set high standards and accept goals that make them stretch.

- Self-aware—They know how their own behavior affects others.

- Future-focused—They organize short-term tasks according to long-term priorities.

These personal traits may be things that people either have or don't have. Some may be developed or modeled through observation of leaders at close range. Biographies of leaders with these traits provide insights into the personal makeup of effective leaders.

While observing what effective leaders *are* is a useful exercise, be equally attentive to what they *do*—how they behave. What they do includes: making decisions even though all the facts are not available; making difficult trade-offs; creating plans that others eagerly follow; taking actions consistent with their values; inspiring ordinary people to do extraordinary things; and balancing the tensions inherent in organizational life. Again, close-range observation of leader behavior can help us model our own behavior as leaders.

The Tensions Leaders Must Balance

One of the behaviors just cited—balancing organizational tensions—is worth investigating here, since it is so rarely considered. Every organization contains internal tensions. Left alone, these could dissipate energy through internal conflict. It is the leader's job to turn the energy within those tensions to good purposes. Among the tensions we find in organizations, two stand out:

1. **The competitive urge.** Even as they collaborate to beat the competition, individual employees, team members, and entire departments inevitably compare themselves to each other. Some try to shine at the expense of others. Their competitive instincts urge them to seek recognition and rewards—often at the expense of their colleagues. The competitive urge is a valuable form of energy. But it cannot be allowed to create internal warfare. Instead, the competitive urge must be channeled into activities that benefit the entire organization. Effective leaders manage to do this.

   The case of T. E. Lawrence provides an engaging example of a leader who accomplished many of his goals by rechanneling internal tensions. Sent out by the British Army to the Arabian Peninsula during World War I, Lawrence's aim was to enlist the area's Bedouin tribes against the Ottoman Turks who controlled strategic parts of the region. These tribes, however, were as eager to attack each other as to fight against the Turks. Lawrence's reputation was made by his success in redirecting the tensions that divided the tribes, turning them into a unified fighting force with a single goal. Business leaders are often faced by the same internecine warfare. It's their job to redirect that energy into productive channels.

2. **Group decision making versus decisiveness.** The idea that leaders share decision making is nothing new. Great generals and kings have always sought the counsel of trusted advisers, often to the point of making key decisions jointly. Does this mitigate the power and influence of the leader? It can, and in the worse cases can lead to suboptimal decisions—"everyone's second choice." While less masterful leaders are defensive about their decision-making rights, astute leaders recognize the benefit of taking counsel, having their assumptions challenged, and hearing alternatives. They know how to make the most of group decision making. Instead of demanding that the inner circle of

leadership accept his solutions, the effective leader demands that the team address critical unresolved issues. For example, rather than telling his team or workgroup, "Here are the cuts that must be made," the leader says, "Our task this morning is to determine the best way to cut the budget, given that the R&D line is untouchable. Tell me your thoughts, the facts that support them, and their likely consequences."

Still, there are times when it is necessary to make a decision by a process other than group consensus. For example, when an emergency demands immediate action a unilateral decision by the leader may be necessary. Team members will accept this as long as they see that their input on other issues is welcomed and considered. A leader who is dismissive of their input quickly loses support.

Crafting a Vision That Others Will Follow

Effective leaders create a vision that others will support with their hands and minds.

A *vision* is a picture of a hoped-for end result: what it will look like, how it will function, what it will produce. A powerful vision is one that resonates with the deep yearning of one's followers. Here's the vision that Hernán Cortés offered to the band of men who followed him from the Caribbean island of Hispañola to the conquest of Mexico in 1519, as recorded by one of his captains:

> [E]very good man of spirit desires and strives, by his own effort, to make himself the equal of the excellent men of his day and even those of the past. And so it is that I am embarking upon a great and beautiful enterprise, which will be famous in times to come, because I know in my heart that we shall take vast and wealthy lands, peoples such as have never before been seen, and kingdoms greater than those of our monarchs.[1]

By twenty-first century standards, Cortés was a freebooter who sought nothing but rank and wealth. Nevertheless, he was a remarkable leader, whose vision sustained his followers through months of

The Elements of an Effective Vision

As you shape your organization's or unit's vision, remember that an effective vision touches people's inner aspirations. Its language can be translated into a realistic strategy. Its fulfillment may be challenging, but achievable. It also has these characteristics: It serves the interests of the company's most important stakeholders and it clearly defines the benefits to them.

The vision must be easy to explain and understand; it must also be focused and straightforward. Even if implementing the vision is a complicated process, explaining it should not be.

danger and privation. Such is the motivating power of a vision. Business leaders must provide the equivalent—a vision that appeals to followers to such a degree that they will muster the creativity or extra effort needed to make it a reality.

David Bradford and Allen Cohen, both scholars of business leadership, have observed that significant change is unlikely without a compelling vision to draw out and channel people's energy. "People need to see that change will be worth all the effort. Sometimes that can be accomplished by a vivid description of the desired future state. . . . It is difficult to visualize interactive changes in the abstract."[2] Their phrase, "vivid description," is worth noting. The vision held up by the leader cannot be abstract or vague; instead, it must be described with sufficient details that followers can see and feel the leader's vision.

Be a Change Agent

More than managers, leaders must be agents for change. They must detect signs in the outer environment that the world is changing, be cognizant of threats and opportunities, and prod others to respond in ways that will lead to success and survival.

Think for a moment about the big, big changes in the world over the centuries. Chances are that you can associate one or a handful of individuals with those changes. Copernicus and Galileo ultimately changed our view of where we stand relative to our neighbors in the solar system and the universe around us. Charles Darwin's theory of natural selection torpedoed the accepted wisdom on humankind's history. That theory has made just about everyone think differently about their origins. Karl Marx, a thinker, and Vladimir Lenin, a doer, created a communist movement that, at its apex, held sway over almost half the world. Henry Ford and his engineers developed a new approach to manufacturing—the assembly line—that fundamentally altered the auto industry and many others. In each of these cases, one or a handful of people who thought differently about the world had a major impact on human history. None began with serious resources or backing. All created change through the power of their ideas. All were what we call change agents.

Change agents are catalysts who get the ball rolling, even if they don't do most of the pushing. Everett Rogers, who has written broadly on change and its diffusion in society, described them as figures with one foot in the old world and one in the new—creators of a bridge across which others can travel. They help others to see what the problems are, and convince them to grapple with those problems. Change agents, in his view, fulfill critical roles.[3] They:

- Articulate the need for change

- Are accepted by others as trustworthy and competent (people must accept the messenger before they accept the message)

- See and diagnose problems from the perspective of their audience

- Motivate people to change

- Work through others in translating intention into action

- Stabilize the adoption of innovation

- Foster self-renewing behavior in others so that they can "go out of business" as change agents

Do you possess these characteristics? If you do, you are already a leader. If you don't, work at developing them. Start looking at your company—or your part of the company—with an "outside-in" perspective. That is, try to stand outside of your situation and look at it with the objectivity of a perceptive stranger. Is what you observe going on in your organization aligned with the world around it, or is it out of touch with larger realities? If it's out of touch, develop some thought leadership on the problem. Discuss the problem with others—both inside and outside your unit—to gain even more perspective. Then find opportunities to alert your peers and your boss to the problem and its perils if they do not change. Be a change agent!

Keep Your Organization Change–Ready

Being a leader and acting like a change agent won't do you much good if your organization isn't prepared for change. Generally, an organization is change-ready if it

- has effective and respected leaders;

- is motivated to change, in that it has a sense of discomfort with the status quo;

- is accustomed to collaborative work.

It's hard for leaders to get people to move in new directions if any of these qualities are absent, and it's the leader's job to keep the organization in a state that reflects these three qualities. For example, if you detect a threat from a new technology or a new competitor, it's your job to challenge complacency and create a sense of urgency. Leaders do this by raising concerns about a current, problematic situation. Harvard Business School professor Michael Beer has recommended four approaches to challenging the complacency that kills so many organizations:[4]

1. Use information about the organization's competitive situation to generate discussion with employees about current and prospective problems. Top management, he says, often fails to understand why employees are not concerned about productivity, customer service, or costs. Too often this is because management

has failed to put employees in touch with the relevant data. In the absence of that data, everything appears to be fine. People say, "Why should we change? Why should we make the effort?"

2. Create opportunities for employees to educate management about the dissatisfactions and problems they experience. In some cases, top management is out of touch with weaknesses of the business or emerging threats—things that front-line employees understand through daily experience on the factory floor or in face-to-face dealings with customers. If this is your company's problem, find ways to improve communications between top management and front-line people so that the message gets through.

3. Create dialogue on the data. Providing data is one thing. Creating dialogue on the data is something entirely different and more productive. Dialogue should aim for a joint understanding of company problems. Dialogue is a means by which both managers and employees can inform each other of their assumptions and their diagnoses.

4. Set high standards and expect people to meet them. The act of stating high standards by itself creates dissatisfaction with the current level of performance. During his tenure as CEO of Hewlett-Packard, John Young periodically challenged employees with "stretch goals" that, on their face, were difficult but achievable. In one case he asked employees for a tenfold cut in the failure rate, which triggered warranty claims, of HP products. Given that the failure rate at the time was only 2 percent (low by U.S. manufacturing standards at the time), this was a Herculean challenge. On another occasion he asked for a 50 percent reduction in the average time-to-market of new product projects. In both cases, HP employees rose to the challenge.

Complacency is a common barrier to change. When people are comfortable with the status quo, they are oblivious to things that need changing. Your job as a leader is to shake them out of their complacency. Table 11-1 details some signs of complacency for which you should be on the lookout.

TABLE 11 - 1

Is Your Organization Complacent?

Signs of Complacency	Examples
No highly visible crisis.	The company is not losing money; no big layoffs are threatened.
The company measures itself against low standards.	The company compares itself to the industry average, not to the industry leader.
Organizational structure focuses attention on narrow functional goals instead of broad business performance.	Marketing has one measurement criterion; manufacturing has another that is unrelated. Only the CEO uses broader measures (return on invested capital, economic value added, etc.).
Planning and control systems are rigged to make it easy for everyone to make their functional goals.	The typical manager or employee can work for months without encountering an unsatisfied or frustrated customer or supplier.
Performance feedback is strictly internal. Feedback from customers, suppliers, and shareholders is not encouraged.	The culture dictates that external feedback is either without value or likely to be uninformed. "Customers really don't know what they want. We do."
Evidence that change is needed results in finger-pointing.	"It's manufacturing's problem, not ours."
Management focuses on marginal issues.	"The ship is sinking. Let's rearrange the deck chairs."
The culture sends subliminal messages of success.	Plush offices, wood paneling, and fine art adorn corporate offices.
Management believes its own press releases and mythology.	"We are the greatest ad agency in the country. We set the standard for our industry."

Source: Adapted from John P. Kotter, *Leading Change* (Boston, MA: Harvard Business School Press, 1996), 39–41.

Leading When You're Not the Boss

If you're like most managers, you regularly find yourself in situations where you have responsibility but not the authority to get things done.[5] Perhaps you head up a cross-functional team whose members don't report to you. Perhaps you manage a set of outside vendors. In other cases you may have nominal authority, but find that your charges are disinclined to respond to directives. In cases where you lack command authority, issuing direct orders is not feasible. Nevertheless, you must lead.

So what works? As it happens, a few students of leadership have sketched out approaches designed for precisely this situation. Jay A. Conger, director of the Leadership Institute at the University of Southern California's business school, advocates management by persuasion, noting that the most effective managers he observed during research and consulting assignments have actually avoided issuing directives.

True leadership, of course, has never been a matter of formal authority. Leaders are effective when the people around them acknowledge them as leaders. A title does not make a leader; a real leader is set apart by his or her attributes, attitudes, and behaviors.

Everyone's familiar with the charismatic leader. But what most aspiring leaders need isn't charisma. They need more mundane virtues: a reputation for hard work, a reputation of integrity, appealing ideas, reliability—someone perceived as having done his homework. Have you always done what you said you'd do? Do your colleagues think of you as someone who always tells the truth and admits his mistakes? Are you the first to figure out what is wrong and to formulate a new approach? These behaviors alone won't make you a leader, but a lack of them will surely eliminate you from contention.

A Five–Step Method

There is no single best way to lead when you are not the boss. Different situations—a crisis, a long-term project, and so forth—call out for different types of leaders. Nevertheless, the following five-step method can help you in many situations where you do not have a boss-subordinate relationship with others. It was developed by Harvard negotiation specialist Roger Fisher and his colleague Alan Sharp, who contend that it can be applied to virtually any project, team, or meeting in which you are a participant.

STEP 1: ESTABLISH GOALS. People accomplish the most when their objectives are clear. It follows that any group's first order of business should be to write down exactly what it hopes to achieve. The person who asks the question, "Can we start by clarifying our goals?" and who then assumes the lead in discussing and drafting those goals is taking a leadership role, whatever his or her position.

STEP 2: THINK SYSTEMATICALLY. Observe your next meeting: People typically plunge into the issue at hand and start arguing over what to do. Effective leaders, in contrast, are more systematic—that is, they gather and lay out the pertinent data, seek out the causes of the situation, and propose actions based on their analysis. Anyone who engages group members in this type of systematic approach, and guides them through it, becomes a de facto leader. Their leadership keeps people focused on the problem-solving process, and they reinforce their leadership by asking appropriate questions.

"Do we have all the information we need to analyze this situation?"

"Can we focus on the causes of the problem we're trying to solve?"

Once they have determined the cause of the problem, they lead people in a similar systematic discussion of potential solutions.

STEP 3: LEARN FROM EXPERIENCE—WHILE IT'S HAPPENING. Most teams plow ahead on a project, and only when it's over do they conduct an after-action review to reflect on what they have learned. It's sometimes more effective to learn as you go along, which means that part of a group's daily work is to conduct minireviews and make any necessary midcourse corrections. Why is this ongoing process more effective than an after-action review? The answer is that the data are fresh in everyone's mind. The reviews engage people's attention because the group can utilize its conclusions to make adjustments. Here, too, anyone who focuses the group on regular review and learning plays a de facto leadership role.

STEP 4: ENGAGE OTHERS. Groups are successful when the skills and efforts of every member are engaged. This doesn't happen naturally;

someone must make it happen. A leader does this by seeking the best fit possible between members' interest and skills and the tasks that need doing. You can fill this role by writing a list of all the tasks that need doing and matching them with individuals or subgroups. If no one wants a particular task, brainstorm ways to make that task more interesting or challenging. Partition the task if necessary into small parts that others can manage. Also, draw out the group's quieter members so that everyone feels like part of the team.

STEP 5: PROVIDE FEEDBACK. Even if you're not the boss, you can provide helpful feedback. Simply indicating your appreciation of the efforts of others will cost you nothing but will win people to your side. "I thought you did a great job in there."

Some team members may appreciate and benefit from coaching. "I had to deal with the same problem a few years ago; can I tell you what worked for me?" (See the section on coaching in chapter 7.)

Given the current popularity of teams, managers at every level can find opportunities to act as leaders without formal authority. Use those opportunities whenever you confront a leadership vacuum or whenever stepping forward can improve the situation. The experience you develop through these situations will help you develop and improve as a manager and leader. And always remember, if you learn to lead successfully *without* formal authority, leading with it will be easy.

Summing Up

- Effective leaders have many common characteristics. They are caring, comfortable with ambiguity, persistent, good communicators and negotiators, politically astute, humorous, and level-headed. They are also effective at engaging people's commitment to challenging goals, aware of how their behavior affects others, and focused on the future.

- Most organizations have internal tensions; for example, from competition between employees. The effective leader turns those tensions into productive activities.

- A vision is a picture of a hoped-for end result. One job of the leader is to articulate a powerful vision that resonates with the deep yearnings of his or her followers.

- When necessary, a leader must act as an agent for change.

- Managers routinely find themselves in situations where they are accountable for results but have no formal authority. In these cases they must lead through persuasion as well as their attributes, attitudes, and behaviors.

Strategy

A Primer

Key Topics Covered in This Chapter

- *How strategy can confer competitive advantage*

- *A five-step process for formulating strategy and aligning activities with it*

- *Why strategic thinking must be ongoing*

MANAGERS are obliged to direct people to do the right things, and to do things right. Doing the right things requires that managers develop strategies. Doing things right is the business of operational effectiveness. The two are bound together in the sense that few organizations succeed with a deficiency in either.

This chapter is concerned with "doing the right things"—which is defined by strategy. If you are a beginning or midlevel manager, strategy formulation may not be part of your job, but it will be as you move higher in the organization. It is never too early to begin thinking strategically about the business. And if you are the owner-manager of a small business, strategy is as important to you as it is to the CEO of a *Fortune* 500 company.

What Is Strategy?

Bruce Henderson, founder of Boston Consulting Group, wrote that "Strategy is a deliberate search for a plan of action that will develop a business's competitive advantage and compound it." Competitive advantage, he went on, is found in differences. "The differences between you and your competitors are the basis of your advantage."[1] Henderson believes that no two competitors can coexist if they seek to do business in the same way. They must differentiate themselves to survive. "Each must be different enough to have a unique advantage." For example, two men's clothing stores on the same block—one featuring formal attire and the other focusing on leisure wear—can potentially survive and prosper. However, if the same two stores sold the same things under the same terms, one or the other would perish. More likely, the one that differentiated itself through price, product mix, or ambiance would have the greater likelihood of survival. Harvard Business School professor Michael Porter concurs: "Competitive strategy is about being different. It means deliberately choosing a different set of activities to deliver a unique mix of value."[2] Consider these examples:

- Southwest Airlines didn't become the most profitable air carrier in North America by copying its rivals. It differentiated itself with a much different strategy, one characterized by low fares, frequent departures, point-to-point service, and a customer-pleasing service.

- eBay created an entirely new way for people to sell and acquire goods: online auctions. Company founders aimed to serve the same purpose of classified ads, flea markets, and formal auctions, but made it simple, efficient, and wide-reaching.

- Toyota's strategy in developing the hybrid-engine Prius passenger car was to create a competitive advantage within an important segment of auto buyers: people who want either a vehicle that is environmentally benign, cheap to operate, or the latest thing in auto engineering. The company also hoped that the learning associated with the Prius would give it leadership in a technology with huge future potential.

Strategies may be based on low-cost leadership, technical uniqueness, or focus. They can also be understood in terms of strategic position. Michael Porter has postulated that strategic positions emerge from three sometimes overlapping sources:[3]

- **Variety-based positioning.** Here, a company chooses a narrow subset of product/service offerings from within the wider set offered in its industry. It can succeed with this strategy if it delivers faster, better, or at lower cost than competitors. Example:

Starbucks offers premium coffee products and locates its outlets in locations that are convenient for potential customers. It doesn't serve breakfast or sell sandwiches. Customers can get those products elsewhere. Its focus is on coffee.

- **Need–based positioning.** Companies that follow this approach, according to Porter, aim to serve all or most of the needs of an identifiable set of customers. These customers may be price sensitive, demand a high-level of personal attention and service, or may want products or services that are uniquely tailored to their needs. Example: USAA is a financial services company that caters exclusively to active-duty and retired military officers and their families. After decades of serving this population, USAA understands its unique banking, insurance, and retirement needs. And it knows how to deal with the fact that military officers are transferred from post to post and around the world with great frequency.

- **Access–based positioning.** Some strategies can be based around access to customers. A discount merchandise chain, for example, may choose to locate its stores exclusively in low-income neighborhoods. This reduces competition from suburban shopping malls and provides easy access for its target market of low income shoppers, many of whom do not have automobiles. Cracker Barrel Old Country Stores, in contrast, locates its restaurants/gift stores along the U.S. expressway system, where it caters to travelers. Its Web site even includes a "trip planner" that identifies the locations of all Cracker Barrel outlets along any "to-from" driving route.

What is your strategy for gaining competitive advantage? Does it differentiate your company in ways that attract customers away from rivals? Is it drawing new customers into the market? Does it provide your company with a tangible advantage?

Simply being different, of course, will not keep you in business. Your strategy must also deliver value. And customers define value in different ways: lower cost, greater convenience, greater reliability, faster delivery, more aesthetic appeal, easier to use. The list of customer-pleasing "values" is extremely long. What value does your strategy aim to provide? Does it deliver?

Steps for Formulating Strategy

If you haven't had much experience with formulating a strategy for your business, don't feel bad. Most managers are in the same position. It's not an everyday activity. Some companies coast along for years with the same strategy, and only address that strategy when it becomes obviously obsolete. Even then, many turn to strategy consultants to do the job. As Harvard Business School professor Clay Christensen once put it, strategic thinking is not a core managerial competence at most companies. "Executives hone their management capabilities by tackling problems over and over again. Changing strategy, however, is not usually a task that managers face repeatedly. Once companies have found a strategy that works, they want to use it, not change it. Consequently, most management teams do not develop a competence in strategic thinking." [4]

So if you are not practiced at formulating strategy, here are steps you can follow. They involve looking outside and inside the organization, since the market to be served is on the outside and the capabilities for making the strategy work are on the inside.

Step 1: Look Outside to Identify Threats and Opportunities

At the highest level, strategy is concerned with the outer environment and how the organization's financial resources, people, and capacity should be allocated to create an exploitable advantage. There are always threats in the outer environment: new entrants, demographic changes, suppliers who might cut you off, substitute products that could undermine your business, and macroeconomic trends that may reduce the ability of your customers to pay. The business may be threatened by a competitor that can produce the same quality goods at a much lower price—or a much better product at the same price.

A strategy must be able to cope with these threats. The outer environment also harbors opportunities: a new-to-the-world technology, an unserved market, and so forth.

The first job of strategists is to scan the outer environment for threats and opportunities. You can do this with the following tasks:

- Form a team of executives, a unit manager, and individuals with special insights. Their job is to identify threats and opportunities. Avoid having anyone on the team who is complacent or wedded to the status quo.

- Gather the views of customers, suppliers, and industry experts. These outside views can be powerful.

Some firms, particularly those in technological fields, enlist teams of scientists and engineers to look outward to markets, competitors, and technical developments. It's their job to look for anything that could threaten their current business or point toward new directions that their business should follow.

The strategist looks within and without, and asks these questions:[5]

- What is the economic environment in which we must operate? How is it changing?

- What are our competencies as an organization? How do these give us an advantage relative to competitors?

- What resources support or constrain our actions?

- What opportunities for profitable action lay before us? What are the risks associated with different opportunities and potential courses of action?

Step 2: Look Inside at Resources, Capabilities, and Practices

Resources and internal capabilities can be a constraint on one's choice of strategy, especially for the larger company that has many employees and fixed assets. And rightly so. A strategy to exploit an unserved market in the electronics industry might not be feasible if your firm lacks the necessary financial capital and the human know-how to exploit it. Likewise, a strategy that would require substantial entrepreneurial behavior on the part of employees, for example, would seem doomed from the beginning if your people practices reward years of service over individual performance.

These internal capabilities—especially the human ones—matter greatly, and are too often overlooked by strategists. A strategy can only succeed if it has the backing of the right set of people and other resources; these must be properly aligned with the strategy.

Step 3: Consider Strategies for Addressing Threats and Opportunities

Clay Christensen has advocated that strategy teams first prioritize the threats/opportunities they find (he calls them "driving forces" of competition), then discuss each in broad strokes. If you follow this advice, and develop strategies to deal with them, be sure to do the following:

- Create many alternatives. There is seldom one way to do things. In some cases, the best parts of two different strategies can be combined to make a stronger third strategy.

- Check all facts and question all assumptions.

- Some information is bound to be missing. Determine what information you need to better assess a particular strategy. Then get the information.

- Vet the leading strategy choices among the wisest heads you know. Doing so will help you avoid "groupthink" within the strategy team.

Step 4: Build a Good "Fit" Among Strategy–Supporting Activities

Michael Porter has made the point that strategy is more than just a blueprint for winning customers; it is also about *combining* activities into a chain whose links are mutually supporting and effective in locking out imitators.[6] He uses Southwest Airlines to illustrate his notion of "fit."

Southwest's strategy is based on rapid gate turnaround. Rapid turnaround allows SWA to make frequent departures and better utilize its expensive aircraft assets. This, in turn, supports the low-cost, high-convenience proposition it offers customers. Thus, each of these activities supports the other and the higher goal. That goal, Porter points out, is further supported by other critical activities, which include highly motivated and effective gate personnel and ground crews, a no-meals policy, and no interline baggage transfers. Those activities make rapid turnarounds possible. "Southwest's strategy," writes Porter, "involves a whole system of activities, not a collection of parts. Its competitive advantage comes from the way its activities fit and reinforce one another."[7]

Step 5: Create Alignment

Once you've developed a satisfactory strategy, your job is only half done. The other half is creating alignment between the people and activities of the organization and its strategy. Alignment is a condition in which every employee at every level (1) understands the strategy, and (2) understands his or her role in making the strategy work. Alignment is a powerful thing. As consultants George Labovitz and Victor Rosansky once wrote, "Imagine working in an organization where every member, from top management to the newly hired employee, shares an understanding of the business, its goals and purpose. Imagine working in a department where everyone knows how he or she contributes to the company's business strategy."[8] That's alignment. As a manager, your role in creating alignment is twofold:

1. **Communicating.** You must help people understand the strategy and how their jobs contribute to it. You want to create a situation in which even the lowest-ranking employee can articulate the goals of the organization and explain how what he or she does every day fits in.

2. **Coordinating work processes.** You must align people's activities with the business's strategic intentions.

Tip: Don't Forget Alignment Between Strategy and Human Capital

Few executives take the time to examine the alignment between their business strategies and their people practices and policies. As Haig Nalbantian, Rick Guzzo, Dave Kieffer, and Jay Doherty explain in *Play to Your Strengths: Managing Your Company's Internal Labor Markets for Lasting Competitive Advantage*, misalignment here can jeopardize the success of even the best strategy.[a] Their research describes several companies whose promotion, retention, and rewards practices were inadvertently encouraging employee behaviors contrary to strategic intentions. In one case, a U.S. manufacturer's policy of building general management skills through frequent, short-term job assignments was undermining its higher goals of product quality and bringing new models to market quickly. Analysis indicated that managers who accepted short-term assignments were rewarded with promotions and higher pay, but they failed to build the technical skills needed to advance the company's higher-level strategy.

[a]See Haig R. Nalbantian, Richard A. Guzzo, Dave Kieffer, and Jay Doherty, *Play to Your Strengths: Managing Your Company's Internal Labor Markets for Lasting Competitive Advantage* (New York: McGraw-Hill Publishing Company, 2003), 17–21.

Be Prepared for Change

Create a winning strategy and implement it well and you might cruise along for years without problems. But no strategy is effective forever. Something in the external environment eventually changes, rendering it ineffective. Your customer-pleasing product is copied and offered at a lower price by a huge company with better distribution than yours. A technological breakthrough undermines your main business and you don't have the technical skills to catch this new wave. Many management teams, unfortunately, are unable to recognize when their strategies have become obsolete. Either through hubris or myopia they fail to recognize how the external environment is changing—through technology, shifting customer needs, or the appearance of cheaper, better substitutes.

The temporary nature of successful strategy should caution you to continually scan the external environment for threats and new opportunities, as described in Step 1. Does your company do this already? If it doesn't, who would be the best people to conduct this duty?

Strategy formulation, then, is an ongoing requirement of good management. It is, to quote Michael Porter, "a process of perceiving new positions that woo customers from established positions or draw new customers into the market."[9] This is a process you must permanently embed in your organization.

Summing Up

- Operational efficiency is about doing things right; strategy is about doing the right things. Don't confuse them.

- Strategy formulation is a search for a plan that will differentiate the enterprise and give it a competitive advantage.

- Per Michael Porter, strategic positions can be found in variety-based, need-based, or access-based positioning.

- The five steps of strategy formulation are: (1) Looking outside the enterprise to identify threats and opportunities; (2) looking inside at resources, capabilities, and practices; (3) considering strategies for addressing threats and opportunities; (4) building a good "fit" among strategy-supporting activities; and (5) creating alignment between the organization's people and activities and its strategy.

- Successful strategies are often short-lived, so keep scanning the horizon for new opportunities and for changes that undermine your current strategy.

Part Three

Mastering the Financial Tools

Budgeting

Seeing the Future

Key Topics Covered in This Chapter

- *Essential functions of budgeting*

- *Types of budgets and their purposes*

- *Creating an operating budget*

- *Creating a cash budget*

- *Applying sensitivity analysis to budgets*

"**G**OOD GRIEF, it's budgeting time again" is a common refrain among managers. Budgeting can cause stress and conflict and can eat up lots of hours. But good budgets are worth the time and trouble.

If you are the owner or manager of a small company with few cash resources, a good budget can be the difference between financial success and insolvency—or the business's inability to expand to its full potential. The budgeting process forces you to estimate how many of each product or service you will produce and sell, the cost of those items, the pace at which receivables will be collected, general expenses, and taxes. These figures provide a forecast of the months or year ahead. A good budget helps you assess whether or not the business will have adequate financial resources to stay the course. For big businesses, forecasting and budgeting provide a similar benefit. And the resulting budget—for individual operation units and for the business as a whole—can be a powerful control mechanism. A budget is also an action plan that guides organizations to their strategic goals.

In this chapter, you'll learn about the many kinds of budgets that serve very different purposes. You'll also learn how to determine which type of budget will most effectively help you meet your business goals.[1]

What Is Budgeting?

Before you go on a trip, you fill your bag with the clothes, food, and money you'll need. Budgeting is conceptually similar—planning your trip and ensuring that you'll have sufficient resources to make it to your destination. An organization plans its journey toward strategic objectives in a similar fashion, and it prepares for the journey with an action plan called a budget. A budget can accomplish various tasks:

- **Cover a short time span.** For example, a start-up company develops a budget to ensure that it will have enough cash to cover operating expenses for twelve months or so.

- **Take a long-term perspective.** For example, a pharmaceutical firm builds a multiyear budget for developing a new product.

- **Focus on required resources for a specific project.** For example, if a manufacturing firm needs to install machinery to achieve production efficiencies, then its budget will anticipate the cost of the installation.

- **Account for income as well as expenditures.** For example, a retailer creates a profit plan based on an expected increase in sales.

So what is a *budget*? It is the translation of strategic plans into measurable quantities that express the expected resources required and anticipated returns over a certain period. A budget functions as an action plan. It may also present the estimated future financial statements of the organization. Finally, a budget is an adaptable tool for management to use to achieve its strategic goals.

Budget Functions

Budgets perform four basic functions, each critical to the success of a company in achieving its strategic objectives. These functions are planning, coordinating and communicating, monitoring progress, and evaluating performance.

Planning

Planning is a three-step process to ensure that the organization will have the resources available to achieve its goals:

1. **Choosing goals.** The goals could be as comprehensive as the strategic mission of the organization. For example, as a manager at an Internet service provider (ISP), your goal could be "to be the most efficient provider of Internet services for our valued customers." Or, as the general manager of a major-league baseball team, your goal could be specific and very focused: to increase revenues by 10 percent during the next quarter.

2. **Reviewing options and predicting results.** Once the goals have been determined, the next step is to look at the options available for attaining the goals and predict what the most likely outcomes would be for each option. For example, if your goal as a manager at an ISP is to become the most efficient provider of Internet services, then you could opt to maintain state-of-the-art equipment at all times, train the most skilled repair teams in the field, or concentrate on providing the most timely customer service. Or, as a baseball team general manager planning to increase revenues by 10 percent, you could consider raising prices or expanding your marketing program. Thus, predicting the costs and benefits of each option is part of planning.

3. **Deciding on options.** After an analysis of the potential costs and benefits of each option, the next step is to decide how to attain the desired goals. Choosing which options to implement establishes the direction the company will take. The budget reflects those decisions. As a manager at an ISP, for example, you may decide that, although the other two options are important, your focus should be on maintaining state-of-the-art equipment to provide the most efficient service for your customers. Or, as manager of the baseball team, you could decide that raising prices would most effectively bring in the specified increase in revenues.

Coordinating and Communicating

Coordination is the act of gathering the pieces together—the individual unit budgets or division budgets—and balancing and combining them to achieve the master budget that expresses the organization's overall financial objectives and strategic goals. In many companies, this is quite a feat!

A master budget compiles the individual budgets from the functional areas of research and development, design, production, marketing, distribution, and customer service into one unit budget. Then the budgets from individual divisions, product lines, and subsidiaries are coordinated and integrated into a larger, cohesive result. Much like a composer weaving the music from many different instruments together to create a symphony, the master budget brings all the pieces together to achieve the organization's overall strategic plan and company mission. Details of the master budget will be discussed later in this chapter.

To achieve this end, communication is essential. Upper management needs to communicate the company's strategic objectives to all levels of the organization, and the individual planners need to communicate their particular needs, assumptions, expectations, and goals to those evaluating the departmental and functional budget pieces.

Additionally, the different groups within the company must always listen to one another. If one division is striving to achieve certain sales goals, then production must have that information to prepare for increased production capacity. If the company is introducing a new product, then the marketing department must be informed early in the planning process. The department will have to include in its budget the marketing efforts for the new product.

Monitoring Progress

Once the plan has been set in motion, the budget becomes a tool that managers can use to periodically monitor progress. They assess progress by comparing the actual results with the budget. This feedback, or monitoring and evaluation of progress, in turn allows for timely corrective action. If, on the one hand, the interim evaluation shows that the organization is right on target, with actual results matching the budget's expected results, then no adjustment to the action plan is required. However, if you discover that the actual results differ from the expected results, then you must take corrective action. For example, if your baseball team's goal is to increase revenues 10 percent by raising prices, but you find after one month that the fans are resistant to higher prices, then you might take corrective action by offering fans bonus packages to offset the negative impact of the higher prices.

The difference between the actual results and the results expected by the budget is called a *variance*. A variance can be favorable, when the actual results are better than expected, or unfavorable, when the actual results are worse than expected. For example, after the first month of the new baseball season, you evaluate how the ticket sales are proceeding (table 13–1).

Overall, unit tickets sales are lower than expected, but you observe that there is a favorable variance for the higher-priced infield box seats (ticket buyers don't seem to mind the price hike for these

TABLE 13-1

Ticket Sales Performance Report for April

	AVERAGE TICKETS SOLD PER GAME		
	Actual Results	Budgeted Amounts	Variance
Infield Box	2,500	2,000	+ 500; favorable
Grandstand	6,850	7,000	– 150; unfavorable
Outfield Grandstand	7,700	9,000	– 1,300; unfavorable
Bleachers	11,850	12,000	– 150; unfavorable
Total	28,900	30,000	– 1,100; unfavorable

Source: HMM Budgeting.

seats). The biggest concern you have is the higher, unfavorable variance for the outfield grandstand seats. This is where you would concentrate your corrective action, because these fans seem to be responding to the higher prices by staying away. Thus, variance analysis can help you identify a problem early in the budget cycle and take the appropriate action.

Note here that we were strictly interested in units, not revenues. Managers could also conduct the budgeting exercise using revenues.

Evaluating Performance

Effective performance-evaluation systems contribute to the achievement of strategic goals, and budgets provide essential tools for measuring management performance. After all, a manager who makes basic planning and implementation decisions should be held accountable for the results. By comparing the actual results to the budget for a given period, an evaluator can determine the manager's overall success in achieving his or her strategic goals. Performance evaluations serve a number of purposes:

- They motivate employees through reward systems based on performance.

- They provide the basis for compensation decisions, future assignments, and career advancement.

- They create a basis for future resource allocations.

Types of Budgets

The notion of the traditional budget has been under growing attack from those who believe that it no longer serves the needs of modern organizations. Critics complain that budgets are timed incorrectly (too long or too short), rely on inappropriate measures, and are either too simplistic (or too complex), too rigid in a changing business environment, or too unchallenging (for instance, the bar is deliberately set so that managers can hit their targets and collect their bonuses). Many budgets we'll explore in this chapter were developed to address some of these difficult planning issues.

Short–Term Versus Long–Term Budgets

Budgets are typically developed to cover a one-year time span. But the period covered by a budget may vary according to the purpose of the budget, particularly as your company defines value creation. If an organization is concerned with the profitability of a product over its expected five-year life, then a five-year budget may be appropriate. If, on the other hand, a company is living hand-to-mouth, which is often the case with start-up companies, then a month-by-month budget that focuses on immediate cash flow might be more useful.

Fixed Versus Rolling Budgets

A fixed budget covers a specific time frame—usually one fiscal year. At the end of the year, a new budget is prepared for the following year. A fixed budget may be reviewed at regular intervals—perhaps quarterly—so that adjustments and corrections can be made if needed, but the basic budget remains the same throughout the period.

In an effort to address the problems of timeliness and rigidity in a fixed budget, some firms, particularly those in rapidly changing industries, have adopted a rolling budget. A *rolling budget* is a plan that is continually updated so that the time frame remains stable while the actual period covered by the budget changes. For example, as each month passes, the one-year rolling budget is extended by one month, so that there is always a one-year budget in place. The advantage of a rolling budget is that managers have to rethink the process and make changes each month or each period. The result is usually a more accurate, up-to-date budget incorporating the most current information.

The disadvantage of a rolling budget is that the planning process can become too time-consuming. Moreover, if a company reviews its budget on a regular basis (say, every quarter for a one-year budget), analyzes significant variances, and takes whatever corrective action is necessary, then the fixed budget truly isn't as rigid as it seems.

Incremental Versus Zero–Based Budgeting

Incremental budgeting extrapolates from historical figures. Managers look at the previous period's budget and actual results as well as expectations for the future in determining the budget for the next period. For example, a marketing department's budget would be based on the actual costs from the previous period but with increases for planned salary raises. The advantage of incremental budgeting is that history, experience, and future expectations are included in the development of the budget.

A disadvantage often cited by critics of the traditional budget is that managers may simply use the past period's figures as a base and increase them by a set percentage for the following budget cycle rather than taking the time to evaluate the realities of the current and future marketplace. Managers can also develop a use-it-or-lose-it point of view, with which managers feel they must use all the budgeted expenditures by the end of the period so that the following period's budget will not be reduced by the amount that would have been saved.

Zero-based budgeting describes a method that begins each new budgeting cycle from a zero base, or from the ground up, as though the budget were being prepared for the first time. Each budget cycle starts with a critical review of every assumption and proposed expenditure. The advantage of zero-based budgeting is that it requires managers to perform a much more in-depth analysis of each line item—considering objectives, exploring alternatives, and justifying their requests. The disadvantage of zero-based budgeting is that although it is more analytic and thorough, developing the budget can be extremely time-consuming, so much so that it may even interfere with actuating that budget. Planning needs to precede, but never overwhelm, action.

Kaizen Budgeting

Kaizen is a Japanese term that stands for continuous improvement, and Kaizen budgeting attempts to incorporate continuous improvement into the budgeting process. Cost reduction is built into the budget on an incremental basis so that continual efforts are made to reduce costs over time. If the budgeted cost reductions are not achieved, then extra attention is given to that operating area. For example, a manufacturing plant may budget a continuous reduction in the cost of components, as shown below, putting pressure on suppliers to find further cost reductions.

January–February	$100.00
February–March	$99.50
March–April	$99.00

This type of incremental budgeting is difficult to maintain because the rate of budgeted cost reduction declines over time, making it more difficult to achieve improvements after the "easy" changes have been achieved.

The Master Budget

The *master budget* is the heart and soul of the budgeting process. It brings all the pieces together, incorporating the operating budget and the financial budget of an organization into one comprehensive picture. In other words, the master budget summarizes all the individual financial projections within an organization for a given period.

For a typical for-profit organization, the operating budget consists of the budgets from each *function*—such as research and development, design, production, marketing, distribution, and customer service—and provides the budgeted income statement. The financial budget includes the capital budget, the cash budget, the budgeted balance sheet, and the budgeted cash flows. The master budget must integrate both the operating budget and the financial budget through an iterative process during which information flows back and forth from each element of the master budget (see figure 13-1).

FIGURE 13-1

Master Budget Flow Chart

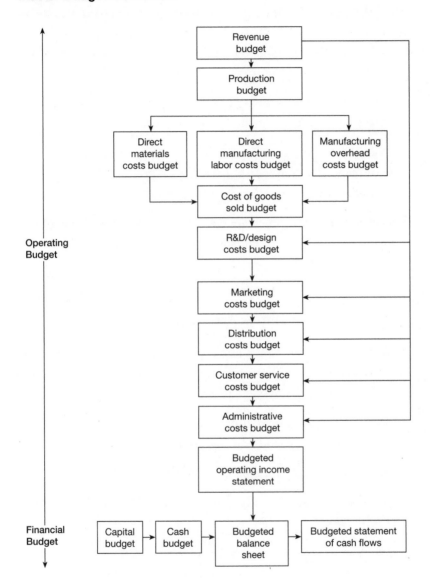

Source: HMM Budgeting. Adapted from Charles T. Horngren, George Foster, and Srikant M. Datar, *Cost Accounting* (New York: Prentice Hall, 2000).

Master budgeting goes hand-in-hand with strategic planning at the highest level. Using the organization's strategic goals as its foundation, the budget-building process is both chronological and iterative, moving back and forth, testing assumptions and options.

Before preparing a master budget, senior managers must ask these three important questions:

1. Do the tactical plans being considered support the larger and longer-term strategic goals of the organization?

2. Does the organization have, or have access to, the required resources—that is, the cash it needs to fund the activities throughout the immediate budget period?

3. Will the organization create enough value to attract adequate future resources—profit, loans, investors, etc.—to achieve its longer-term goals?

Setting Assumptions

The first step in developing a budget is establishing a set of assumptions about the future. The assumptions that managers make will be directly affected by the answers to questions such as these:

- What are sales and marketing's expectations for unit sales and revenues from new and existing products?

- Are supplier prices anticipated to rise or fall?

- What will be the cost of the company's health-care plan for the coming year?

- If the unemployment rate is expected to decline, will the company need to raise salaries to ensure an adequate work force in a tight labor market?

- What will competitors do to gain market share?

Assumptions should be sought from the sources that have the best information. For example, top management has a clear view of the strategic goals, and the finance group has records of past financial performance and future economic trends. Look to the human resource group for information on shifts in the labor market, and the sales representatives for the best information about sales prospects. Likewise, the purchasing department has the latest information about suppliers and price trends. Developing assumptions is a companywide endeavor in which communication and coordination play a key role.

Tips for Setting Assumptions

- Use historical data as a starting point. Even when times are changing quickly, information about past performance can establish a base from which to begin.

- Trust your own experience. Make educated guesses where necessary about what is likely to happen in the future.

- Listen to your intuition. Even though you can't verify those gut feelings, you can take them into account.

- Conduct due diligence. Seek out the information you need. This may involve doing research, reading trade journals, collecting industry statistics, and so on. And don't forget that the Internet is a growing information resource.

- Talk with and listen to knowledgeable people. Discuss your ideas with team members, colleagues, mentors. Seek out industry participants, suppliers, concerned community leaders, and experts in the field. Engage in discussions with competitors.

- Learn when to be a risk taker and when to be conservative. In a volatile market, conservative assumptions may be the safest.

- Test your assumptions. If possible, try out your assumptions in small experiments before you accept them.

Preparing the Operating Budget

An *operating budget* is nothing more than an agreed-upon pact between top management and other members of the management
team. It is a target, not a forecast. It specifies revenues and costs for
the coming period. These are expressed in a statement that resembles
the income (or profit and loss) statement that every company gener-
ates. The essential difference is that we are building the statement
from expected versus actual quantities. In a nutshell, the operating
budget is structured as follows:

> Revenues − (Cost of Goods Sold + Sales, General, and
> Administrative Costs) = Operating Income

We have divided the operating budget process into five simple steps.

STEP 1: CALCULATE YOUR EXPECTED REVENUES For the first
step in preparing an operating budget, managers must apply some assumptions to forecast revenue growth (or decline). For our hypothetical for-profit company, Amalgamated Hat Rack, the managers
of the Moose Head division translate their assumptions about revenue growth based on past performance and future expectations of
sales for their products during the fiscal year (table 13-2).

If they take an incremental-budgeting approach, the managers
will use the prior year's actual sales of $1,228,100 as the base for de-
veloping their projections for the next year. If, on the other hand,
they follow the zero-based budgeting method, they will make their
sales projections for each model from the ground up, using forecasted
economic data, predicted consumer behavior, and other information. These will take recent experience with customer behavior, economic forecasts, and other information into account.

Establishing projected revenue figures can create internal tensions. If managers are evaluated and rewarded on their achieving
budgeted revenue targets, then they may be tempted to develop conservative revenue targets that will be easy to reach. This budgetary
slack, or padding, provides a hedge for managers, making it more
likely that actual revenues will be higher than budgeted revenues.
With such results, the managers appear very effective.

TABLE 13-2

Moose Head Division, Amalgamated Hat Rack, Year 1 Budget

	Prior Year's Actual	Year 1 Budget	Rate of Change
Sales by Model			
Moose Antler Deluxe	$201,000	$205,000	2.0%
Moose Antler Standard	$358,000	$381,000	6.4%
Standard upright	$515,500	$556,000	7.9%
Electro-revolving	$72,400	$60,250	(16.8%)
Hall/wall model	$81,200	$80,000	(1.5%)
Total sales	$1,228,100	$1,282,250	4.4%
Cost of Goods Sold			
Direct labor	$92,325	$96,500	4.5%
Factory overhead	$6,755	$7,200	7.0%
Direct materials	$211,000	$220,284	4.4%
Total cost of goods sold	$310,080	$323,984	4.5%
Marketing and Administrative Costs			
Sales salaries	$320,000	$331,200	3.5%
Advertising expenses	$145,000	$151,000	4.1%
Miscellaneous selling expenses	$4,200	$3,900	(7.1%)
Administrative expenses	$92,000	$94,500	2.7%
Total SG&A	$561,200	$580,600	3.46%
Operating Income	$355,820	$377,666	6.14%

Source: HMM Budgeting.

Production constraints (the availability of qualified people for service firms and production capacity for manufacturers) may affect the revenue budget. If, for example, sales demand is expected to exceed the company's ability to manufacture and distribute, then the revenue budget must be adjusted to match the production constraints rather than the actual demands of the market. Otherwise, the budget must add funds for building the capacity needed to meet demand.

STEP 2: CALCULATE THE EXPECTED COST OF GOODS SOLD Once the revenue budget has been established, managers can then develop the budget for the cost of goods sold. The total number of units to be produced will form the basis for determining the direct costs, including labor and materials. In the same way, the Moose Head division calculates the indirect factory costs or overhead as part of the cost of goods sold budget. Remember here that sales are budgeted to rise 4.4 percent to $1,282,250.

STEP 3: CALCULATE THE EXPECTED OTHER COSTS Other non-production costs include costs generated by research and development, product design, marketing, distribution, customer service, and administration. For the Moose Head division, only various sales-related and administrative expenses make up the other-costs budget.

STEP 4: CALCULATE THE EXPECTED OPERATING INCOME Finally, you can calculate the budgeted income statement. The difference between expected sales and expected costs results in the expected operating income. The managers of the Moose Head division provide their expected income statement to the top management of Amalgamated Hat Rack so that top management, in turn, can determine how the Moose Head division's budget fits with the company's master budget and overall strategic goals.

STEP 5: DEVELOP ALTERNATIVE SCENARIOS Testing different scenarios is the "what if" iterative process of budgeting. How will a change in one area affect the expected outcome? What if we increase advertising? How much would that increase sales? What if the Moose Head employees decide to go on strike? How can we incorporate that risk into the budget?

For example, Amalgamated's management may decide to shift its strategic emphasis from increasing profits to developing a new product line in the Moose Head division. Moose Head managers would then develop another set of budget figures indicating research and development costs that would reduce the current budgeted operating income. Alternatively, Moose Head managers could decide to accept bids from a new group of suppliers that would in turn reduce materials expenditures and increase the budgeted operating income.

Creating Financial Budgets

Once managers of operations have developed their operating budgets, or expected income statements, financial managers then plan for the capital required to support those operating budgets. You can't anticipate a 10 percent increase in sales, for example, without creating a parallel plan for the extra working capital and other inputs that will be required if the anticipated increase is realized. Three other budgets are developed:

1. A cash budget that includes estimated cash from operations as well as other sources of cash (accounts payable, borrowing, or equity). The cash budget predicts and plans for the level and timing of cash inflow and outflow.

2. An operating asset investment plan that ensures that adequate capital will be available for assets such as inventory and accounts receivable.

3. A capital investment plan that budgets for proposed investments in long-term productive assets such as property, plant, and equipment expenditures and extended R&D programs.

These financial plans support the strategic objectives of the organization, planning for both the near-term (cash budget) and the long-term (capital investment plan) financial needs. They are expressed in forecasted (or pro forma) balance sheet and cash flow statements to form a complete picture of the organization's expected financial position during the budget period.

The *cash budget* is particularly important for the firm's financial managers since it indicates shortages or surpluses of cash in each period (usually months). No business can afford a shortfall of cash, as the company would be unable to pay bills as they come due. The cash budget shown in table 13-3 is one company's simplified cash budget for a five-month period (January through May). Notice that it identifies all cash inflows and outflows for each month. The ending cash balance of a given month becomes the beginning balance for the next month. Thus, December's $220 ending balance becomes January's beginning cash balance. By adding the monthly surplus (or deficit) and the beginning cash balance, the budget finds the ending balance for the month. A glance across the bottom line indicates when the enterprise will encounter a cash shortfall, as happens here in April and becomes

TABLE 13-3

A Simplified Cash Budget (in Thousands of Dollars)

	Dec.	Jan.	Feb.	March	April	May
Cash Inflows						
Sales revenues		1,100	875	600	500	600
Other revenues		250	225	200	200	0
Interest income			34	34	34	
Total inflows		1,350	1,134	834	734	600
Cash Outflows						
Purchases		400	380	320	300	350
Salaries		200	200	200	200	200
Hourly wages		170	165	150	195	220
Health-care payments		20	20	20	20	20
Retirement contributions		25	23	25	23	25
Interest payments		15	15	15	15	15
Taxes		305	295	270	260	240
Utilities		20	18	15	20	25
Total cash outflows		1,155	1,116	1,015	1,033	1,095
Cash Surplus or Deficit		195	18	(181)	(299)	(495)
Beginning Balance		220	415	433	252	(47)
Ending Balance	220	415	433	252	(47)	(542)

larger in May. Companies whose businesses are heavily seasonal—agricultural producers, garment makers, ski manufacturers, and so forth—routinely experience wide swings in ending cash balances.

During months of surplus, financial managers store cash in interest-bearing money market instruments such as short-term bank certificates of deposit (CDs), commercial paper, and U.S. Treasury bills. As surpluses disappear, they convert those instruments back into cash and draw on lines of credit and short-term bank loans to eliminate any cash deficits. As you can see in table 13-3, managers must begin drawing on past surpluses in March. The surpluses have evaporated by April, forcing them to seek outside sources of cash. Seasonal and cyclical businesses use periods of heavy cash inflows to pay off their lines of credit and to build money market positions in anticipation of the next cash-consuming cycle.

Here are the steps to follow in building your own cash budget:

1. **Add receipts.** Determine the expected receipts—collections from customers and other sources—that will flow into the cash account each period. Cash collections may vary during the budget period. For example, many retail stores expect to receive most of their receipts during holiday seasons.

2. **Deduct disbursements.** Based on expected activity, calculate how much cash will be required to cover disbursements—cash payouts—during the period. Disbursements could include payment for materials, payroll, taxes due, and so on. Some of these expenditures may be evenly distributed throughout the budget period, but some, such as payroll and materials costs, may fluctuate as part of the production process.

3. **Calculate the cash surplus or deficiency.** To calculate the cash surplus or deficiency for a period, subtract the disbursements from the sum of the beginning cash balance and the receipts expected during that period.

4. **Add the beginning cash balance.** The beginning cash balance is the ending balance from the previous period. By adding them together, you have a new ending balance.

5. **Determine financing needed.** The ending balance will be positive or negative. A positive balance indicates that you have more than enough cash to cover operations during that period. A negative balance indicates that the company must develop a plan for financing the shortfall from other sources, such as a bank loan. Repayment of any such loan must be reflected among the cash outflows of subsequent budget periods.

The Human Side of Budgeting

To some degree, preparing a budget is a matter of crunching numbers, a process being left more and more to financial modeling software, computers, and technology. But behind those numbers are real people like you—people who make assumptions, people who think about future situations, people who understand the idiosyncrasies of customers and competitors. Ideally, everyone involved in the budget process has the same goal in mind—achieving the organization's strategic objectives.

What some may see as a straightforward, even mechanical, process, however, is in reality complicated by genuine disagreements over assumptions about future trends and events, by conflicting needs, and by individual agendas that overshadow the larger corporate good. For this reason, the budget process can be defined as a series of negotiations between disparate interests. Top management wants the highest possible economic value in terms of profit. Middle management may have contrary needs, such as new equipment or new personnel. The human element is what can make the budget process so engaging and, at times, so frustrating.

Top-Down Versus Participatory Budgeting

Top-down budgeting describes the process whereby upper management sets budget goals—revenue, profit, and so on—and imposes these goals on the rest of the organization. Thus, for example, the CEO of Amalgamated Hat Rack gives Moose Head manager Claude Cervidés the goal of attaining an operating profit—or earnings before interest and taxes—of $400,000 for the upcoming fiscal year. It's then up to

Claude to shape his operating budget with $400,000 as the operating profit target.

Top-down budgeting has many advantages. Since senior management has a clearer concept of the organization's strategic objectives, top-down budgeting ensures the following benefits for senior management:

- Budget goals that reflect management's larger strategic objectives

- Better coordination of the budget requirements for all the elements of the organization

- The discouragement of "padding" managers' unit budgets

- High goals that challenge managers to stretch

Top-down budgeting has two main disadvantages. First, upper management may be out of touch with the realities of the individual divisions' production processes or markets. As a result, the goals they set may be inappropriate or unattainable. Second, middle managers may feel left out of the decision-making process and, consciously or unconsciously, may not fully participate in achieving the budgeted goals.

With participatory budgeting, the people responsible for achieving the budget goals are included in goal setting. Cervidés, for instance, would develop the budget for his own division, with the active participation of the heads of purchasing, human resources, production, marketing, and administration. Once his team had completed the budget, Cervidés would send it to Amalgamated Hat Rack's senior management. After review and possible feedback to Cervidés, they would incorporate Moose Head's budget, along with all the other budgets, into the master budget.

One advantage of participatory budgeting is that the people closest to the line activities—people who presumably have the best information—make the budget decisions. Also, participants in this type of budget process are more likely to make the extra effort to achieve the budgeted goals. The disadvantages of participatory budgeting are also twofold. First, the people closest to the line activities may not see the larger strategic picture. Second, if performance evaluations are tied to budget achievement, then the managers will have an incentive to pad their budgets either by underestimating revenues or by overestimating costs.

Tips for Negotiating Your Team's Budget

Effective budgeting requires a certain organizational savvy. Here are some tips for dealing with organizational issues that surround the budgeting process:

- Understand your organization's budgeting process. What guidelines must you follow? What is the timing of the budget process? How is the budget used in the organization?

- Communicate often with the controller or finance person in your department. Ask questions about points you don't understand. Get that person's advice about the assumptions your team is making.

- Know what real concerns are driving the people making the decisions about your budget. Be sure to address those concerns.

- Get buy-in from the decision makers. Spend time educating the finance person or decision maker about your area of the business. This will lay the groundwork for implementing changes later.

- Understand each line item in the budget you're working on. If you don't know what something means or where a number comes from, find out yourself. Walk the floor. Talk to people on the line.

- Have an ongoing discussion with your team throughout the budget period. The more you plan, the more you will be able to respond to unplanned contingencies.

- Avoid unpleasant surprises. As the numbers become available, compare actual figures to the budgeted amounts. If there is a significant or an unexpected variance, find out why. And be sure to notify the finance person who needs to know.

Iterative budgeting is an attempt to combine the best of both top-down and participatory budgeting. In the initial step, senior management provides the unit heads with a clear understanding of the organization's strategic goals. The unit heads then work with their teams to develop operating budgets that incorporate both their own tactical goals and the organization's larger strategic goals. After the unit heads send their budget proposals to upper management, upper management reviews the individual budgets and may ask for adjustments. And the negotiating process continues back and forth until a final master budget is achieved. The key to success in this and other budgeting processes is communication. Senior management has to communicate strategic goals in a way that makes sense. In turn, the unit heads communicate their resource needs and concerns when presenting budget proposals to management. All participants in the budget process have an obligation to listen to the various and sometimes conflicting positions.

Slack

Budgetary slack, or padding, occurs when managers believe they are going to be evaluated on their performance relative to the budget. To ensure that they will achieve their budgeted figures and be rewarded, they budget revenues conservatively or exaggerate anticipated costs, or do both. Both actions make the budget "game" easier to win. Budgetary slack also provides these managers with a hedge against unexpected problems, reducing the risk that they will fail to "make their numbers." It's an old game that managers at all levels learn to play. The big losers, of course, are the owners of the business.

What–If Scenarios and Sensitivity Analysis

Budgets are only as good as the future assumptions on which they are based. But assumptions are often wrong. We assume that customer A will purchase ten thousand units from us next year—and we have the sales agreement to back it up. But if customer A experiences a major business collapse, then that sales agreement isn't worth much.

We assume that our energy bills will increase at roughly the current rate of inflation. But guess what? A cold winter and huge demand for energy could push prices through the roof.

Sensitivity analysis is an approach to dealing with assumptions and alternative options. As a budgetary tool, this analysis can greatly enhance the value of budgets as instruments for planning, feedback, and course correction. A sensitivity analysis applies a what-if situation to

---

Tips for Effective Budgeting

If you want to use budgeting as a planning and team-building tool, you need to develop a game plan. Even if you recently finished this year's budget, it's not too early to start thinking about next year. Here are a few points to keep in mind:

- If you're a new manager, become familiar with your company's budgeting process.

- Spend time learning and understanding company priorities, as well as helping your team understand them.

- Make sure that any request for funds is in sync with the objectives set by senior management.

- Determine your unit's cost per output, however defined.

- Ask for volunteers to research line items. This will make your job easier and give subordinates opportunities to learn about the budgeting process.

- If you need to reduce costs, identify the activities that add value for the customer and those that don't. Analyze the cost of each, and begin by cutting non-value-added activities.

- Show how your budget request will generate income for the company. In other words, your budget should not be so much a request for funds as a proposal showing how you will help the company realize its goals.

TABLE 13-4

Moose Head Division, Amalgamated Hat Rack, Sensitivity Analysis of Several Options

What-If Scenarios	Units Sold	Direct Materials Cost	Operating Income
Budget model	21,400	$214,000	$383,950
Scenario 1: increase unit sales 10%	23,540	$235,000	$422,730
Scenario 2: decrease unit sales 5%	20,330	$203,300	$360,900
Scenario 3: decrease materials cost 5%	21,400	$203,300	$398,700

Source: HMM Budgeting.

the budget model to see the effect of the potential change on the original data. For example, what if the cost of materials rises 5 percent, or what if sales rise 10 percent? Software packages for financial planning are available and commonly used to perform these calculations, giving managers a powerful tool to estimate the costs and benefits of various options and possibilities.

For example, if the Moose Head division wanted to test its assumptions with what-if scenarios, it could determine the effect of some likely alternative scenarios (table 13-4). Given the results of these analyses, Claude Cervidés may decide to direct his efforts toward lowering materials costs to achieve the best bottom-line result.

Summing Up

- The four basic functions of budgets are planning, coordinating and communicating, monitoring progress, and evaluating performance.

- Budgets help an organization move forward and keep on track. And they make the time and trouble associated with budgeting worthwhile.

- The master budget brings together operating and cash budgets and various financial projections into a comprehensive picture.

- What-if scenarios and sensitivity analysis can help budget makers predict the effects of specific changes in any important assumptions built in to the budget.

Understanding
Financial Statements

Making More Authoritative Decisions

Key Topics Covered in This Chapter

- *Balance sheets*

- *Income statements*

- *Cash flow statements*

- *Financial leverage*

- *The financial structure of the firm*

- *Interpreting financial statements*

WHAT DOES your company own, and what does it owe to others? What are its sources of revenue, and how has it spent its money? How much profit has it made? What is the state of your company's financial health? This chapter will help you answer those questions by explaining the three essential financial statements: the balance sheet, the income statement, and the cash flow statement. The chapter will also help you understand some of the managerial issues implicit in these statements and broaden your financial know-how through discussion of two important concepts: financial leverage, and the financial structure of the firm.

If you're a line manager, you might be thinking "I don't need to know about that stuff. That's for senior management, not me." If you believe this, think again. The ability to read and interpret financial statements has become more and more necessary as accountability and decision-making authority are pushed down to lower levels. The language of financial statements is also important to managers at every level. When the conversation turns to "current liabilities," "profit margin," "financial leverage," and "working capital," you must know precisely the meaning of these terms. Indeed, the language of modern business draws heavily on the accounting terminology used in financial statements. Familiarity with the language and meaning of financial statements will make you a valued colleague in the higher circles of your organization. For the small business owner-manager, this understanding of financial statements is an absolute must.

Why Financial Statements?

Financial statements are the essential documents of business. Managers use them to assess performance and identify areas in which intervention is required. Shareholders use them to keep tabs of how well their capital is being managed. Outside investors use them to identify opportunities. And lenders and suppliers routinely examine financial statements to determine the creditworthiness of the companies with which they deal.

Publicly traded companies are required by the Securities and Exchange Commission (SEC) to produce financial statements and make them available to everyone as part of the full-disclosure requirement the SEC places on publicly owned and traded companies. Companies not publicly traded are under no such requirement, but their private owners and bankers expect financial statements nevertheless.

Financial statements—the balance sheet, income statement, and cash flow statement—follow the same general format from company to company. And though specific line items may vary with the nature of a company's business, the statements are usually similar enough to allow you to compare one business's performance against another's.

The Balance Sheet

Most people go to a doctor once a year to get a checkup—a snapshot of their physical well-being at a particular time. Similarly, companies prepare balance sheets as a way of summarizing their financial positions at a given point in time, usually at the end of the month, the quarter, or the fiscal year.

In effect, the *balance sheet* describes the assets controlled by the business and how those assets are financed—with the funds of creditors (liabilities), with the capital of the owners, or with both. A balance sheet reflects the following basic accounting equation:

Assets = Liabilities + Owners' Equity

Assets in this equation are the things in which a company invests so that it can conduct business. Examples include cash and financial instruments, inventories of raw materials and finished goods, land, buildings, and equipment. Assets also include monies owed to the company by customers and others—an asset category referred to as *accounts receivable.*

Now look at the other side of the equation, starting with liabilities. To acquire its necessary assets, a company often borrows money or promises to pay suppliers for various goods and services. Monies owed to creditors are called *liabilities.* For example, a computer company may acquire $1 million worth of motherboards from an electronic parts supplier, with payment due in thirty days. In doing so, the computer company increases its inventory assets by $1 million and its liabilities—in the form of *accounts payable*—by an equal amount. The equation stays in balance. Likewise, if the same company were to borrow $100,000 from a bank, the cash infusion would increase its assets by $100,000 and its liabilities by the same amount.

Owners' equity, also known as shareholders' or stockholders' equity, is what is left over after total liabilities are deducted from total assets. Thus, a company that has $3 million in total assets and $2 million in liabilities would have owners' equity of $1 million.

Assets − Liabilities = Owners' Equity
$3,000,000 − $2,000,000 = $1,000,000

If $500,000 of this same company's uninsured assets burned up in a fire, its liabilities would remain the same, but its owners' equity—what's left after all claims against assets are satisfied—would be reduced to $500,000:

Assets − Liabilities = Owners' Equity
$2,500,000 − $2,000,000 = $500,000

Thus, the balance sheet "balances" a company's assets and liabilities. Notice, for instance, how the total assets equal total liabilities plus owners' equity in the balance sheet of Amalgamated Hat Rack, our example company (table 14-1). The balance sheet also describes how much the company has invested in assets, and where the money is

TABLE 14-1

Amalgamated Hat Rack Balance Sheet as of December 31, 2002

	2002	2001	Increase (Decrease)
Assets			
Cash and marketable securities	$355,000	$430,000	$(75,000)
Accounts receivable	$555,000	$512,000	$43,000
Inventory	$835,000	$755,000	$80,000
Prepaid expenses	$123,000	$98,000	$25,000
Total current assets	$1,868,000	$1,795,000	$73,000
Gross property, plant, and equipment	$2,100,000	$1,900,000	$200,000
Less: accumulated depreciation	$333,000	$234,000	$(99,000)
Net property, plant, and equipment	$1,767,000	$1,666,000	$101,000
Total assets	$3,635,000	$3,461,000	$174,000
Liabilities and Owner's Equity			
Accounts payable	$450,000	$430,000	$20,000
Accrued expenses	$98,000	$77,000	$21,000
Income tax payable	$17,000	$9,000	$8,000
Short-term debt	$435,000	$500,000	$(65,000)
Total current liabilities	$1,000,000	$1,016,000	$(16,000)
Long-term debt	$750,000	$660,000	$90,000
Total liabilities	$1,750,000	$1,676,000	$74,000
Contributed capital	$900,000	$850,000	$50,000
Retained earnings	$985,000	$935,000	$50,000
Total owner's equity	$1,885,000	$1,785,000	$100,000
Total liabilities and owner's equity	$3,635,000	$3,461,000	$174,000

Source: HMM Finance.

invested. Further, the balance sheet indicates how much of those monetary investments in assets comes from creditors (liabilities) and how much comes from the owners (equity). Analysis of the balance sheet can give you an idea of how efficiently a company is utilizing its assets and how well it is managing its liabilities.

Balance sheet data is most helpful when compared with the same information from one or more previous years. Consider the balance sheet of Amalgamated Hat Rack. First, this statement represents the company's financial position at a moment in time: December 31, 2002. A comparison of the figures for 2001 against those for 2002 shows that Amalgamated is moving in a positive direction: It has increased its owners' equity by nearly $100,000.

Assets

You should understand some details about this particular financial statement. The balance sheet begins by listing the assets most easily converted to cash: cash on hand and marketable securities, receivables, and inventory. These are called *current assets*. Generally, current assets are those that can be converted into cash within one year.

Next, the balance sheet tallies other assets that are tougher to convert to cash—for example, buildings and equipment. These are called plant assets or, more commonly, *fixed assets* (because it is hard to change them into cash).

Since most fixed assets, except land, depreciate—or become less valuable—over time, the company must reduce the stated value of these fixed assets by something called accumulated depreciation. Gross property, plant, and equipment minus accumulated depreciation equals the current book value of property, plant, and equipment.

Some companies list *goodwill* among their assets. If a company has purchased another company for a price above the fair market value of its assets, that so-called goodwill is recorded as an asset. This is, however, strictly an accounting fiction. Goodwill may also represent intangible things such as brand names or the acquired company's excellent reputation. These may have real value. So too can other intangible assets, such as patents.

Finally, we come to the last line of the balance sheet, total assets. Total assets represents the sum of both current and fixed assets.

Liabilities and Owners' Equity

Now let's consider the claims against those assets, beginning with a category called current liabilities. *Current liabilities* represent the claims of creditors and others that typically must be paid within a year; they include short-term IOUs, accrued salaries, accrued income taxes, and accounts payable. This year's repayment obligation on a long-term loan is also listed under current liabilities.

Subtracting current liabilities from current assets gives you the company's net working capital. *Net working capital* is the amount of money the company has tied up in its current (short-term) operating activities. Just how much is adequate for the company depends on the industry and the company's plans. In its most recent balance sheet, Amalgamated had $868,000 in net working capital.

Long-term liabilities are typically bonds and mortgages—debts that the company is contractually obligated to repay, with respect to both interest and principal.

According to the aforementioned accounting equation, total assets must equal total liabilities plus owners' equity. Thus, subtracting total liabilities from total assets, the balance sheet arrives at a figure for the owners' equity. Owners' equity comprises *retained earnings* (net profits that accumulate on a company's balance sheet after any dividends are paid) and contributed capital (capital received in exchange for shares).

Historical Values

The values represented in many balance sheet categories may not correspond to their actual market values. Except for items such as cash, accounts receivable, and accounts payable, the measurement of each classification will rarely be equal to the actual current value or cash value shown. This is because accountants must record most items at their historic cost. If, for example, XYZ's balance sheet indicated land worth $700,000, that figure would represent what XYZ paid for the land way back when. If the land was purchased in downtown San Francisco in 1960, you can bet that it is now worth immensely more than the value stated on the balance sheet. So why do accountants use historic instead of market values? The short answer is that it represents the lesser of two evils. If market values were mandated, then every public company would be required to get a professional appraisal of every one of it properties, warehouse inventories, and so forth—and would have to do so every year. And how many people would trust those appraisals? So we're stuck with historic values on the balances sheet.

Managerial Issues

Though the balance sheet is prepared by accountants, it represents a number of important issues for managers.

WORKING CAPITAL Financial managers give substantial attention to the level of working capital, which naturally expands and contracts with sales activities. Too little working capital can put a company in a bad position: The company may be unable to pay its bills or to take advantage of profitable opportunities. Too much working capital, on the other hand, reduces profitability, since that capital has a carrying cost—it must be financed in some way, usually through interest-bearing loans.

Inventory is one component of working capital that directly affects many managers who are not involved in finance. Like working capital in general, inventory must be balanced between too much and too little. Having lots of inventory on hand solves many business problems: The company can fill customer orders without delay, and a robust inventory provides a buffer against potential production stoppages and strikes. The flip side of plentiful inventory is financing cost and the risk of deterioration in the market value of the inventory itself. Every excess widget in the stockroom adds to the company's financing costs, which reduces profits. And every item that sits on the shelf may become obsolete or less salable as time goes by—again, with a negative impact on profitability. The personal computer business provides a clear example of how excess inventory can wreck the bottom line. Some analysts estimate that the value of finished-goods inventory melts away at a rate of approximately 2 percent *per day*, because of technical obsolescence in this fast-moving industry.

FINANCIAL LEVERAGE You have probably heard someone say, "It's a highly leveraged situation." Do you know what "leveraged" means in the financial sense? *Financial leverage* refers to the use of borrowed money in acquiring an asset. We say that a company is highly leveraged when the percentage of debt on its balance sheet is high relative to the capital invested by the owners. For example, suppose that you paid $400,000 for an asset, using $100,000 of your own money and $300,000 in borrowed funds. For simplicity, we'll ignore loan payments, taxes, and any cash flow you might get from the investment. Four years go by, and your asset has appreciated to $500,000. You decide to sell. After paying off the $300,000 loan, you end up with $200,000 in your pocket (your original $100,000 plus a $100,000 profit). That's a gain of 100 percent on your personal capital, even though the asset increased in value by only 25 percent. Financial leverage made this possible. In contrast, if you had financed the purchase entirely with your own funds ($400,000), then you would have ended up with only a 25 percent gain. (*Operating leverage*, in contrast, refers to the extent to which a company's operating costs are fixed versus variable. For example, a company that relies heavily on machinery and very few workers to produce its goods has a high operating leverage.)

Financial leverage creates an opportunity for a company to gain a higher return on the capital invested by its owners. In the United States and most other countries, tax policy makes financial leverage even more attractive by allowing businesses to deduct the interest paid on loans. But leverage can cut both ways. If the value of an asset drops (or fails to produce the anticipated level of revenue), then leverage works against its owner. Consider what would have happened in our example if the asset's value had dropped by $100,000, that is, to $300,000. The owner would have lost his or her entire $100,000 investment after repaying the initial loan of $300,000.

FINANCIAL STRUCTURE OF THE FIRM The negative potential of financial leverage is what keeps CEOs, their financial executives, and board members from maximizing their debt financing. Instead, they seek a financial structure that creates a realistic balance between debt and equity on the balance sheet. Although leverage enhances a company's potential profitability as long as things go right, managers know that every dollar of debt increases the riskiness of the business—both because of the danger just cited, and because high debt results in high interest payments, which must be paid in good times and bad. Many companies have failed when business reversals or recessions reduced their ability to make timely payments on their loans.

When creditors and investors examine corporate balance sheets, they look carefully at the debt-to-equity ratio. They factor the riskiness of the balance sheet into the interest they charge on loans and the return they demand from a company's bonds. Thus, a highly leveraged company may have to pay 14 percent on borrowed funds instead of the 10 to 12 percent paid by a less leveraged competitor. Investors also demand a higher rate of return for their stock investments in highly leveraged companies. They will not accept high risks without an expectation of commensurately large returns.

Where Are the Human Assets?

As people look to financial statements to gain insights about companies, many are questioning the traditional balance sheet's ability to reflect the value of human capital and profit potential. This is particularly true for knowledge-intensive companies, for which the workforce know-how, intellectual property, brand equity, and customer relationships are the real productive assets. Unfortunately, these intangible assets are not found on the balance sheet.

The growing irrelevance of balance sheets to reflect real value prompted Federal Reserve Board chairman Alan Greenspan to complain in January 2000 that accounting failed to track investments in "knowledge assets." Former SEC chairman Arthur Levitt echoed Greenspan's concern: "As intangible assets grow in size and scope, more and more people are questioning whether the true value—and the drivers of that value—are being reflected in a timely manner in publicly available disclosure." Indeed, a study by Baruch Lev of New York University found that 40 percent of the market valuation of the average company was missing from its balance sheet. For high-tech firms, the figure was more than 50 percent.

The implication of these findings for investors and managers is that they must look beyond the bricks and mortar, the equipment, and even the cash that traditionally constitute balance sheet assets and focus on the undisclosed assets that produce the greatest value for shareholders. In most cases, those assets are the people who create the bonds between the enterprise and its customers, who create innovations that customers are eager to pay for, and who know how to get others to work together productively. The accounting profession is beginning to debate the pros and cons of including these intangible assets in financial statements. Watch for future developments.

The Income Statement

The *income statement* indicates the results of operations over a specified period. Those last two words are important. Unlike the balance sheet, which is a snapshot of the enterprise's position at a point in time, the income statement indicates cumulative business results within a defined time frame. It tells you if the company is making a profit—that is, whether it has positive or negative net income (net earnings). This is why the income statement is often referred to as the *profit-and-loss statement*, or P&L. It shows a company's profitability at the end of a particular time—typically at the end of the month, the quarter, or the company's fiscal year. In addition, the income statement tells you how much money the company spent to make that profit—from which you can determine the company's *profit margin*.

As we did with the balance sheet, we can represent the contents of the income statement with a simple equation:

Revenues − Expenses = Net Income (or Net Loss)

An income statement starts with the company's *revenues*: the amount of money that results from selling products or services to customers. A company may have other revenues as well. In many cases, these are from investments or interest income from its cash holdings.

Various costs and expenses—from the costs of making and storing goods, to depreciation of plant and equipment, to interest expense and taxes—are then deducted from revenues. The bottom line —what's left over—is the *net income*, or net profit or net earnings, for the period of the statement.

Consider the meaning of various line items on the income statement for Amalgamated Hat Rack (table 14-2). The *cost of goods sold* is what it cost Amalgamated to manufacture its hat racks. This figure includes the cost of raw materials, such as lumber, as well as the cost of turning them into finished goods, including direct labor costs. By deducting the cost of goods sold from sales revenue, we get a company's *gross profit*—the roughest estimation of the company's profitability.

The next major category of cost is *operating expenses*. Operating expenses include administrative employee salaries, rents, sales and marketing costs, as well as other costs of business not directly attributed to the cost of manufacturing a product. The lumber for making hat racks would *not* be included here; the cost of the advertising and the salaries of Amalgamated employees would.

Depreciation is counted on the income statement as an expense, even though it involves no out-of-pocket payments. As described earlier, depreciation is a way of estimating the "consumption" of an asset, or the diminishing value of equipment, over time. A computer, for example, loses about a third of its value each year. Thus, the company would not expense the full value of a computer in the first year of its purchase, but as it is actually used over a span of three years. The idea behind depreciation is to recognize the diminished value of certain assets.

TABLE 14-2

Amalgamated Hat Rack Income Statement for the Fiscal Year Ending December 31, 2002

Retail Sales	$2,200,000
Corporate Sales	$1,000,000
Total Sales Revenue	$3,200,000
Less: Cost of Goods Sold	$1,600,000
Gross Profit	$1,600,000
Less: Operating Expenses	$800,000
Depreciation Expense	$42,500
Earnings Before Interest and Taxes	$757,500
Less: Interest Expense	$110,000
Earnings Before Income Tax	$647,500
Less: Income Tax	$300,000
Net Income	$347,500

Source: HMM Finance.

By subtracting operating expenses and depreciation from the gross profit, we get *operating earnings*. These earnings are often called earnings before interest and taxes, or EBIT.

We're now down to the last reductions in the path that revenues follow on their way to the bottom line. Interest expense is the interest charged on loans a company has taken out. Income tax, tax levied by the government on corporate income, is the final charge.

What revenues are left are referred to as net income, or earnings. If net income is positive—as it is in the case of Amalgamated—we have a profit, what the for-profit company lives for.

Making Sense of the Income Statement

As with the balance sheet, our analysis of a company's income statement is greatly aided when presented in a multiperiod format. This allows us to spot trends and turnarounds. Most annual reports make multiperiod data available, often going back five or more years. Amalgamated's income statement in multiperiod form is depicted in table 14–3.

TABLE 14-3

Amalgamated Hat Rack Multiperiod Income Statement

	FOR THE PERIOD ENDING DECEMBER 31			
	2002	**2001**	**2000**	**1999**
Retail Sales	$2,200,000	$2,000,000	$1,720,000	$1,500,000
Corporate Sales	$1,000,000	$1,000,000	$1,100,000	$1,200,000
Total Sales Revenue	$3,200,000	$3,000,000	$2,820,000	$2,700,000
Less: Cost of Goods Sold	$1,600,000	$1,550,000	$1,400,000	$1,300,000
Gross Profit	$1,600,000	$1,450,000	$1,420,000	$1,400,000
Less: Operating Expenses	$800,000	$810,000	$812,000	$805,000
Depreciation Expense	$42,500	$44,500	$45,500	$42,500
Earnings Before Interest and Taxes	$757,500	$595,500	$562,500	$552,500
Less: Interest Expense	$110,000	$110,000	$150,000	$150,000
Earnings Before Income Tax	$647,500	$485,500	$412,500	$402,500
Less: Income Tax	$300,000	$194,200	$165,000	$161,000
Net Income	$347,500	$291,300	$247,500	$241,500

In this multiyear format, we observe that Amalgamated's annual retail sales have grown steadily, while its corporate sales have stagnated and even declined slightly. Operating expenses have stayed about the same, however, even as total sales have expanded. That's a good sign that management is holding the line on the cost of doing business. The company's interest expense has also declined, perhaps because it has paid off one of its loans. The bottom line, net income, has shown healthy growth.

The Cash Flow Statement

The *cash flow statement*, the last of the three essential financial statements, is the least used and understood. This statement details the reasons why the amount of cash (and cash equivalents) changed during the accounting period. More specifically, it reflects all changes in cash as affected by operating activities, investments, and financing activities. Like the bank statement you receive for your checking account, the cash flow statement tells how much cash was on hand at the beginning of the period, and how much was on hand at the end. It then describes how the company acquired and spent cash in a particular period. The uses of cash are recorded as negative figures, and sources of cash are recorded as positive figures.

If you're a manager in a large corporation, changes in the company's cash flow won't typically have an impact on your day-to-day functioning. Nevertheless, it's a good idea to stay up-to-date with your company's cash flow projections, because they may come into play when you prepare your budget for the upcoming year. For example, if cash is tight, you will probably want to be conservative in your spending. Alternatively, if the company is flush with cash, you may have opportunities to make new investments. If you're a manager in a small company or its owner, you're probably keenly aware of your cash flow situation and feel its impact almost every day.

The cash flow statement is useful because it indicates whether your company is turning accounts receivable into cash—and that ability is ultimately what will keep your company solvent. *Solvency* is the ability to pay bills as they come due.

As we did with the other statements, we can conceptualize the cash flow statement in terms of a simple equation:

Cash Flow from Profit + Other Sources of Cash − Uses of Cash = Change in Cash

Again using the Amalgamated Hat Rack example, we see that in its year 2002 cash flow statement, the company generated a positive cash flow of $377,900 (table 14-4). The statement shows that cash flows from operations ($283,900), plus those from investing activities ($92,000), and from financing ($2,000) produced $377,900 in additional cash.

The cash flow statement doesn't measure the same thing as the income statement. If there is no cash transaction, then it cannot be reflected on a cash flow statement. Notice, however, that net income at the top of the cash flow statement is the same as the bottom line of the income statement—it's the company's profit. Through a series of adjustments, the cash flow statement translates this net income into a cash basis.

The statement's format reflects the three categories of activities that affect cash. Cash can be increased or decreased because of (1) operations, (2) the acquisition or sale of assets, that is, investments, or (3) changes in debt or stock or other financing activities. Let's consider each in turn, starting with operations:

- Accounts receivable and finished-goods inventory represent items the company has produced, but for which it hasn't received payment. Prepaid expenses represent items the company has paid for but has not consumed. These items are all subtracted from cash flow.

- Accounts payable and accrued expenses represent items the company has already received or used, but for which it hasn't yet paid. Consequently, these items add to cash flow.

Now, consider investments. Investment activities include the following:

- Gains realized from the sale of plant, property, and equipment—in other words, gains realized from converting investments into cash.

TABLE 14-4

Amalgamated Hat Rack Cash Flow Statement, 2002

Net Income	$347,500
Operating Assets and Liabilities	
Accounts receivable	$(75,600)
Finished-goods inventory	$(125,000)
Prepaid expenses	$(37,000)
Accounts payable	$83,000
Accrued expenses	$25,000
Income tax payable	$(23,000)
Depreciation expense	$89,000
Total changes in operating assets and liabilities	$(63,600)
Cash flow from operations	$283,900
Investing Activities	
Sale of property, plant, and equipment	$267,000
Capital expenditures	$(175,000)
Cash flow from investing activities	$92,000
Financing Activities	
Short-term debt increase	$27,000
Long-term borrowing	$112,000
Capital stock	$50,000
Cash dividends to stockholders	$(187,000)
Cash flow from financing activities	$2,000
Increase in cash during year	$377,900

Source: HMM Finance.

Cash Flow Versus Profit

Many people think of profits as cash flow. Don't make this mistake. For a particular period, profit may or may not contribute positively to cash flow. For example, if this year's profit derives from a huge sale made in November, the sale may be booked as revenues in the fiscal period—thus adding to profit. But if payment for that sale is not received until the next accounting period, it goes on the books as an account receivable, which reduces cash flow.

- Cash that the company uses to invest in financial instruments and plant, property, and equipment (such investments in plant, property, and equipment are often shown as capital expenditures).

The cash flow statement shows that Amalgamated has sold a building for $267,000 and made capital expenditures of $175,000, for a net addition to cash flow of $92,000.

Finally, we come to cash flow changes from financing activities. Amalgamated has raised money by increasing its short-term debt, by borrowing in the capital markets, and by issuing capital stock, thereby increasing its available cash flow. The dividends that Amalgamated pays, however ($187,000) must be paid out of cash flow and thus represent a decrease in cash flow.

Where to Find It

As mentioned earlier, all firms that trade their shares in U.S. public financial markets are required by the Securities and Exchange Commission to prepare and distribute their financial statements in an annual report to shareholders. Most annual reports go beyond the basic disclosure requirement of the SEC, providing discussion of the year's operations and the future outlook. Most public companies also issue quarterly reports.

If you are looking for even more material on your company—or on one of your competitors—obtain a copy of the company's form 10-K, which must be filed with the SEC. The 10-K often contains abundant and revealing information about a company's strategy, its view of the market and its customers, its products, its important risks and business challenges, and so forth. You can obtain 10-K reports and annual and quarterly reports directly from a company's investor relations department, or online at http://www.sec.gov/edgar/search edgar/formpick.htm.

Summing Up

- The balance sheet shows a company's financial position at a specific point in time. That is, it gives a snapshot of the company's financial situation—its assets, equity, and liabilities—on a given day.

- The income statement shows the bottom line: It indicates how much profit or loss was generated over a period—a month, a quarter, or a year.

- The cash flow statement tells where the company's cash came from and where it went—in other words, the flow of cash in, through, and out of the company.

- In a nutshell, the income statement tells you whether your company is making a profit. The balance sheet tells you how efficiently a company is utilizing its assets and managing its liabilities in pursuit of profits. The cash flow statement tells you how cash has been increased or decreased through operations, the acquisition or sale of assets, and financing activities.

Net Present Value and Internal Rate of Return

Accounting for Time

Key Topics Covered in This Chapter

- *Present and future value*

- *Net present value*

- *Internal rate of return*

- *Hurdle rate and discount rate*

T HIS CHAPTER will introduce you to financial decision-making tools that account for time value: specifically, present and future value, net present value, and internal rate of return. These are among the most powerful and useful decision tools available to managers. Whether you're considering the development of a new product, the purchase of a new asset, or any other type of investment, these time-value tools can greatly enhance your decisions. Best of all, they account for your company's cost of capital in those decisions.

Time Value—and Why It Matters

Some managers use the concept of return on investment (ROI) to make decisions and assess performance. They say, "We invested $10 million in the development of this technology and sold it four years later for $15 million. So our ROI was 50 percent." Unfortunately, the calculation of ROI has an important weakness: It fails to account for the timing of cash flows. The timing of cash flows matters, and should be factored into management decisions. To understand why, consider two different investments—A and B.

Investment A

Purchased a piece of land for $1 million; sold it four years later for $1.5 million.

Investment B

Purchased a piece of land for $1 million; sold it two years later for $1.5 million.

Each produced a 50 percent return on investment, but B is clearly superior because its return was captured in half the time.

The utility of ROI as a decision-making tool is rather limited. It pays to understand it and its weakness, however, since many business people use it.

Calculating Return on Investment

Returns from an investment can take the form of cost savings, incremental profit, or value appreciation. You begin by determining the "net return." To calculate the net return from an investment, subtract the total cost of the investment from the total benefits received. Then, to calculate the ROI, divide the net return by the total cost of investment. For example, using Investment A above:

Total Benefits − Total Cost = Net Return
$1.5 million − $1 million = $0.5 million

Net Return / Total Cost = ROI
$0.5 million / $1 million = 50%

The time value of money is a mathematically based recognition that money received today is worth more than an equal amount of money received months or years in the future. If you have any doubts about this statement, consider the following example:

Your father-in-law takes you aside and says, "The grim reaper is going to catch up with me one of these days. And as much as I'd like to take all of my money with me, I've decided to give you youngsters a bundle of it before I go—say $300,000 dollars."

Naturally, you're pleased to learn of his generous intention. You are also eager to learn when the money will be coming your way. "I'm not *sure when I'll give you the money," he continues. "It might be this year, next year, or five years down the road. But that shouldn't matter since it will be $300,000 in any case."*

Your father-in-law got that last point dead wrong. *When* you receive the money does matter. Thanks to the effect of compounding interest, $300,000 put today into a bank CD or savings account with a 5 percent annual interest rate would be worth almost $383,000 five years from now—and slightly more than $483,000 if your investment compounded at a 10 percent annual rate! Let's look at how compounding works over time using the $300,000 in our example, with annual compound interest at 10 percent per year over five years (table 15-1).

This example demonstrates the importance of time in the receipt of cash amounts. If your father-in-law were to give you the $300,000 today, you'd be $183,153 better off (assuming a 10 percent compounded return) than if he delayed his gift to you by five years. (Note: This analysis assumes that you reinvest the interest you earn at the same rate.)

The example also introduces a number of important terms in the language of finance:

- **Present value.** The $300,000 is a *present value* (PV), that is, an amount received today.

TABLE 15-1

Time Value of an Investment with 10 Percent Compounded Interest

Period	Beginning Value	Interest Earned	Ending Value
1	$300,000	+ $30,000	$330,000
2	$330,000	+ $33,000	$363,000
3	$363,000	+ $36,300	$399,300
4	$399,300	+ $39,930	$439,230
5	$439,230	+ $39,930	$483,153

- **Future value:** The $483,153 is a *future value* (FV)—the amount to which a present value, or series of payments, will increase over a specific period at a specific compounding rate.

- **Periods:** Time is measured by periods. The number of periods (n) in this example is five years.

- **Rate:** The rate (i) is the compounding percentage.

Understand these terms, and use them properly, and you'll rise a notch or two in the estimation of your company's CFO.

Generations of business students have been forced to learn how to calculate present and future values using tables like the one in table 15-2. This table indicates the present value of $1, given various compounding rates and compounding periods. Each cell in the table is commonly referred to as a present-value interest factor, or PVIF. For example, the PVIF for $1 received at the end of five periods at 10 percent (i) is 0.621 according to the table. In other words, $1 received at

TABLE 15-2

Present Value of $1 (PVIF)

Period	2%	4%	6%	8%	10%	12%
1	0.980	0.962	0.943	0.926	0.909	0.893
2	0.961	0.925	0.890	0.857	0.826	0.797
3	0.942	0.889	0.840	0.794	0.751	0.712
4	0.924	0.855	0.792	0.735	0.683	0.636
5	0.906	0.822	0.747	0.681	0.621	0.567
6	0.888	0.790	0.705	0.630	0.564	0.507
7	0.871	0.760	0.665	0.583	0.513	0.452
8	0.853	0.731	0.627	0.540	0.467	0.404
9	0.837	0.703	0.592	0.500	0.424	0.361
10	0.820	0.676	0.558	0.463	0.386	0.322

the end of a five-year period is worth only $0.621, assuming that you could invest funds today at a 10 percent compound rate.

Tables for determining future values are also available. Tables such as these are easy to use, but thanks to today's preprogrammed business calculators and electronic spreadsheets, you don't need them. A business calculator like the ubiquitous Hewlett-Packard 12C has several keys programmed to make these solutions simple. Its keyboard has keys for present value (PV), future value (FV), compounding rate (i), and number of compounding periods (n). If you know any three of these variables, the calculator will solve for the fourth. The instruction book explains the sequence to follow in entering the values and obtaining the solution. Likewise, PC spreadsheet programs such as Microsoft's Excel have built-in formulas that make time-value problems easy to solve.

Net Present Value

Future value is an easy idea to grasp, since most of us have been exposed to the principle of compound interest. Put money in an interest-bearing account, leave it alone, and it will grow to a larger amount over time. The longer you leave it alone, or the higher the compounding rate, or both, the larger the future value. The idea of the present value of a future sum is less familiar and less intuitive, but financial people and other savvy managers use it all the time. You can, too.

Present value is the monetary value today of a future payment discounted at some annual compound interest rate. To understand the concept of present value, let's go back to our initial example—the bequest from your father-in-law. In that example, the present value of $483,153 is $300,000. This is calculated through a process of discounting, or reverse compounding, at a rate of 10 percent per year over a period of five years. In the parlance of finance, 10 percent is the *discount rate*. If your father-in-law had said, "Look, I'm planning on giving you $483,153 five years from now, but if you'd rather have the money today I'm willing to give you $300,000," he'd be giving you an equivalent value, assuming you could invest it at 10 percent.

In short, you would see no difference between getting $300,000 now or $483,153 in five years—unless you worried about your father-in-law's not making good on his promise.

Note that the PVIF in table 15-2 for five periods at 10 percent is 0.621. We can use this factor to calculate the present value of your father-in-law's $483,153 gift received five years in the future:

Future Value x PVIF = Present Value
$483,153 x 0.621 = $300,038

We're off by just a little as a result of rounding of the PVIF in the table.

The PVIF table clearly indicates how the present value of money received in the future shrinks with time. Your financial calculator and PC spreadsheet can handle this same calculation. You simply enter the known values (future value, discount rate, and number of compounding periods) and solve for the unknown value, PV.

Now that you understand present value, let's move on to a typical business situation and see how time-value calculations can help your decision making. But first let's broaden the concept of present value to *net present value* (NPV), which is the present value of one or more future cash flows *less* any initial investment costs. To illustrate this concept, let's say that Amalgamated Hat Rack expects its new product line to start generating $70,000 in annual profit (or, more specifically, net cash flows) beginning one year from now. For simplicity, we'll also say that this level of annual profit will continue for the succeeding five years (totaling $350,000). Bringing the product line on stream will require an up-front investment of $250,000. The questions for the company can thus be phrased as follows: Given this expected profit stream and the $250,000 up-front cost required to produce it, is a new line of coat racks the most productive way to invest that initial $250,000? Or would Amalgamated be better off investing it in something else?

A net-present-value calculation answers this question by recognizing that the $350,000 in profit that Amalgamated expects to receive over five years is not worth $350,000 in current dollars. Because of discounting, it is worth less than that. In other words, that future sum of $350,000 has to be discounted back into an equivalent of today's dollars. How much it is discounted depends on the rate of return Amalgamated could reasonably expect to receive had it chosen to put the initial $250,000 investment into something other than the line of coat racks (but similar in risk) for the same period. As explained earlier, this rate of return is often called the discount rate. We define the *discount rate* as the annual rate, expressed as a percentage, at which a future payment or series of payments is reduced to its present value. In our Amalgamated example, let's assume a discount rate of 10 percent. But before we describe the calculation, let's lay out the situation as follows, with the values in thousands of dollars:

Year	0	1	2	3	4	5
Cash flows	−250	+70	+70	+70	+70	+70

Here we see a negative cash flow of $250,000 in year zero, the starting point of our investment project. This is the cash outflow required to get the project off the ground. The company then experiences a positive cash flow of $70,000 *at the end* of each of the next five years.

To find the net present value of Amalgamated's stream of cash flows, we need to find the present value of *each* of the $70,000 cash flows, discounted at 10 percent for the appropriate number of years. If we add together the present values of the five annual inflows and

Beginning or End of the Period?

In solving for net present value and other time-value problems, it is important to know if the cash flows take place at the beginning or end of the period. The present value of a cash flow received in early January is worth more than the same amount received in late December of the same year. Your financial calculator and electronic spreadsheet are set up to accommodate this important difference.

then subtract the $250,000 initially invested, we will have the NPV of the investment. We can determine the NPV for this set of cash flows using our PVIF table (see table 15-2) and its present value interest factors. The cash flow quantities are in thousands of dollars.

Calculations such as this one can be laborious, but the financial calculators and computer spreadsheets now available make them faster and more accurate. All that you have to do is plug in the right numbers in the right sequence. The NPV function on your calculator or spreadsheet takes into consideration your initial investment, each periodic cash flow, your discount rate, and the number of years over which you will receive the cash flows.

If the resulting NPV is a positive number, and no other investments are under consideration, then the investment should be pursued. In the Amalgamated case depicted in table 15-3, the NPV for the line of coat racks is a positive $15,300, which suggests that it would be an attractive investment for Amalgamated. Its compound annual return is at least 10 percent. While this outcome is positive, company managers should only move forward with the project if it is superior to alternative projects. Every vibrant company has a number of investment alternatives, and all should be subjected to the same NPV analysis before any decisions are made.

TABLE 15-3

Net Present Value of Amalgamated's Cash Flow

	Cash Flows (in $1,000)	PVIF	PV (in $1,000)
Year 0	− 250		− 250.00
Year 1	+ 70	0.909	+ 63.63
Year 2	+ 70	0.826	+ 57.82
Year 3	+ 70	0.751	+ 52.57
Year 4	+ 70	0.683	+ 47.81
Year 5	+ 70	0.621	+ 43.47
Total			+ 15.30

Complications

Of course, business situations are almost always more complex than the conveniently simple one we've contrived in the Amalgamated example. Project investments are rarely made in a single lump sum at the very beginning, and cash flows are almost always irregular—some positive, others negative—over time. What's more, it is often difficult or impossible to accurately estimate what cash flows will look like far in the future, or when they will finally end. Some investments end abruptly with the sale of the product line or factory building—the net sale value of which must be entered as a terminal-value cash flow. Other cash flows may go on for decades and gradually fade to nothing.

With this complexity in mind, we will try to present a slightly more realistic picture of a business situation using NPV analysis. Let's deliberately make Amalgamated's new product line investment project slightly more complex. We'll do this in three ways and then show how you could assess the investment project through the same NVP analysis framework:

1. We'll spread the $250,000 investment over three periods instead of one. This is more typical of business practice in developing a new product line.

2. Cash flows will be made more irregular, with a negative cash flow in the first full year and growing cash flows in later years.

3. We'll arbitrarily plan for Amalgamated to sell the product line at the end of five years for $170,000, and we'll treat the sale price as a terminal value.

Table 15-4 shows the results of these assumptions. Using 10 percent once again as the discount rate, we calculate a NPV of about $69,800 for this series of negative and positive cash flows. If 10 percent is the cost of capital to Amalgamated, we could say that this investment would (1) earn its cost of capital *and* (2) make a positive present-value contribution of $69,800.

TABLE 15-4

Net Present Value of Amalgamated's Cash Flow, with Complications (Values in Thousands)

	Year					
	0	1	2	3	4	5
Cash Investments	− 150	− 75	− 25	0	0	0
Cash Flow from Operations		− 15	+ 40	+ 80	+ 90	+ 100
Terminal Value						+ 170
Net Cash Flow	− 150	− 90	+ 15	+ 80	+ 90	+ 270
PVIF		0.909	0.826	0.751	0.683	0.621
PV	− 150	− 81.81	+ 12.39	+ 60.08	+ 61.47	+ 167.67
NPV	+ 69.80					

More Complications

Our presentation makes NPV analysis seem as straightforward as the mathematics on which it rests. It is straightforward, but the cash flows we use are, unfortunately, merely estimates of what we expect to happen in the future. One has to ask, "How realistic are those estimates?" Consider Amalgamated's $250,000 investment. Where did that number come from? Chances are it is an agreed-upon estimate produced by people in Amalgamated's R&D and manufacturing units. Those people have experience in designing new products and setting up the manufacturing equipment needed to crank them out. But past experience is an uncertain guide to the future. The only thing that you can say with certainty is that the cost of the investment will be more or less than $250,000!

Estimates of the net cash flows from operations are bound to be even less certain. Consider how cash flow from operations is determined. The product line manager no doubt asks the marketing department three questions:

1. How many of these new products (in units) can your people sell in each of the next five years?

2. What would be our net revenues from each sale?

3. What level of marketing budget would you need to achieve those sales at those prices?

The manager would likewise get a unit production and labor and materials cost estimate from the manufacturing unit. In effect, the new-product manager would have to develop a detailed "mini" income statement. This statement would detail the revenues and costs (materials, labor, marketing, and all other costs) associated with the new product line over the five-year span of the analysis. The sum of the revenues and costs would be the cash flow from operations.

Taken together, these annual estimated cash flows from operations would be used in determining the NPV of the project. Obviously, there are lots of assumptions here, and plenty of room for error—especially as people attempt to forecast sales further and further into the future. There is even a chance that sales of the new product line will cannibalize the sales of existing product lines. As a consequence, opponents of a particular investment can usually find lots of opportunities to attack the numbers, and experienced decision makers usually insist on fairly conservative sales forecasts and cost estimates.

Nevertheless, careful NPV analysis based on sound assumptions is an excellent decision-making tool—and it's certainly better than the alternatives. Its value can be improved if the NPV of an investment is presented in worst-case, most-likely-case, and best-case scenarios. This approach captures a broader range of opinions in the organization about future unit sales, various costs of production, and other assumptions.

Internal Rate of Return

Farnsworth Dabble, vice president of product development for Amalgamated Hat Rack, was just wrapping up his presentation of the new-product-line proposal to senior management. He directed his audience's attention to the five-year series of cash flows that he and his colleagues anticipated from the proposed new product line. "And so you see that we anticipate negative cash flows in each of the first two years of the project, mostly due to R&D expenditures and production ramp-up. But over the next three years, we anticipate healthy cash flows, particularly if we sell the product line and its production facilities at the end of year five."

Dabble went on to explain the assumptions made in determining those cash flows, the internal debates underlying them, and his team's wish to err on the side of conservative projections. "As you can see," he concluded with satisfaction, "the proposed product line has a positive net present value."

The CFO was the first to respond. "So, what's the internal rate of return for this project?"

Dabble stiffened. Internal rate of return? He'd heard that term used before and had a sense of its meaning, but he was clueless about how to do the actual calculation or respond to the CFO's question. In the end, he was forced to utter the three dreaded words, hoping that none of his subordinates—or his boss—were within earshot: "I don't know."

The *internal rate of return* (IRR) is another time-value tool that managers can use to decide whether to commit to a particular investment opportunity, or use to rank the desirability of various opportunities. IRR is defined as the discount rate at which the NPV of an investment equals zero. Let's consider what that means in terms of our more complicated version of Amalgamated's cash flow projection for its new product line:

Year	0	1	2	3	4	5
Net cash flow	−150	−90	+15	+80	+90	+270

As calculated earlier, the NPV of this stream of cash flows discounted at 10 percent was a positive $69,800. That told us that these numbers, if realized, would cover Amalgamated's cost of capital (10 percent) *and* contribute an additional present value of $69,800. IRR tells us something more. It captures the discount rate *and* the additional present value contribution in a single number. To calculate it, we need to determine the discount rate that would reduce NPV to exactly zero. IRR is that discount rate.

We know right from the beginning that the IRR for our example must be greater than 10 percent since the cash flow discounted at 10 percent produced a positive NPV. But how much more? Well, if we had a few blackboards and several hours, we could calculate the IRR through an iterative process that used higher and higher discount rates. Eventually, we'd get to the one that produced an NPV of zero. But financial calculators and electronic spreadsheets again come to the rescue, making IRR calculations very easy. All we need to do is enter the values for each of the cash flows and solve for the discount rate (i). The IRR calculation is based on the same algebraic formula as the NPV calculation. With the NPV calculation, you know the discount rate, or the desired rate of return, and are solving the equation for the NPV of the future cash flows. In contrast, with IRR, the NPV is set at zero and the discount rate is unknown. The equation solves for the discount rate. For the Amalgamated project just described, the IRR is about 17.7 percent.

Typically, when the IRR is greater than the opportunity cost (the expected return on a comparable investment) of the capital required, the investment under consideration should be undertaken. You can also use your company's *hurdle rate* as the IRR target. The CFO usually prescribes the hurdle rate, which is a minimal rate of return that all investments of the enterprise must achieve. The IRR of the investment under consideration must exceed the hurdle rate in order for the company to go forward with it.

What's a reasonable hurdle rate for a business? It varies from company to company. Typically, the hurdle rate is set well above what could be obtained from a risk-free investment, such as a U.S. Treasury bond. You can, in fact, think of the hurdle rate as this:

Hurdle Rate = Risk-Free Rate + Premium that
Reflects the Enterprise's Risk

Like any investor, a business entity expects to be rewarded for the uncertainty to which it is subjected. And new product lines and other such activities are, by nature, filled with uncertainty. For this reason, they demand that prospective projects show particularly good promise.

Some companies use different hurdle rates for different types of investments, with low-risk investments having to clear a lower hurdle than that imposed on the higher-risk type. For example, a company might require that replacement of an existing assembly line or a specialized piece of equipment use a hurdle rate of 8 percent, whereas the expansion of an existing product line would have a 12 percent hurdle rate. The development of a new product line, which is riskier still, might require a 15 percent hurdle rate.

Summing Up

- Net present value (NPV) is the monetary value today of a future stream of positive and negative future cash flows discounted at some annual compound interest rate. You can use NPV analysis for any number of decision-making purposes.

- Internal rate of return (IRR) is another tool that you can use to decide whether to commit to a particular investment opportunity, or to rank the desirability of various opportunities. IRR is the discount rate at which the NPV of an investment equals zero.

- The hurdle rate is a minimal rate of return that all investments for a particular enterprise must achieve. In most cases it is used as the discount rate in time-value calculations.

Breakeven Analysis and Operating Leverage

Understanding Cash Flow

Key Topics Covered in This Chapter

- *The concepts of fixed costs, variable costs, and contribution margin*

- *How to determine breakeven on a fixed investment*

- *The benefits and dangers of operating leverage*

THIS CHAPTER explains breakeven analysis, another financial tool that many managers find useful in making decisions. Explaining this tool introduces several other financial concepts that every manager should understand: fixed costs, variable costs, contribution margin, and operating leverage.

Breakeven analysis indicates how much (or how much more) you need to sell in order to pay for a fixed investment—in other words, at what point you will break even on your cash flow. With that information in hand, you can look at market demand and competitors' market shares to determine whether it's realistic to expect to sell that much. Breakeven analysis can also help you think through the impact of changing price and volume relationships.

More specifically, the breakeven calculation helps you determine the volume level at which the total after-tax contribution from a product line or an investment covers its total fixed costs. But before you can perform the calculation, you need to understand the components that go into it. These components are handy terms for every manager to know:

- **Fixed costs.** These are costs that stay mostly the same no matter how many units of a product or service are sold—costs such as insurance, management salaries, and rent or lease payments. For example, the rent on the production facility will be the same, whether the company makes ten thousand or twenty thousand units, and so will the company's fire and liability insurance.

- **Variable costs.** Variable costs are those that change with the number of units produced and sold; examples include the cost of utilities, labor, and raw materials. The more units you make, the more you consume of these items.

- **Contribution margin.** This is the amount of money that every sold unit contributes to paying for fixed costs. It is defined as follows:

Net Unit Revenue − Variable (or Direct) Costs per Unit

With these concepts understood, we can make the calculation. We are looking for the solution to this straightforward equation:

Breakeven Volume = Fixed Costs / Unit Contribution Margin

And here's how we do it. First, find the unit contribution margin by subtracting the variable costs per unit from the net revenue per unit. Then divide total fixed costs, or the amount of the investment, by the unit contribution margin. The quotient is the breakeven volume, that is, the number of units that must be sold in order for all fixed costs to be covered.

To see breakeven analysis in practice, let's look at a plastic extruder used to produce hat racks for Amalgamated, Inc. The cost of the extruder is $100,000. Suppose that each hat rack produced by the extruder sells for $75, and that the variable cost per unit is $22. Then

$75 (Price per Unit) − $22 (Variable Cost per Unit) =
$53 (Unit Contribution Margin)

therefore

$100,000 (Total Investment Required) / $53 (Unit
Contribution Margin) = 1,887 hat racks.

The preceding calculations indicate that Amalgamated must sell 1,887 hat racks to break even on its $100,000 investment.

At this point, Amalgamated must decide whether the breakeven volume is achievable: Is it realistic to expect to sell 1,887 additional hat racks, and if so, how quickly?

A Breakeven Complication

Our hat rack breakeven analysis represents a simple case. It assumes that costs are distinctly fixed or variable, that costs and unit contributions will not change as a function of volume (in other words, that the sale price of the item under consideration will not change at different levels of output). These assumptions may not hold in your more complicated world. Rent may be fixed up to a certain level of production, then increase by 50 percent as you rent a secondary facility to handle expanded output. Labor costs may in reality be a hybrid of fixed and variable costs. And as you push more and more of your product into the market, you may find it necessary to offer price discounts—which reduces contribution per unit. You will need to adjust the breakeven calculation to accommodate these untidy realities.

Operating Leverage

Your goal as a businessperson, of course, is not to break even but to make a profit. Once you've covered all your fixed costs with the contributions of many unit sales, every subsequent sale contributes directly to profits. As we observed above,

Unit Net Revenue − Unit Variable Cost = Unit Contribution to Profits

You can see at a glance that the lower the unit variable cost, the greater the contribution to profits will be. In the pharmaceutical business, for example, the unit cost of cranking out and packaging a bottle of a new wonder drug may be less than a dollar. Yet if the company can sell each bottle for $100, a whopping sum of $99 contributes to corporate profits once sales have gotten beyond the breakeven point! The trouble is that the pharmaceutical company may have invested $400 million up front in fixed product development costs just to get the first bottle out the door. It will have to sell many bottles of the new medication just to break even. But once it does, the profits can be extraordinary.

The relationship between fixed and variable costs is often described in terms of *operating leverage*. Companies whose fixed costs are high relative to their variable costs are said to have high operating leverage. The pharmaceutical business, for example, generally operates with high operating leverage. So too does the software industry—the greater percentage of its costs are fixed product development outlays; the variable cost of the plastic compact discs on which programs are distributed is measured in pennies per copy.

Now consider the opposite: *low* operating leverage. Here fixed costs are low relative to the total cost of producing every unit of output. A law firm is a good example of an enterprise with low operating leverage. The firm has a minimal investment in equipment and fixed expenses. The bulk of its costs are the fees it pays its attorneys, which vary depending on the actual hours they bill to clients.

Operating leverage is a great thing once a company passes its breakeven point, but it can cause substantial losses if breakeven is never achieved. In other words, it's risky. This is why managers give so much thought to finding the right balance between fixed and variable costs.

Summing Up

- Breakeven analysis indicates how much (or how much more) you need to sell in order to pay for a fixed investment.

- Fixed costs are costs that stay mostly the same, no matter how many units of a product or service are sold.

- Variable costs change with the number of units produced and sold.

- Contribution margin is the amount of money that every sold unit contributes to paying for fixed costs.

- The breakeven volume is fixed costs divided by the contribution margin of each unit sold.

- Operating leverage describes the relationship between fixed and variable costs.

Useful Implementation Tools

This appendix contains five forms you may find useful (figures A-1, A-2, A-3, A-4, and A-5) throughout your career as a manager. All the forms are adapted from Harvard ManageMentor, an online product of Harvard Business School Publishing. For the convenience of readers, downloadable versions of these and other checklists, worksheets, and tools can be found on the Harvard Business Essentials series Web site: www.elearning.hbsp.org/businesstools.

1. **Interview Preparation Form (figure A-1).** This form will help you prepare for a hiring interview, review the job profile, and make a list of the key responsibilities and tasks of the job, associated training and/or experience, and personal attributes required to do the job well. For each of the areas you need to explore with the candidate, prepare several questions in advance. After the interview, rate the candidate in each of the key areas on the Decision-Making Matrix.

2. **Decision-Making Matrix (figure A-2).** Complete this form after you interview each job candidate for a particular position. Enter a score for each of the key areas. By tallying the total scores and reviewing your notes from the interviews, you can begin to evaluate which candidate is the right person for the job.

3. **Planning a Feedback Session (figure A-3).** Use this tool to organize before giving feedback to anyone.

4. **Rewards Worksheet (figure A-4).** Use this worksheet to think through what really motivates you at work. You can also rate

each item from low (1) priority to high (5). Review these ratings as you assess your degree of satisfaction with your current
job, or as a guide to what you'd be looking for in your next
position.

5. **Skills Assessment (figure A–5).** Use this form to develop a
baseline assessment of your skills, including those that are transferable from one position to another, or those that you want
to develop. Rate your current level of proficiency, if desired,
from 1 (low, beginning level) to 5 (high, expert level). You may
want to supplement this form with skills-assessment tools that
relate directly to your position; these may be available from your
company. You can also use this form to solicit peer feedback on
your skill level.

FIGURE A - 1

Interview Preparation Form

Job Title:

Key Responsibilities and Tasks	Associated Training and/or Experience
1.	1.
2.	2.
3.	3.
4.	4.

Personal Attributes to Look for:

Key Areas to Explore	Questions to Ask	Notes
Education	1. 2. 3.	
Previous Experience	1. 2. 3.	
Job Accomplishments	1. 2. 3.	
Skills and Knowledge	1. 2. 3.	
Personal Attributes	1. 2. 3.	
Previous Appraisal or Rating	1. 2. 3.	

Decision-Making Matrix

Job Title:

Candidate Name	Key Area Ratings (poor) 1 to 5 (excellent)						TOTAL
	Education	Previous Experience	Job Accomplishments	Skills and Knowledge	Personal Attributes	Previous Appraisal or Rating	
	Notes:						
	Notes:						
	Notes:						
	Notes:						
	Notes:						
	Notes:						
	Notes:						

FIGURE A - 3

Planning a Feedback Session

Name the issue or behavior that needs to be corrected or reinforced.

What is the organizational and personal significance of this issue?

What is the purpose of the feedback?

What details do you have to describe the behavior accurately? (who, what, when)

What is the impact of the behavior?

What results do you want to produce?

Who is the best person to give the feedback and why?

What communication style will be the most effective and why?

Describe possible barriers to giving this feedback. What can you do to overcome them?

What behavior on the other person's part would be more constructive? Why?

Source: © 1998 by the President and Fellows of Harvard College and its licensors. All rights reserved. Adapted from *Giving and Receiving Feedback,* 32.

FIGURE A - 4

Rewards Worksheet

	Level of Importance or Value				
	Low 1	2	3	4	High 5
Financial gain This position provides an excellent opportunity for financial reward.					
Power and influence The position offers the opportunity to exercise power and influence, and the chance to be an influential decision maker.					
Lifestyle The position fits with my desired lifestyle. It lets me balance work and life demands and interests.					
Autonomy The position offers me autonomy and independence—the ability to work without a lot of close supervision.					
Affiliation The position lets me work with colleagues I enjoy and admire, and gives me a sense of belonging to a group.					
Workspace The location and physical workspace are desirable and offer me benefits such as a pleasing environment, an easy commute, or accessibility to day care.					
Intellectual stimulation or challenge The position is interesting and challenging, and offers learning and development opportunities.					
Competence This position offers me the opportunity to build competence or expertise in an area.					
Recognition and support In this position and work environment, my contributions are recognized and valued. My development is supported as well.					

Other
List additional specific rewards that you value.

Assessment
Reviewing your ratings above, what jumps out at you as most important? Least important? How well does your current job meet your reward needs?

Are there some actions you can take so that your work better satisfies your needs, such as modifying your work, taking on a "stretch" assignment, or spending more time with colleagues you enjoy?

FIGURE A - 5

Skills Assessment

Date of Assessment:

Skill	Level of Proficiency Low 1 2 3 4 5 High				Transferable Yes No	Key Skill I Want to Develop
Communication Skills						
Business Writing						
Proposal Writing						
Presentation						
Facilitation						
Running a Meeting						
Listening						
Interviewing						
Influencing						
Giving and Receiving Feedback						
Conflict Resolution						
Negotiating						
Creative or Promotional Writing						
E-mail Communication						
Editing or Copyediting						
Proofreading						
Writing Job Descriptions						
Other:						
Technology and Computer Skills						
Keyboarding						
Word Processing						
Spreadsheet						
HTML						
XML						
Project Management						
E-mail						
Presentation Software						
Graphics Software						
Other:						
Financial Skills						
Budgeting						
Financial Analysis						
Cost Accounting						
Forecasting						

(continued)

Skills Assessment

Skill	Level of Proficiency Low 1 2 3 4 5 High		Transferable Yes No	Key Skill I Want to Develop
Financial Skills *(continued)*				
Tracking and Management				
Preparing a Business Plan				
Preparing an Investment Initiative				
Cash-Flow Analysis				
Breakeven Analysis				
Quantitative Analysis				
Other:				
Supervisory Skills				
Hiring				
Coaching				
Delegating				
Setting Goals and Objectives				
Directing				
Assessing Performance				
Leading				
Motivating				
Training and Support Development				
Analyzing Work Flow and Processes				
Recruiting and Retention				
Administrative Management				
Other:				
Management Skills				
Managing Change				
Managing Customers, Internal and/or External				
Project Management				
Production or Implementation Management				
Managing Upward				
Solving Business Problems				

FIGURE A - 5

Skill	Level of Proficiency Low 1 2 3 4 5 High		Transferable Yes No	Key Skill I Want to Develop
Management Skills (continued)				
Business Analysis, Critical Thinking				
Internal Consulting and Networking				
Vendor Management				
Strategic Planning				
Tactical Planning				
Creative Thinking, Brainstorming				
Managing for Innovation				
Managing a Diverse Workforce				
International Marketing				
Other:				
Teamwork Skills				
Leading a Team				
Group Problem Solving				
Keeping Teams on Target				
Working with a Virtual Team				
Assuming Team Membership Roles				
Collaborating				
Other:				
Self-Management Skills				
Self-Awareness				
Emotional Intelligence				
Time Management				
Balancing Work and Life				
Career Development				
Stress Management				
Limit Setting and Goal Setting				
Using Power and Authority Positively				
Seeing Multiple Perspectives				
Other:				

(continued)

FIGURE A - 5 *(continued)*

Skills Assessment

Skill	Level of Proficiency Low 1 2 3 High 4 5	Transferable Yes No	Key Skill I Want to Develop
Sales and Marketing Skills			
Product Marketing			
Direct Marketing			
Market Research (perform or direct)			
Telemarketing			
Promotions			
Publicity			
Electronic Marketing			
Trade Show/Exhibits Management			
Consumer Marketing			
Business-to-Business Marketing			
Competitive Analysis and Planning			
Direct Sales			
Sales Forecasting			
Telesales			
Consultative Selling			
Other:			
Physical and Manual Dexterity Skills			
Assembling, Constructing, or Building			
Operating Tools or Machinery			
Fixing or Repairing			
Ability to Train Others on Tasks			
Other:			
Other Industry and/or Job-Specific Skills (list)			

Legal Landmines in Hiring

Note: This appendix applies to U.S. hiring situations only.

Employment in the United States is governed by many laws on hiring, firing, discrimination, sexual harassment, benefits and pension, and union activities, to name just a few. Hiring discrimination laws protect job applicants from questions that are not directly related to the applicant's ability to do the job.

The relevant laws applying to hiring are

- the Civil Rights Act of 1964, which forbids the use of arbitrary and artificial requirements that would create de facto barriers to employment because of a person's race, gender, national origin, ethnicity, or religion;

- the Age Discrimination in Employment Act, which prohibits workplace discrimination against persons of forty years and older;

- the Pregnancy Discrimination Act of 1978, which forbids workplace discrimination on the basis of pregnancy or a related medical problem;

- the Americans with Disabilities Act of 1990, which forbids discrimination against physically and mentally disabled people;

- the Immigration Reform and Control Act of 1986, which forbids discrimination against individuals based on national origin and citizenship.

This appendix offers suggestions on how you, as a job interviewer, can obtain the information you need while remaining on the right side of these various laws. It is by no means complete, nor is it intended as a source of legal advice. Its only purpose is to alert you to aspects of the hiring process where care must be exercised.

When hiring, there are some questions you cannot ask without fear of legal liability. Human resource departments are knowledgeable about these questions and make sure that none appear on job application forms. Questions prohibited on these forms are also prohibited during job interviews. Here are the areas where you must either *not* ask questions, or observe great care:

- **Age or date of birth.** This could run you afoul of the Age Discrimination in Employment Act. However, certain public safety positions have age limits for hiring. Questions about age may be asked if necessary to satisfy provisions of state or federal law. For example, you *can* ask "If hired, can you show proof that you are at least eighteen years old?" You will need the actual age and date of birth to comply with benefits and other company plans; however, these can only be obtained *after* the individual is hired.

  Other age-related *illegal* questions include: "How soon do you plan to retire?" "Can you work for a younger manager?" "Do you think you could keep up with the rest of the younger employees?"

- **The applicant's religion.** No inquiries on this subject may be asked except by religious organizations as provided by certain statutes. Nor may you inquire about the following: "Do you intend to take time off for your religious holidays?" "Do you have any unusual religious practices that we should be aware of?" "Do you think you can fit into our mostly (fill in the religion) department?"

  It is appropriate to ask "This position requires weekend work (travel). Do you have any responsibilities that conflict with these requirements?"

- **Marital status.** Never ask if the applicant is single or married. Also, avoid any question that would be construed as an indirect attempt to determine marital status, such as "What does your husband/wife do for a living?"

- **Intention to have children.** This is another forbidden area. Do not ask "Do you have children?" or "Do you intend to have children?" Indirect questions in this area are also off-limits, such as "What child-care arrangement would you have to make if you took this job?"

- **Race.** Never ask the applicant about his/her race or ethnicity. Nor can you require an individual to submit a photograph with his or her job application or résumé.

- **Gender or sexual orientation.** Another off-limits area.

- **National origin, ethnicity, and/or ancestry.** Do not ask any questions about these; nor may you inquire about the national origins of the applicant's parents, spouse, or other close relatives. And don't make the innocent mistake of saying, "Draculaskov is an interesting last name. What kind of name is that?" Other questions not to ask are: "Do you speak English at home?" "Will you wear American clothes or your native dress to work?"

- **Citizenship.** You may *not* ask "Are you a U.S. citizen?" Nor may you inquire into the citizenship of the applicant's parents or spouse. However, you may ask "Are you legally authorized to work in the United States?" Or, "If hired, can you show proof of your eligibility to work in the United States?"

- **Disability or handicap.** Make no inquiry as to whether the applicant has a physical or mental disability or handicap or about the nature or severity of either. The same applies to questions about alcoholism, drug addition, and AIDS. Other illegal questions include: "Are you taking any medications?" "Do you have frequent doctor appointments?" "Have you ever been hospitalized or received worker's compensation?"

    You may, however, ask "Are you able to perform the essential functions of this job with or without reasonable accommodation?"

- **Education.** Make no inquiry unless educational background is demonstrably related to the ability to do the job. For example, someone applying for a position as a financial analyst would need to meet certain educational requirements in mathematics, finance, and statistics; a mail-room employee would not. However, avoid questions designed to determine the age of the applicant.

- **Arrests and conviction records.** Unless the person is applying for a security-sensitive job, you cannot ask about these.

- **Garnishment of wages.** Never ask "Are your wages being garnished?"

If there is any simple advice in this maze of "don't ask" categories it is this: If your question does not relate *directly* to the job at hand, don't ask it.

Notes

Chapter 1

1. The content of this chapter is drawn in part from the "Setting Goals" module of Harvard ManageMentor, an online product of Harvard Business School Publishing.

2. Robert H. Schaffer, "Demand Better Results—And Get Them," *Harvard Business Review*, March–April 1991.

Chapter 2

1. The five-step hiring process presented in this chapter is adapted from Harvard ManageMentor, an online product of Harvard Business School Publishing.

2. Subrata Chakravarty, "A Model of Superb Management: Hit 'Em Hardest with the Mostest," *Forbes*, 16 September 1991, 48–51.

3. Pierre Mornell, *Hiring Smart!* (Berkeley, CA: Ten Speed Press, 1998), 123.

Chapter 3

1. Ed Michaels, Helen Handfield-Jones, and Beth Axelrod, *The War for Talent* (Boston: Harvard Business School Press, 2001), 47.

2. See Frederick Herzberg, "One More Time: How Do You Motivate Employees?" *Harvard Business Review*, September–October 1987, 109–120.

3. Peter Cappelli, "A Market-Driven Approach to Retaining Talent," *Harvard Business Review*, January–February 2000, 103–111.

4. Stewart D. Friedman, Perry Christensen, and Jessica DeGroot, "Work and Life: The End of the Zero-Sum Game," *Harvard Business Review*, November–December 1998, 119–129.

5. See <http:// www.att.com/telework/article_library/survey_results_ 2003.html> for AT&T research and experience with telework.

6. Mahlon Apgar IV. "The Alternative Workplace: Changing Where and How People Work," *Harvard Business Review*, May–June, 1998, 121–136.

7. See "Flexibility Works" at <http://www.deloitte.com/dtt/e_library/0,2321,sid%253D1021,00.html> (accessed 21 August 2003).

Chapter 4

1. This chapter is based on the "Delegating" module of Harvard ManageMentor, an online product of Harvard Business School Publishing.

Chapter 5

1. William Oncken Jr. and Donald L. Wass, "Management Time: Who's Got the Monkey?," *Harvard Business Review*, November–December, 1999, 178–186.

2. Ibid., 183.

Chapter 7

1. Materials in this chapter draw heavily on the "Coaching" and "Performance Evaluation" modules of Harvard ManageMentor, an online product of Harvard Business School Publishing.

Chapter 8

1. Frederick Herzberg, "One More Time: How Do You Motivate Employees?" *Harvard Business Review*, January 2003, 87–96. Note: Herzberg's original article was printed by HBR in 1968, but was reissued in 2003.

2. Nigel Nicholson, "How to Motivate Your Problem People," *Harvard Business Review*, January 2003, 56–65.

3. Beth Axelrod, Helen Handfield-Jones, and Ed Michaels, "A New Game Plan for C Players," *Harvard Business Review*, January 2002, 83.

4. This section is based on the "Dismissals" module of Harvard ManageMentor, an online product of Harvard Business School Publishing.

Chapter 9

1. This chapter is adapted from the "Crisis Management" module in Harvard ManageMentor, an online product of Harvard Business School Publishing.

2. Norman Augustine, "Managing the Crisis You Tried to Prevent," *Harvard Business Review*, November–December 1995, 147–158.

Chapter 10

1. Timothy Butler and James Waldroop, "Job Sculpting: The Art of Retaining Your Best People," *Harvard Business Review*, September–October 1999, 144–152.

2. Ibid., 144–152.

3. Ibid., 149.

Chapter 11

1. Bernal Díaz de Castillo, *The True History of the Conquest of New Spain*, trans. J. M. Cohen (Harmondsworth: Penguin Books, Ltd, 1963), 38.

2. David Bradford and Allen Cohen, *Power Up* (New York: John Wiley & Sons, Inc., 1998), 232.

3. Everett M. Rogers, *Diffusion of Innovation*, 3rd ed. (New York: The Free Press, 1983), 315–316.

4. Michael Beer, "Leading Change," Class note 9-488-037 (Boston: Harvard Business School, 1988; revised 1991), 2.

5. This section is adapted from "How to Lead When You're Not the Boss," *Harvard Management Update*, March 2000, 1–3.

Chapter 12

1. Bruce Henderson, "The Origin of Strategy," *Harvard Business Review*, November–December 1989, 139–143.

2. Michael E. Porter, "What Is Strategy?" *Harvard Business Review*, November–December 1996, 61–78.

3. Ibid.

4. Clayton M. Christensen, "Making Strategy: Learning by Doing," *Harvard Business Review*, November–December 1997, 141–156.

5. These questions were articulated many years ago by Kenneth Andrews in his classic book, *The Concept of Corporate Strategy*, 3rd ed. (Homewood, IL: Dow Jones-Irwin, 1978).

6. Porter, "What Is Strategy?" 72–73.

7. Ibid., 72.

8. George Labovitz and Victor Rosansky, *The Power of Alignment* (New York: John Wiley & Sons, Inc., 1997).

9. Porter, "What Is Strategy?" 65.

Chapter 13

1. This chapter is adapted from Harvard ManageMentor, an online product of Harvard Business School Publishing.

Glossary

ACCOUNTS PAYABLE A category of balance sheet liabilities representing monies owed by the company to suppliers and other short-term creditors.

ACCOUNTS RECEIVABLE A category of balance sheet assets representing monies owed to the company by customers and others.

ACCRUAL ACCOUNTING An accounting practice that records transactions as they occur, whether or not cash changes hands.

ASSETS The balance sheet items that a company invests in so that it can conduct business. Examples include cash and financial instruments, inventories of raw materials and finished goods, land, buildings, and equipment. Assets also include monies owed to the company by customers and others—an asset category referred to as *accounts receivable*.

AVAILABLE-TO-PROMISE A scheduling tool, usually set up on an electronic spreadsheet, which tells a scheduler the volume of production capacity available in any given time period to accept additional orders. This tool can be adapted to an individual's work schedule.

BALANCE SHEET A financial statement that describes the assets owned by a business and how those assets are financed—with the funds of creditors (liabilities) and/or the equity of the owners. Also know as the statement of financial position.

BUDGET The translation of strategic plans into measurable quantities that express the expected resources required and returns anticipated over a certain period.

CAREER DEVELOPMENT The process of assessing where you are in your work life, deciding where you want to be, and then making the changes necessary to get there.

CAREER LADDER   A logical series of stages that move a talented and dedicated employee through progressively more challenging and responsible positions.

CASH BUDGET   A budget that predicts and plans for the level and timing of cash inflows and outflows.

CASH FLOW STATEMENT   A financial statement that details the reasons for changes in cash (and cash equivalents) during the accounting period. More specifically, it reflects all changes in cash as affected by operating activities, investments, and financing activities.

CASH-BASIS ACCOUNTING   An accounting practice that records transactions only when cash changes hands.

CLOSED QUESTIONS   Questions that lead to "yes" or "no" answers.

COACHING   A two-way activity in which the parties share knowledge and experience in order to maximize the coaching recipient's potential and help him or her achieve agreed-upon goals.

CORE BUSINESS INTERESTS   From a career perspective, these interests are long-held, emotionally driven passions. They derive from an individual's personality, and influence what kinds of activities make people happy.

COST OF CAPITAL   The opportunity cost that shareholders and lenders could earn on their capital if they invested in the next best opportunity available to them at the same level of risk, calculated as the weighted average cost of the organization's different sources of capital.

COST OF GOODS SOLD   On the income statement, what it costs a company to produce its goods and services. This figure includes raw materials, production, and direct labor costs.

CRISIS   A change—either sudden or slowly evolving—that results in an urgent problem that management must address immediately.

CURRENT ASSETS   Assets that are most easily converted to cash: cash equivalents such as CDs and Treasury bills, receivables, and inventory. Under generally accepted accounting principles, current assets are those that can be converted into cash within one year.

CURRENT LIABILITIES   Liabilities that must be paid in a year or less; these typically include short-term loans, salaries, income taxes, and accounts payable.

DELEGATION   The assignment of a specific task or project by one person to another, and the assignee's commitment to complete the task or project.

DEPRECIATION   A noncash expense that effectively reduces the balance sheet value of an asset over its presumed useful life.

DISCOUNT RATE   The annual rate, expressed as a percentage, at which a future payment or series of payments is reduced to its present value.

DISCOUNTED CASH FLOW (DCF)   A method based on time-value-of-money concepts that calculates value by finding the present value of a business's future cash flows.

ECONOMIC VALUE ADDED (EVA)   A measure of real economic profit calculated as net operating income after tax *less* the cost of the capital employed to obtain it.

EQUITY BOOK VALUE   The value of total assets less total liabilities.

FINANCIAL LEVERAGE   The degree to which borrowed money is used in acquiring assets. A corporation is said to be highly leveraged when its balance sheet debt is much greater than its owners' equity.

FIXED ASSETS   Assets that are difficult to convert to cash—for example, buildings and equipment. Sometimes called plant assets.

FUNCTION   A group of tasks and projects that are all related to one ongoing activity such as sales, marketing, or training.

FUTURE VALUE (FV)   The amount to which a present value, or series of payments, will increase over a specific period of time at a specific compounding rate.

GANTT CHART   A chart that illustrates the duration and chronological order of discrete activities.

GENERALLY ACCEPTED ACCOUNTING PRINCIPLES (GAAP)   In the United States, a body of conventions, rules, and procedures sanctioned by the Financial Accounting Standards Board, an independent self-regulating body. All entities must follow GAAP in accounting for transactions and representing their results in financial statements.

GOAL SETTING   A process for defining targets you plan to achieve.

GOODWILL   An intangible balance sheet asset. If a company has purchased another company for a price in excess of the fair market value of its assets, that "goodwill" is recorded as an asset. Goodwill may also represent intangible things such as the acquired company's excellent reputation or brand names. These may have real value. So, too, can other intangible assets, such as patents.

GROSS PROFIT   Sales revenues less the cost of goods sold. The roughest measure of profitability.

HURDLE RATE   The minimal rate of return that all investments for a particular enterprise must achieve.

INCOME STATEMENT   A financial statement that indicates the cumulative results of operations over a specified period of time. Also referred to as the profit and loss statement, or P&L.

INCREMENTAL BUDGETING   A budgeting practice that extrapolates from historical figures. Managers look at the previous period's budget and actual results as well as expectations for the future in determining the budget for the next period.

INFLUENCE   The exercise of power to change behavior, attitudes, and values.

INTERNAL RATE OF RETURN (IRR)   The discount rate at which the net present value of an investment equals zero.

INVENTORY   The supplies, raw materials, components, etc., that a company uses in its operations. It also includes work-in-process—goods that are in various stages of production—as well as finished goods waiting to be sold and/or shipped.

LIABILITY   A claim against a company's assets.

MASTER BUDGET   A budget that incorporates the operating budget and the financial budget of an organization into one comprehensive picture. In other words, the master budget summarizes all the individual financial projections within an organization for a given period.

NET INCOME   The "bottom line" of the income statement. Net income is revenues less expenses less taxes. Also referred to as net earnings or net profits.

NET PRESENT VALUE   The present value of one or more future cash flows *less* any initial investment costs.

NET WORKING CAPITAL   Current assets less current liabilities. Net working capital is the amount of money a company has tied up in short-term operating activities.

OPEN-ENDED QUESTIONS Questions that invite participation and idea sharing.

OPERATING BUDGET A projected target for performance in revenues, expenses, and operating income.

OPERATING EARNINGS Gross margin less operating expenses and depreciation. Also called earnings before interest and taxes, or EBIT.

OPERATING EXPENSES On the balance sheet, a category that includes administrative expenses, employee salaries, rents, sales and marketing costs, as well as other costs of business not directly attributed to the cost of manufacturing a product.

OPERATING LEVERAGE The extent to which a company's operating costs are fixed versus variable. For example, a company that relies heavily on machinery and very few workers to produce its goods has a high operating leverage.

OWNERS' EQUITY What, if anything, is left over after total liabilities are deducted from total assets. Owners' equity is the sum of capital contributed by owners plus their retained earnings. Also known as shareholders' equity.

PERFORMANCE APPRAISAL A formal method for assessing how well people are doing with respect to their assigned goals.

PREFERRED STOCK An equity-like security that pays a specified dividend and has a superior position to common stock in case of distributions or liquidation.

PRESENT VALUE The monetary value today of a future payment discounted at some annual compound interest rate.

PROFIT AND LOSS STATEMENT See *income statement*.

PROFIT MARGIN The percent of every dollar of sales that makes it to the bottom line. Profit margin is net income after tax divided by net sales. Sometimes called the return on sales, or ROS.

RETAINED EARNINGS Annual net profits left after payment of dividends that accumulate on a company's balance sheet.

REVENUES The amount of money that results from selling products or services to customers.

ROLLING BUDGET A plan that is continually updated so that the time frame remains stable while the actual period covered by the budget changes.

SCHEDULE   A written commitment to accomplish tasks within a time frame.

SELF–DIRECTED WORK TEAM   A self-managed unit with a specific objective.

SHAREHOLDERS' EQUITY   See *owners' equity*.

SOLVENCY   The ability to pay bills as they come due.

STRATEGY FORMULATION   A search for a plan that will differentiate the enterprise and give it a competitive advantage.

STRETCH GOAL   A goal that goes beyond routine responsibilities, and instead concentrates on some particular skill or project that a manager and employee agree to be of major importance and worthy of extra effort.

TEAM   A small number of individuals with complementary skills committed to a common purpose with collective accountability.

TELEWORK   Work that is done by employees in locations other than their regular offices, and is facilitated by telecommunications and Internet capabilities.

VARIANCE   The difference between actual results and the results expected in the budget.

VISION   A picture of a hoped–for end result: what it will look like, how it will function, what it will produce.

WORKING CAPITAL   See *net working capital*.

ZERO–BASED BUDGETING   A budgeting practice that begins each new budget cycle from a zero base, or from the ground up as though the budget was being prepared for the first time.

For Further Reading

This book has covered the "essentials" of many and diverse subjects that matter to managers. If you'd like to learn more, consult any of the publications listed below.

Becoming a Manager

Hill, Linda A. *Becoming a Manager: Mastery of a New Identity*. 2nd ed. Boston: Harvard Business School Press, 2003. The transition from individual contributor to manager can be trying—even traumatic—for many people. Hill traces the experiences of nineteen new managers to unravel the complexity of the process. As these personal interviews reveal, becoming a manager represents a profound psychological transformation—one that all too many individuals fail to make. Hill provides concrete, practical suggestions for companies to help managers survive their first year and become major contributors to their organizations.

Mintzberg, Henry. "The Manager's Job: Folklore and Fact." *Harvard Business Review*, March–April 1990. Managerial work involves interpersonal roles, informational roles, and decisional roles, Mintzberg notes. These in turn require specific skills—for example, developing peer relationships, carrying out negotiations, motivating subordinates, resolving conflicts, establishing information networks and disseminating information, making decisions with little or ambiguous information, and allocating resources. Applying the principles of adaptive work can make a manager more effective in all his or her roles, but especially in dealing with people and providing information.

Goals

Brown, Tom. "Turning Mission Statements into Action." *Harvard Management Update*, September 1997. Corporations love to author mission statements because they help an organization figure out its purpose, and help employees work toward that goal. But if management fails to create commitment to the statement, then action toward the statement cannot occur. In order to make your mission statement happen, you must complete five steps: (1) iteration, (2) awareness, (3) understanding, (4) commitment, and (5) action.

Schaffer, Robert H., and Harvey A. Thomson. "Successful Change Programs Begin with Results." *Harvard Business Review*, January–February 1992. Most corporate improvement efforts have negligible impact, the authors maintain, because they bear little relationship to a company's goals and have long, indeterminate time horizons. Moreover, they equate measures of activities with actual improvements in performance. An activity-centered program confuses ends with means, processes with outcomes. It assumes, for example, that once the company has benchmarked its performance against the competition, assessed customers' expectations, and trained its staff in problem solving, that quality, sales, and profits will automatically improve. A results-driven approach, by contrast, bypasses lengthy preparations. Instead, the focus is on specific, measurable goals for performance improvement that can be achieved in the short term. Process innovations are introduced only as they are needed for better results. By committing to measurable change, managers can not only see results faster, they can also determine more quickly what's working and what isn't.

Smith, Douglas K. *Make Success Measurable!* New York: John Wiley & Sons, 1999. This book shows how to avoid activity-based goals that can go on indefinitely, and articulate aggressive outcome-based goals that are specific, measurable, achievable, relevant, and time-bound. This is a how-to book, emphasizing outcomes as opposed to actions in setting goals. Lessons include how to set goals that matter to customers, shareholders, and funders; set nonfinancial as well as financial goals and link them together; understand and use outcome-based goals that support success while avoiding activity-based goals that produce failure; and select and use management disciplines needed to achieve your goals.

Hiring and Retention

Cappelli, Peter. "Making the Most of On-Line Recruiting." *Harvard Business Review* OnPoint Enhanced Edition. Boston: Harvard Business School Publishing, 2001. Ninety percent of large U.S. companies are already recruiting via the Internet. By simply logging on to the Web, company recruiters can locate vast numbers of qualified candidates for jobs at every level, screen them in minutes, and contact the most promising ones immediately. The payoffs can be enormous: It costs substantially less to hire someone online, and the time saved is equally great. In this article, Peter Cappelli examines some of the emerging service providers and technologies—matchmakers, job boards, hiring management systems software, and applicant-screening mechanisms that test skills and record interests. He also looks at some of the strategies companies are adopting as they enter online labor markets. Integrating recruiting efforts with overall marketing campaigns, especially through coordination and identification with the company's brand, is the most important thing companies can do to ensure success in online hiring. Along the way, Cappelli sounds two cautionary notes. First, a human touch, not electronic contact, is vital in the last steps of a successful hiring process. Second, companies must make sure that online testing and hiring criteria do not discriminate against women, disabled people, workers over forty, or members of minority groups. When competition for talent is fierce, companies that master the art and science of online recruiting will be the ones that attract and keep the best people.

Harvard Business Review. *Harvard Business Review on Finding and Keeping the Best People*. Boston: Harvard Business School Press, 2001. This collection of *Harvard Business Review* articles reveals how to hire and retain top employees in today's fiercely competitive job market. The articles show you not only how to find good people but also how to use their skills even if they leave.

Mornell, Pierre. *45 Effective Ways for Hiring Smart! How to Predict Winners and Losers in the Incredibly Expensive People-Reading Game*. Berkeley, CA: Ten Speed Press, 1998. Presents strategies for measuring candidates, emphasizing behavior, not words. Covers all stages of the hiring process from pre-interview screening to interviewing to checking references and background.

Delegating

Homes, Carl, and Regina Fazio Maruca. "Fighting the Urge to Fight Fires." *Harvard Business Review*, November–December 1999. Face it: Delegating responsibility is hard. But not delegating can be disastrous. In this article, former Oklahoma City fire chief Carl Homes shares his best practices for efficient leadership. Even the most dedicated corporate micromanager can benefit from Homes's outlook on the value of delegating.

Schwartz, Andrew E. *Delegating Authority*. New York: Barron's Business Success Series, 1992. This handy pocket guide to delegation provides both new and experienced managers with an overview of the essential skills and techniques needed to delegate effectively. It discusses delegation in terms of five key components: goal setting, communication, motivation, supervision, and evaluation. There are recommendations for specific techniques and approaches within each component.

Time Management

Ferner, Jack D. *Successful Time Management: A Self-Teaching Guide*. New York: John Wiley & Sons, 1995. This book provides a broad overview of the principles of time management. The author maintains that time management is a management process that involves analysis, planning, and commitment. He includes exercises and references that can be incorporated into everyday professional and personal situations to help you manage your time successfully.

Oncken, Jr., William, and Donald L. Wass. "Management Time: Who's Got the Monkey?" *Harvard Business Review* OnPoint Enhanced Edition. Boston: Harvard Business School Publishing, 2000. Many managers feel overwhelmed. They have too many problems—too many monkeys—on their backs. All too often, they say, they find themselves running out of time while their subordinates are running out of work. Such is the common phenomenon described by the late William Oncken, Jr., and Donald L. Wass in this 1974 HBR classic. This article describes how the manager can reverse this phenomenon and delegate effectively. In his 1999 commentary, Stephen R. Covey discusses both the enduring power of this message and how theories of time management have progressed beyond these ideas.

Managing Teams

Billington, Jim. "The Three Essentials of an Effective Team." *Harvard Management Update*, January 1997. The author discusses three essentials that distinguish an effective team: commitment, competence, and a common goal. The author states that commitment comes from a shared sense of ownership of what the team hopes to accomplish. He believes that builders of teams must look for technical competence, problem-solving skills, and interpersonal skills in team members. The common goal of the team must be explored, shaped, and agreed on by all team members.

Gary, Loren. "Managing a Team vs. Managing the Individuals on a Team." *Harvard Management Update*, March 1997. Managing a team is not the same thing as managing the individuals who make up the team. To maximize team effectiveness, managers should ask themselves four questions, particularly in the early stages of assembling a team: (1) Is a team the best organizational structure for this effort? (2) Have I established collective goals that the team members can make their own? (3) What signals am I sending to members about how the team should interact? (4) Does my performance management system actually reward interdependence and mutual accountability?

Katzenbach, Jon R., and Douglas K. Smith. "The Discipline of Teams." *Harvard Business Review* OnPoint Enhanced Edition. Boston: Harvard Business School Publishing, 2000. The essence of a team is shared commitment. Without it, groups perform as individuals; with it, they become a unit of collective performance. The fundamental distinction between teams and other forms of working groups turns on performance. A working group relies on the individual contributions of its members for group performance. But a team strives for something greater than its members could achieve individually. The best teams invest a tremendous amount of time shaping a purpose, and they translate their purpose into specific performance goals. Team members also pitch in and become accountable with and to their teammates. The authors identify three basic types of teams: teams that recommend things, teams that make or do things, and teams that run things. The key is knowing where in the organization real teams should be encouraged. Team potential exists anywhere hierarchy or organizational boundaries inhibit good performance. (This article is based on a book by the same authors: *The Wisdom of Teams: Creating the High-Performance Organization*. Boston: Harvard Business School Press, 1993.)

Parcells, Bill. "The Tough Work of Turning Around a Team." *Harvard Business Review*, November–December 2000. How do you reverse the fortunes of a troubled team? Bill Parcells—one of the NFL's most successful coaches—offers managers three rules: (1) Make it clear from day one that you're in charge, (2) view confrontation as healthy, and (3) identify small goals and hit them. As Parcells maintains, if you get people on your team who share the same goals and passion—and then push them to achieve their highest potential—the team is bound to come out on top.

"Why Some Teams Succeed and So Many Don't." *Harvard Management Update*, January 2000. Teams—sometimes they have great results, and sometimes they are huge failures. What makes the difference? Research shows that it's how teams are managed—and whether your company as a whole really supports teamwork. Includes six keys to successful teams, and an annotated list of resources.

Performance Appraisal and Coaching

Carney, Karen. "Successful Performance Measurement: A Checklist." *Harvard Management Update*, November 1999. Does your performance measurement system actually boost performance? Here's a checklist for ensuring meaningful performance measurement. Includes an annotated "If you want to learn more" section and a sidebar on "soft" metrics entitled "Measuring the Soft Stuff."

Waldroop, James, and Timothy Butler. "The Executive as Coach." *Harvard Business Review* OnPoint Enhanced Edition. Boston: Harvard Business School Publishing, 2000. How do you deal with the talented manager whose perfectionism paralyzes his direct reports or the high-performing expert who disdains teamwork? What about the sensitive manager who avoids confrontation of any kind? Get rid of them? The authors suggest that you coach them; helping to change the behaviors that threaten to derail a valued manager is often the best way to help that manager succeed. Executives increasingly recognize that people management skills are the key to both their personal success and the success of their business. And being an effective coach is a crucial part of successful people management.

Handling Problem Employees

Delpo, Amy, and Lisa Guerin. *Dealing with Problem Employees: A Legal Guide.* Berkeley, CA: Nolo, 2001. Problem employees pose an enormous number of legal and other challenges. This book shows you how to recognize who is and isn't a problem employee, help problem employees get back on track, investigate problems and complaints, conduct effective performance evaluations, apply progressive discipline, and handle the many complex aspects of dismissals.

Weeks, Holly. "Taking the Stress Out of Stressful Conversations." *Harvard Business Review* OnPoint Enhanced Edition. Boston: Harvard Business School Publishing, 2002. Dismissing an employee can be one of the most stressful conversations a manager can face. That's because such conversations are emotionally loaded. Weeks explains the emotional dynamics that take place in stressful conversations and emphasizes the importance of preparation before delivering painful news to an employee. She describes a method for identifying your vulnerabilities during stressful conversations and practicing more effective delivery styles and behaviors.

Managing Crises

Augustine, Norman R. "Reshaping an Industry: Lockheed Martin's Survival Story." *Harvard Business Review*, November–December 1997. In this behind-the-scenes story about the effects of the end of the Cold War on industry, Augustine draws important lessons about what managers can do to avoid crises, and how they can manage them once they begin.

Burrough, Bryan, and John Helyar. *Barbarians at the Gate: The Fall of RJR Nabisco.* New York: Harper Collins, 1991. This thoroughly researched story reveals how power, greed, and ego all combined to create a crisis, and explains the do's and don'ts of crisis management.

Fink, Steven. *Crisis Management: Planning for the Inevitable*. New York: American Management Association, 1986. Considered by many to be the definitive work on crisis management, this book is well written and practical. Using numerous highly readable case studies, Fink tracks the seeds of crisis, analyzing what mistakes were made, and how the crisis was either exacerbated or contained by the decisions of management. He draws conclusions from his research and observations and gives direct, practical advice.

Managing Your Career

Ibarra, Herminia. *Working Identity*. Boston: Harvard Business School Press, 2003. The author presents a new model for career reinvention that flies in the face of conventional thinking on career change and development. While common wisdom holds that we must first know what we want to do before we can act, Ibarra argues that this advice is backward. Knowing, she says, is the result of doing and experimenting. Career transition is not a straight path toward some predetermined identity, but a crooked journey of discovery.

Moses, Barbara. *The Good News about Careers: How You'll Be Working in the Next Decade*. San Francisco, CA: Jossey-Bass, 1999. With its emphasis on freedom and flexibility, the new economy provides us with incredible opportunities for self-experimentation and expansion. This savvy guide shows you how to construct a new-economy career—including ways you can benefit from current work trends. Includes advice on building necessary skills.

Waldroop, James, and Timothy Butler. *The 12 Bad Habits That Hold Good People Back: Overcoming the Behavior Patterns That Keep You from Getting Ahead*. New York: Doubleday, 2000. These career specialists describe twelve behaviors that keep people from being successful at work. They present case studies of failure and describe problems of character that impede success. Remedies are shown to begin with self-understanding.

Leading

Farkas, Charles M., and Suzy Wetlaufer. "The Ways Chief Executive Officers Lead." *Harvard Business Review*, May–June 1996. The authors conducted 160 interviews with executives around the world. Instead of finding 160 different approaches, they found five, each with a singular focus: strategy, people, expertise, controls, or change. For leaders whose focus is organizational change, the fundamental principles for leading adaptive work are particularly relevant.

Harvard Business Review. *Harvard Business Review on Leadership*. Boston: Harvard Business School Press, 1998. This collection gathers together eight of HBR's most influential articles on leadership, challenging many long-held assumptions about the true sources of power and authority.

Heifetz, Ronald A., and Loren Gary. "The Work of a Modern Leader: An Interview with Ron Heifetz." *Harvard Management Update*, April 1997. This interview explores organizational and individual resistance to the work of adaptive leadership, examining Heifetz's principles of "getting on the balcony" and "regulating distress" in some detail.

Kotter, John P. "What Leaders Really Do." *Harvard Business Review* OnPoint Enhanced Edition. Boston: Harvard Business School Publishing, 2000. Leadership and management are two distinctive and complementary systems of action, each with its own function and characteristic activities. Management involves coping with complexity, while leadership involves coping with change. Most U.S. corporations actively seek out people with leadership potential and expose them to career experiences designed to develop that potential.

Zaleznik, Abraham. "Managers and Leaders: Are They Different?" *Harvard Business Review* OnPoint Enhanced Edition. Boston: Harvard Business School Publishing, 2001. Managers tend to exercise their skills in diplomacy and focus on decision-making processes within an organization. Managers wish to create an ordered corporate structure and are emotionally detached from their work. Leaders, in contrast, direct their energies toward introducing new approaches and ideas. Leaders engender excitement through their work and often realize their potential through one-to-one relationships with mentors. Business organizations can foster development of leaders by establishing such relationships between junior and senior executives. This article includes a retrospective commentary by the author.

Strategy

Harvard Business Review. *How to Create Effective Strategy*. Boston: Harvard Business School Publishing, Product #39105. Contains a collection of popular articles on strategy formulations by a number of experts, including Michael Porter and Clayton Christensen.

Harvard Business Review. *Making Strategy Work*. Boston: Harvard Business School Publishing, Product #49567. More popular articles on strategy and strategy implementation, featuring such well-known authors as Clayton Christensen, Henry Mitzberg, and Gary Hamel.

Porter, Michael. *Competitive Strategy*. New York: Free Press, 1986. Considered by many as the bible of corporate strategy, Porter's widely read tome introduces his three generic strategies: lowest cost, differentiation, and focus. Each can bring structure to the task of strategic positioning. Porter also presents a framework for predicting the behavior of competitors, which has given rise to the discipline of competitor assessment. If you could read only one book on this important subject, this would be it.

Financial Tools

Bruns, Jr., William J. "Introduction to Financial Ratios and Financial Statement Analysis." Harvard Business School Case Note 9-193-029. Boston: Harvard Business School Publishing, 1996. Introduces and describes financial ratios, which are used to assess profitability, activity, solvency and leverage, and returns to shareholders.

Bruns, Jr., William J. "The Accounting Framework, Financial Statements, and Some Accounting Concepts." Harvard Business School Case Note 9-193-028. Boston: Harvard Business School Publishing, 1997. Introduces the accounting framework, basic financial statements, and eleven accounting concepts.

Kaplan, Robert, and David P. Norton. "The Balanced Scorecard: Measures that Drive Performance." *Harvard Business Review* OnPoint Enhanced Edition. Boston: Harvard Business School Publishing, 2000. The balanced scorecard performance measurement system allows executives to view a company from several perspectives simultaneously. The scorecard includes financial measures that reveal the results of actions already taken, as well as three sets of operational measures that assess customer satisfaction, internal processes, and the organization's ability to learn and improve.

Index

About the Subject Adviser

CHRISTOPHER BARTLETT is the Thomas D. Casserly, Jr., Professor of Business Administration, Emeritus at Harvard Business School. He received master's and doctorate degrees in business administration from Harvard University (1971 and 1979). Prior to joining the faculty of Harvard Business School in 1979, he was a marketing manager with Alcoa in Australia, a management consultant in McKinsey & Company's London office, and general manager at Baxter Laboratories' subsidiary company in France. Among his eight books are *Managing Across Borders: The Transnational Solution* and *The Individualized Corporation* (coauthored with Sumantra Ghoshal), each of which has been translated into more than ten languages.

About the Writer

RICHARD LUECKE is the writer of this and several other books in the Harvard Business Essentials series. Based in Salem, Massachusetts, Mr. Luecke has authored or developed over thirty book and dozens of articles on a wide range of business subjects. He has an M.B.A. from the University of St. Thomas.